Student Politics in Argentina

STUDENT MOVEMENTS—PAST AND PRESENT
General Editor: Seymour Martin Lipset

1. STUDENT POLITICS, edited by Seymour Martin Lipset
2. STUDENT POLITICS IN ARGENTINA, by Richard J. Walter

Student Politics in Argentina

The University Reform and Its Effects, 1918–1964

RICHARD J. WALTER

BASIC BOOKS, INC., PUBLISHERS
New York / London

To the memory of my grandfather,

PROFESSOR JOHN VAN HORNE

Introduction

The increasingly important role of university students in the national affairs of many countries has been one of the most noticeable factors in world politics since the end of World War II. This increased activism has been particularly evident in the developing areas of Asia, Africa, and Latin America. In the early 1960's university students in South Vietnam, through public demonstrations and the use of force, caused governments to topple in the unstable atmosphere of that country. Students and young intellectuals in Africa, many of whom received their university training in Europe or the United States, provided much of the leadership for the anti-colonial and independence movements which swept that continent in the postwar years. Student activity in Latin America, whether supporting Fidel Castro's revolution in Cuba (1958–1959), contributing to the overthrow of dictator Marcos Pérez Jiménez in Venezuela (1958), or leading anti-American demonstrations in the Panama Canal Zone (1964), has been an issue of growing concern for North American political officials and scholars.

Increased student activism has not been restricted to the developing areas. By the mid-1960's it was clear that the United States, often pointed to as a country where students have been apathetic and lacking in influence, was undergoing a significant change with regard to the role of the university youth. In the early 1960's, thousands of students and recent graduates entered the Peace Corps, serving with low pay and under harsh conditions in foreign countries. At home, many youths participated in the civil rights movement, often risking their lives to register Negro voters in the American South. On many campuses groups arose to discuss matters of university and national concern, often echoing in their statements many of the sentiments and aims which have long been current among the student movements of the developing areas.[1] In Latin America the participation of students and young university graduates in national affairs has a long tradition, dating back to the early nineteenth century. The graduates of both European and American institutions of higher learning provided much of the intellectual, military, and political leadership during the Latin American Wars for Independence against Spain (1810–1825). A dozen years later, a group of young Argentine intellectuals, the "Generation of 1837," led the liberal movement which eventually overthrew the dictator Juan Manuel de Rosas in 1852. Although Brazil did not have a full-fledged university until the twentieth century, students from the law school in São Paulo composed much of the leadership for the campaigns which abolished slavery (1888) and replaced the empire with a republic (1889). Venezuela's university youth formed one of the principal groups opposing and, finally, bringing to an end the dictatorship of Antonio Guzmán Blanco (1888).

Nevertheless, it was not until the early twentieth century, after the significant economic development, population increase, and urban growth of the 1850–1900 period, that student politics became formalized, institutionalized, and consistently influential in Latin America. These developments, in the first two decades of the twentieth century, were marked by the formation of student federations in several republics and the holding of various continent-wide student meetings. The most important single event underscoring the emergence of the Latin American university youth into national political life was the University Reform movement, begun in Argentina's University of Córdoba in 1918. The Reform, which spread rapidly from Argentina to most of Latin America, established the principle of student participation in the administrative councils of the area's universities. This participation, along with other factors related to the Reform program, was largely responsible for stimulating among Latin America's university students a widespread, consistent, and continuing interest in national and continental political affairs.

Against this background, my purpose is to examine the history of student political activity in one of Latin America's most important countries, Argentina, and to determine the nature and extent of student influence on the social, economic, and political life of the Republic between 1918, the year of the Reform, and 1964. I shall pay particular attention to the role of Argentina's university youth in the important political changes that have occurred in the nation's twentieth-century history, analyzing the significance of student participation in these historical events. I shall also consider carefully the attitudes of the university groups with regard to the outstanding national issues current in Argentina between 1918 and 1964. I believe that a study of the historical contributions, actions, and opinions of the Argentine youth can provide some explanations of the contemporary behavior of the Republic's university students.

It should be noted that this work is a study in history, undertaken by a historian. The bulk of the work produced to date (1966) on students in developing areas has been done by political scientists and sociologists and has concentrated on developments since World War II. The aim of my book is to supply background information for contemporary studies and to show that student activity in Argentina and Latin America is much more than a phenomenon of the past two decades. I shall stress the historical continuities which are evident in the Argentine student movement from 1918 on and shall also underscore the importance of a historical tradition of political activism as a factor in explaining present-day student behavior.

Although I have considered these issues as a historian, I have also addressed myself to some of the questions raised by political scientists and sociologists who have done work on student activities in developing areas.[2] With these broader concerns in mind, I have attempted to look at factors in the historical material which relate to the larger questions and concerns dealing with student activities in general. Below I have listed eight of the problems which have occupied social scientists in recent studies and have mentioned some of the interpretations which other scholars have provided with regard to students in developing countries.

1. *What have been the ages and socio-economic backgrounds of student leaders?*

In Argentina, has the leadership and motivating force for university political activity come from the "professional students," those who remain in the universities past the normal time needed to gain a degree, intent more on political activism than on academic pursuits? Or, have the students between the ages of twenty and twenty-five, the average time span for the pursuit of a university career, been the principal leaders of student activity? Moreover, has the student leadership in Argentina come predominantly from the middle classes, as seems to have been the case in most of Latin America? If not, has student leadership been recruited from either the more privileged groups or, at the other end of the scale, from the working classes?

2. *What factors have made students politically influential?*

Why have university groups been important elements in promoting political change? Several scholars have suggested that university students are strong politically because Latin American governments themselves are weak. Kalman H. Silvert has noted that Latin American students have demonstrated power "in inverse relation to the strength of governments and the efficacy of the university administrations themselves. The relative influence of organized student movements must be heightened by the essential fragility of societies in transition toward modern nationhood."[3] However, students have been influential not only when weak and unstable governments have prevailed, but also under dictators, when, as S. Walter Washington has observed for Venezuela and Cuba, "the youth have been the repositories of the ideals of the nations and . . . have given expression to the grievances of the people." [4]

As most observers have pointed out, students in Latin America and the emerging nations of Africa and Asia wield power because they represent an educated elite in countries with high rates of illiteracy and narrow bases of leadership. In these areas the university youth are looked to as the future leaders of their respective countries, and as such they are treated with unusual deference and respect. E. Wight Bakke has suggested that the prestige of the student position considerably increases the political potency of the university youth:

If to the influence on his blood relatives is added the influence he is likely to have on his godparents and their families, and on his friends unable to attend the university, it would seem to be within the realm of possibility to assume an impact of a student on from 5 to 10 votes. Even taking the lower figure of 5, the 65,000 students in the National University in Mexico City alone would carry some weight with 325,000 satellite voters. No politician can afford to ignore that number of potential voters.[5]

3. *Have there been connections between national political parties and university organizations?*

Have students in Argentina been "used" by national parties as in Cuba and Venezuela?

Their [student] proclivities are fully exploited by the political parties. It is an old practice of opposition leaders to place students in the forefront of demonstrations that might provoke violence on the part of the powers-that-be. In both Cuba and Venezuela all political parties have had youth directors to organize the students. On occasion party leaders have induced students to make political demands that the former did not dare to make.[6]

Or, have the Argentine students been more independent of political party direction, comparing more closely with their colleagues in Chile?

The University political groups enjoy considerable independence within the broad framework of basic party policy and organization. They are able to influence party decisions through their dominance of youth sections and by allying themselves with sympathetic elements in the party hierarchy.[7]

4. *How influential have been professors, national political leaders, and intellectuals on student thought and action?*

What kind of men have had the greatest impact upon Argentina's students? Has there been in Argentina any development similar to that noted by Edward Shils in other areas?

From the 1920's to the 1940's, the example of the late Professor Harold Laski elicited and fortified the socialistic disposition of many young intellectuals of the English-speaking underdeveloped countries; Jean-Paul Sartre has played a parallel role among the French-speaking intellectuals from 1945 onward.[8]

Has Argentina been like Colombia, where writers, student leaders, and politicians have been most influential in the formation of student opinion? [9]

5. *What percentage of the university youth have participated in political activities?*

The popular impression is that the great majority of Latin American students constantly and actively take part in political affairs, at both the university and national levels. Evidence gathered from several countries, however, questions this assumption. A 1963 survey of 1,250 law students in Brazil revealed that, "Queried on their current participation in student politics, 36 per cent of the students replied that they participated; 59 per cent did not." [10] Similarly, in Chile:

The vast majority of students are indifferent to Fech [national student federation] affairs. Although between 55 and 60 per cent of those eligible voted in the 1956 and 1957 elections of executive officers, the proportion who take a lively interest and participate actively in federation affairs is far smaller. On a day-to-day basis, those involved in actual Fech operations number no more than 50 to 60 individuals, and even within this inner circle the participation of many is marginal. In the year 1956–1957, there were at most 500 students from the University of Chile in Santiago enrolled in youth organizations of political parties.[11]

In Cuba and Venezuela not all students engage actively in politics, although "in the universities there is a large and vociferous minority which does expend its energies in politics and in times of crisis this minority expands rapidly into a majority." [12]

6. *Has the student movement been of one defined political tendency?*

Have the Argentine university groups been closely identified with one particular political party or one particular set of political ideas? S. Walter Washington has stated: "In Venezuela articulate student opinion is leftist, hostile to the United States government's policies and tolerant of Communists." [13] The Chilean Student Federation, according to Frank Bonilla, has based its program of action on the following principles:

the courage to hold and defend a point of view on fundamental issues, a readiness for self-sacrifice, loyalty in friendship, love of country, hatred of dictators and distrust of the military, a sentimental identification with the working classes, and solidarity with the youth of other Latin American countries.[14]

However, might these prevailing characteristics overshadow the fact that significant segments of the student population do not hold expressly to these views? Seymour Martin Lipset, reviewing the literature on student activities in developing areas, has remarked upon the presence of moderate and conservative elements among the university groups. Not only are many students not liberal, he has concluded, but many are also politically apathetic:

> The discrepancy between the image of university students in developing countries as predominantly leftist, and the data reported in various opinion surveys, points to the existence of large numbers of students who are indifferent to politics or who, whatever their preferences, do not have intense feelings about political things.[15]

7. *What has been the relationship between the quality of education and student political activity in national affairs?*

What has been the connection between the quality of education in Argentina and student involvement in politics? What role have conditions endemic to twentieth-century Latin American universities, such as the lack of extracurricular university activities, the small numbers of full-time professors, and the low percentage of national funds allocated to education, played in the development of student political activity in Argentina?

8. *What have been the political attitudes and activities of student leaders after graduation from the university?*

The popular answer to this question has been that, after sowing their political wild oats, students who are liberal and leftist become more moderate and conservative when they leave the university and face the necessities of earning a living. Daniel Goldrich has observed that in Panama "many student reformers in the past have been coopted or at least neutralized by being given (relatively lucrative) government positions." [16] However, Lipset has warned of overgeneralizing this concept, noting that in many of the developing countries university graduates enter naturally into the political and economic elites and identify with leftist ideologies "because these political tendencies are symbolically associated with modernization, rapid economic development and ultimately with equality, all of these being objectives favored by the well educated." [17]

It is my intention in examining the history of student activity in

Argentina to provide information for the general body of literature dealing with the role of university youth in Latin America and the developing areas and to suggest some answers to the problems just mentioned. Many of the conclusions concerning the Argentine students can be applied to and compared with the activities of university youth in other nations; there are many similarities, but also many differences. Student activity takes place within the broader framework of the national history. Consequently, just as the development of Argentina has differed in many ways from the history of the other Latin American republics, so too has the history of student politics in Argentina differed in important respects from the experiences of youth movements in other countries.

NOTES

1. For information on the most significant "student revolution" in the United States during this period, see Seymour Martin Lipset and Sheldon S. Wolin, eds., *The Berkeley Student Revolt: Facts and Interpretations* (New York, 1965).

2. A partial list of works concerned with student activities in the developing areas, which I have consulted in establishing a framework for my study, includes the following articles and monographs: E. Wight Bakke, "Students on the March: The Cases of Mexico and Colombia," *Sociology of Education*, XXXVII (Spring 1964), 200–228; Frank Bonilla, "The Student Federation of Chile: 50 Years of Political Action," *Journal of Inter-American Studies*, II (July 1960), 311–334; Daniel Goldrich, *Radical Nationalism: The Political Orientations of Panamanian Law Students* (East Lansing, Mich., 1962); Seymour Martin Lipset, "University Students and Politics in Underdeveloped Countries," in Seymour Martin Lipset, ed., *Student Politics* (New York, 1967), pp. 3–53; Ronald L. Scheman, "The Brazilian Law Student: Background, Habits, Attitudes," *Journal of Inter-American Studies*, V (July 1963), 333–356; Edward Shils, "The Intellectuals in the Political Development of the New States," in John H. Kautsky, ed., *Political Change in Underdeveloped Countries: Nationalism and Communism* (New York, 1962), pp. 195–234; Kalman H. Silvert, "The University Student," in John J. Johnson, ed., *Continuity and Change in Latin America* (Stanford, Calif.,

1964), pp. 206–226; S. Walter Washington, "The Political Activity of Latin American Students," in Robert D. Tomasek, ed., *Latin American Politics: Studies of the Contemporary Scene* (Garden City, N.Y., 1966), pp. 115–127; and Robert C. Williamson, *El estudiante colombiano y sus actitudes, un análisis de psicología social en la universidad nacional* (Bogotá, Colombia, 1962).
3. Silvert, *op. cit.*, p. 207.
4. Washington, *op. cit.*, p. 115.
5. Bakke, *op. cit.*, p. 225.
6. Washington, *op. cit.*, p. 119.
7. Bonilla, *op. cit.*, p. 330.
8. Shils, *op. cit.*, pp. 212–213.
9. Williamson, *op. cit.*, p. 25.
10. Scheman, *op. cit.*, p. 349.
11. Bonilla, *op. cit.*, p. 316.
12. Washington, *op. cit.*, pp. 117–118.
13. *Ibid.*, p. 125.
14. Bonilla, *op. cit.*, p. 315.
15. Lipset, *op. cit.*, p. 53.
16. Goldrich, *op. cit.*, p. 23.
17. Lipset, *op. cit.*, p. 55.

Acknowledgments

This work could not have been completed without the generous aid and support of many organizations and persons, both in the United States and Argentina. I wish to express my deep gratitude to the Henry L. and Grace Doherty Charitable Foundation for financing a twelve-month stay in Buenos Aires, Argentina, in the year 1964, during which time I gathered the bulk of the material for this study. Thanks are also due to the Graduate Division and the Latin American Studies Committee of Washington University, St. Louis, Missouri, for the financial support they gave to me to complete my research.

Field research in Latin America is often a difficult and frustrating experience, particularly when dealing with a subject as volatile as student politics. For me, these difficulties and frustrations were largely overcome through the help and encouragement of a number of persons in Buenos Aires. I wish to pay special thanks to Gerardo A. Andújar, Gabriel del Mazo, José Luis Romero, and Florentino V. and Horacio J. Sanguinetti for their invaluable assistance.

Thanks are also due to the many North Americans who read and commented upon my work. Professors Richard Fagen, David M. Potter, and John D. Wirth of Stanford University provided many insightful and thought-provoking criticisms of my study. My colleagues at Washington University, Professors William N. Chambers and Merle Kling, and Professor Seymour Martin Lipset of Harvard University, editor of this series, also read my work and provided me with valuable comments and support.

I owe a special debt of gratitude to my graduate advisor at

Stanford University, Professor John J. Johnson, who read this manuscript in both its original and revised form and provided me the benefits of his advice and constant encouragement.

A final word of thanks is due to my parents, Mr. and Mrs. David O. Walter, and to my grandmother, Mrs. John Van Horne, all three of whom helped me proofread this manuscript in its original form and shared with me the agonies and pleasures of its creation.

The responsibility for any errors in fact or interpretation in what follows is entirely mine.

Washington University   Richard J. Walter
St. Louis
June 1968

Contents

1 Argentina's Universities and Students 3

2 Antecedents to the University Reform 23

3 The University Reform of 1918 39

4 Reform and Counterreform, 1918–1930 63

5 Students and Conservatives, 1930–1943 87

6 Students and Perón, 1943–1955 119

7 Students and Reconstruction, 1955–1964 155

8 Conclusions 187

Bibliography 209

Index 225

Student Politics in Argentina

Argentina's Universities and Students

1

Before considering the actual historical development of the Argentine student movement, it is necessary to provide some brief but essential background information about the university system and the life of the student in Argentina. In both these respects, Argentina and Latin America are strikingly different from the United States. Keeping these differences in mind, I shall therefore discuss in this chapter the development of institutions of higher education in Argentina, the organization and administration of the Republic's universities, and some important characteristics of that country's student life and student organization. Wherever appropriate, these remarks will be related to explanations of student political activism. Finally, I shall summarize the most prevalent criticisms of higher learning in Argentina, criticisms which have a direct bearing on student political activity. The material for this chapter comes not only from written sources, but also from my own observations during a year's visit to Argentina in 1964.

The University of Córdoba was Argentina's first institution of higher learning. It was established in the city of Córdoba in 1613 by the Bishop of Tucumán, Jesuit Father Fernando Trejo y Sanabria. The University developed under Jesuit guidance until the expulsion of that order from Spanish America in 1767. The school then passed to the control of the Franciscans until 1858, at which time the national government under Justo José Urquiza assumed responsibility for its administration. Because of a tradition of Jesuit and Franciscan control and the strong Catholic position in Córdoba, the University remained closely connected with the church for many years after national jurisdiction was effected and religious influences in the professorial body, the administration, and the curriculum continued to be evident into the first decades of the twentieth century.

The Republic's second university, that of Buenos Aires, was founded in 1821. Bernardino Rivadavia, energetic minister of government and foreign affairs in the Buenos Aires provincial administration, was the principal force in the foundation and organization of the new institution. The University of Buenos Aires (UBA) at first remained quite limited in scope and enrollment. Under the dictator Juan Manuel de Rosas (1835–1852), who greatly restricted the exercise of academic freedom and did not promote the growth of the University, the UBA suffered two decades of stagnation. However, after the fall of Rosas the UBA began to develop into an important intellectual and cultural center. Its expansion during the last half of the nineteenth century was strongly supported by Presidents Bartolomé Mitre (1862–1868), Domingo Faustino Sarmiento (1868–1874), and Nicolás Avellaneda (1874–1880), all of whom recognized the importance of education for the social, economic, and political development of the Republic. In the twentieth century, the UBA paralleled the growth in size and influence of the capital city, Buenos Aires. By 1960 UBA was the largest and most influential university in the Republic, with an impressive reputation and prestige throughout Latin America.[1]

Argentina's third university was founded in 1890 in La Plata, capital city of Buenos Aires Province. In 1905 the University of La Plata (ULP) was placed under national jurisdiction. Under the dynamic leadership of its founder and first president, Joaquín V. González, the ULP soon attracted many able professors and students. A steady growth continued throughout the twentieth century, and by 1960 the ULP was second only to the University of Buenos Aires in number of students and academic reputation.

In the twentieth century, after a period of significant economic development and population growth, Argentina moved to diffuse culture and learning, which were tending to concentrate in and around the capital city. In response to this need, six new universities were established in the interior provinces between 1919 and 1958. These schools had their beginnings as small and loosely organized institutions, which were eventually placed under the control of the national government and strengthened in structure and administration.

The first of these was the National University of the Littoral (1919), with branches located in the cities of Santa Fe, Rosario, Paraná, and Corrientes. The University of the Littoral was followed by the National University of Tucumán (1921); the National University of Cuyo (1939), located in Mendoza; the National University of the South (1956), located in Bahía Blanca; the National University of the Northeast (1956), located in Resistencia; and the National University of La Pampa (1958), located in Buenos Aires Province.[2]

Each of these universities is under the auspices of the national government. This means that the federal administration in Buenos Aires is responsible for their financing and maintenance and has some controls over their administration. For most of the twentieth century Argentina had no private universities. Finally, by enactment of controversial legislation in 1958, the national government allowed the establishment of private Catholic universities in

Buenos Aires, Mendoza, Córdoba, and Santa Fe. Although their enrollments were only a small percentage of the nation's total student body in the early 1960's, by 1964 these new schools seemed firmly established and flourishing concerns.[3] Reviewing the historical development of Argentina's university system, the newness and the rapid growth of this system stand out as significant characteristics. Seven of the nine institutions were established as national universities in the twentieth century. The enrollment in Argentina's universities has paralleled and even outstripped the rapid population growth of the Republic. From 1918 to 1960, the number of university students increased ten times, from 14,745 to 155,004.[4] In 1918, of the Republic's approximately eight million citizens, only one in 571 was enrolled in a university. By 1960, of the nation's twenty million inhabitants, one in 129 was attending an institution of higher learning. In 1960 Argentina led all Latin America in total number of university students, claiming some 70,000 more than its nearest competitor, Brazil.[5]

In general, all of Argentina's universities are organized and administered along similar lines. These similarities stem from the fact that the Latin American university originally was modeled on the University of Salamanca in Spain, whose structure was adapted by Spanish colonial administrators to New World conditions. This pattern of organization has continued in most aspects down to the mid-twentieth century. Consequently, the University of Buenos Aires can serve as the model of the organization and administration of each of Argentina's institutions of higher education.

The University of Buenos Aires is divided into individual schools. These are called "faculties" and correspond roughly to the colleges of a university in the United States. A student chooses the academic career he desires to follow and enters the appropriate faculty. Ordinarily there is no interdisciplinary study. A student usually follows his program in only one faculty, which specializes exclusively in his particular course of study. In 1960, the UBA comprised ten faculties. These were the Faculties of Law and Social Sciences, Medical Sciences, Engineering, Philosophy and Letters, Agronomy, Economic Sciences, Dentistry, Architecture, Exact and Natural Sciences, and Pharmacy and Biochemistry. There is no central campus as we know it in the United States; the faculties are scattered throughout the city, each one commonly located in a single building. Nor is there a central library; instead each faculty has its own individual collection of books and research materials.

The administrative body of each faculty is the Directive Council (*Consejo Directivo*), composed of eight professors, four alumni, and four students. The administrative organ of the entire university is the Superior Council (*Consejo Superior*). This Council includes the deans of each faculty, five professors, five alumni, and five students. The final important administrative body is the University Assembly (*Asamblea Universitaria*), which represents the total membership of the university and is composed of the members of the Superior and Directive Councils. The University Assembly elects the presiding officers of the university, the rector and the vice-rector, both of whom serve four-year terms. The Assembly, among other responsibilities, deals with university legislation, financial matters, and disciplinary problems.

Moving from the university level back to the faculty, the dean is the executive head of this branch and he, along with the vice-dean, is elected every four years by the Directive Council. The latter are themselves selected in university-wide elections in which students, professors, and alumni participate. To insure that policy making reflects the changing composition and needs of the university, the various categories of representatives to the Directive Councils are chosen at different times: Professorial representatives are elected every four years, alumni representatives every two years, and student representatives every year. In addition to electing administrative officers, the Directive Councils choose new professors and periodically review the situation of established faculty members.[6] The relationship of Argentina's universities with the federal government was defined in 1885 by National Law Number 1597, the so-called "Ley Avellaneda." In the year of its enactment this law was applied to the Universities of Córdoba and Buenos Aires. As other universities were created, the legislation was extended to include them in its provisions. The "Ley" remained in effect until 1947, at which time President Juan D. Perón passed new legislation to insure his personal control over the universities. However, the basic provisions granted by the law were restored and strengthened after Perón's overthrow in 1955. From its inception the "Ley Avellaneda" has proved quite flexible. Consisting of only seven basic sections, the "Ley" has allowed for modifications and reforms which permit the Argentine educational system to adjust to modern conditions and needs without sacrificing the law's original spirit and purpose.

According to the "Ley Avellaneda," the Argentine university is theoretically free from state control. The law provides that the university should enjoy the right to govern itself and administer its own affairs, including the establishment of policing and disciplinary measures, the election of officials, and the management of internal funds. Police are not allowed to enter the university and federal intervention is prohibited, except under extraordinary circumstances or with the written request of a university official.

Despite the university's legal autonomy, the president of the Republic, usually acting through the minister of education, maintains various controls over the institution. For example, the president approves all new university statutes and the appointments of new professors. The most effective control is the annual approval of the university budget by the legislative and executive branches. Through this power of the purse string the national government has often been able to turn autonomy more into a concept than into a reality. It is difficult for a university to maintain an independent position if it must rely on the government for almost all its funds.

Defense of university autonomy has been one of the principal areas of concern for student politics in Argentina and all of Latin America. As is true of most legislation in Latin America, in Argentina the effectiveness of a law depends not so much on the fact that it has been enacted, but rather on the will of the controlling powers to respect and enforce it. For example, the colonial university in Latin America was legally entitled to freedom from governmental interference. But as Luis Alberto Sánchez remarks, when the university became a cauldron of revolutionary ideas in the late eighteenth century, governmental intervention in educational affairs increased.[7] So, too, as will be seen, university independence in twentieth-century Argentina has depended more on the willingness of the government to respect this privilege than on the provisions of the "Ley Avellaneda."

Student life in Argentina, as are university organization and administration, is more or less uniform throughout the Republic. Therefore, the example of the UBA can once again be applied generally to students in all of the nation's institutions of higher learning.

In Argentina, university careers normally begin at the age of eighteen. To enter the university a youth must possess a "bachelor's" degree, which certifies his graduation from a *colegio*. The *colegio* corresponds generally to the advanced years of a North American high school and the first two years of a North American university. It is designed to provide a broad-gauged education to prepare the student for his chosen career. To enter a particular faculty, the applicant must pass the required entrance examination. He then follows his academic program, which varies in length, depending on the faculty—usually from five to six years.

Most university students come from urban middle-class families, live at home, and commute to classes. A survey conducted in the Faculties of Philosophy and Letters, Exact Sciences, and Economic Sciences of the UBA in 1956 revealed that approximately 90 per cent of the students interviewed were from the middle and upper classes.[8] Two years later, a university-wide census in Buenos Aires indicated that about 91 per cent of the 58,684 university students polled belonged to middle-class families. The 1958 census also found that 72 per cent of the youths were living at home with their parents, that 85 per cent were unmarried, that 90 per cent were Argentine nationals, and that 65 per cent had been born in greater Buenos Aires.[9]

Finances play an important role in Argentine student life. The student pays no tuition in the national universities. But books and materials, particularly in law and medicine, are costly, and there are other "hidden" expenses for such items as clothing and transportation. Most of the university youth in Buenos Aires hold part-time or even full-time jobs. In 1958, according to the university census, only 12,406 of the 58,684 students interviewed were able to devote all their time to their studies; 32,102 replied that they worked five or more days a week.

There is very little campus social life in Argentina, especially in comparison with North American universities. Rarely are there university-sponsored dances, parties, or athletic events. There are no fraternities and sororities, nor are there dormitories or concentrated student housing. The lack of campus activities has often been mentioned as an explanation of political activism among the youth, the argument being that energies which ordinarily would be directed toward social affairs are channeled into political participation. Nonetheless, it should be noted that the social life of the Argentine student outside the university, particularly in Buenos Aires, is quite active. In my opinion, there are fewer "bored" or "beat" students in the UBA than on the average North American campus.

Within the university, the Argentine student elects a career-oriented course of study which has a considerable influence on his social status and political activism. A very large number of youths enter faculties of law and medicine. According to statistics for 1960 from the Statistical Section of the Argentine Ministry of Education in Buenos Aires, the UBA Faculty of Medicine had 16,627 students and the Faculty of Law 10,502, a total of 27,129 which represents about 40 per cent of the University's enrollment. Since colonial times law and medicine have held first rank as prestige professions in Latin America, and the acquisition of the university degree in these academic disciplines continues to have importance for the Argentine. The possession of the degree, especially in these two professions, means more than just a key to professional practice and economic livelihood. It represents also an important step up on the ladder of social mobility. In a culture that does not look upon manual work with high regard, as has been the case not only in Argentina, but in Latin America generally, the possession of credentials which prove intellectual achievement is extremely important for social status. The significance of the university degree in Argentina can be seen, for example, in the common practice of calling the graduate by his title, "Doctor," rather than by his family name.[10]

Throughout Argentina's history there has been a close connection between university or scholarly achievements and national leadership, and most men in public life have been able to point with pride to professional degrees, informal intellectual activity, or both. Nineteenth-century Presidents Sarmiento and Mitre were outstanding journalists and authors of significant historical works in addition to being political leaders. Between the years 1853 and 1962, thirteen of the nation's twenty-seven presidents were lawyers (ten were military men).

The clear relationship between higher education and national leadership contributes to the formation of an acute political consciousness among many Argentine university students. A large number of students, particularly in the faculties of law and medicine, expect to enter eventually into the national political leadership—an expectation that stimulates their activism within the university. Many see their university experience as a testing ground for postgraduate activities on the larger national scene.

All these factors—the prestige of the university degree, the connection between a professional title and political leadership, and the large number of students who enter law and medicine—help to explain student political activity. It should be noted, however, that the importance of the university degree for economic and social success also acts as a negative influence by discouraging students from engaging in activities which might interrupt their important academic careers for long periods. In addition, the 1958 census of the UBA revealed that only 8,784 students could claim parents who were university graduates. Assuming that most Argentine parents plan for their children to rise above their own achievements, this is another factor which would tend to limit any activities likely to divert time from studies leading to a career.

An important characteristic of Argentine student life is the large percentage of "older" students within the university. According to Ministry of Education statistics for 1960, out of a total of 17,657 students enrolled in the UBA Faculty of Economic Sciences, 6,458 were over twenty-five years of age. In the same year, out of a total of 10,502 students enrolled in the UBA Faculty of Law, 3,615 were over twenty-five. The high percentage of students twenty-five years of age or older results from certain aspects of university life, primarily compulsory military service and the necessity for many students to earn an income while pursuing their studies. Flexibility in the taking of examinations and in the arrangement of schedules permits the student considerable freedom as to the time spent on his studies. Political interruptions, which often result in the closing of the university for long periods, may delay graduation. For example, between 1943 and 1955 student strikes against the national government frequently led to the postponement of examinations and constant delays in the beginning of classes. Moreover, the leaders of the disturbances during this period were often imprisoned or exiled for political reasons, actions that greatly lengthened the time it would take them to obtain a university degree.

The Argentine university is coeducational. Since 1918, women have constituted a significant percentage of the student body. By 1960 they represented almost one-third of the total number of students enrolled in the nation's institutions of higher education. Although women tend to concentrate in faculties of philosophy and letters, where they dominate numerically, they also enter faculties of law, medicine, and economic sciences in impressive numbers. Ministry of Education statistics for 1960 give the following female enrollment figures in the UBA: 3,386 out of a total of 4,567 in Philosophy and Letters; 3,136 out of 10,502 in Law; 3,995 out of 16,627 in Medicine; and 4,811 out of 17,657 in Economic Sciences.

Student political activity is carried on through organizations which co-ordinate actions within and among the universities of the Republic. The primary unit in this structure is the student center (*centro*). Each faculty has its own center, which is managed by and for the students. This organization usually provides a variety of student services: a library, a cafeteria which serves food and drinks at lower prices than do public restaurants, books at discount prices, athletic activities, round-table discussions, cinemas, representation of the student before the university authorities, and orientation for the entering student. One of the most important functions of many centers is the publication of a periodical. These publications are often among the best scientific and professional reviews in the nation. One such periodical is the *Revista de derecho y ciencias sociales* of the student center of the Faculty of Law in the University of Buenos Aires. Begun in 1906, the *Revista* publishes articles on legal, social, and political problems in addition to considering issues of university politics.[11]

The student center is administered through a general assembly and a directive council, the officers of which are elected annually by the members. The students at a faculty are not compelled to belong to the center, but most of them do; membership fees are nominal. Within a faculty there often are various smaller groups (*agrupaciones*), which may belong to the center or remain independent. Ordinarily these groups appear for specific political reasons and enjoy only a short life span.

Another important student organization is the university federation, which theoretically is representative of all students in the university. All faculty centers are represented in the federation, which also consists of a general assembly, a directive council, and elective officials chosen annually.[12] As of 1960, each major university in the nation had a student federation. Hereafter, these federations will be frequently referred to by their abbreviations, such as FUBA (*Federación Universitaria de Buenos Aires*). The others are FUC (Córdoba), FUS (Sur–Bahía Blanca), FUC (Cuyo –Mendoza), FUN (North–Tucumán), FUNE (Northeast–Resistencia), FUL (Littoral), and FULP (La Plata).

Theoretically, the *Federación Universitaria Argentina* or FUA (University Federation of Argentina) is representative of all the university youth in the nation. Founded in 1918, the FUA is one of the world's oldest student federations. It is ruled by a representative junta, made up of two delegates from each university federation. Officers of the organization are selected from its junta, and the junta and the officers act as the FUA's directive body. They meet in ordinary session every month, and in extraordinary session whenever necessary. Headquarters are located in Buenos Aires. Delegates and officials are elected each year and are allowed to serve consecutive terms. The functions of the FUA are to co-ordinate student activities in the nation and to represent Argentine student interests both at home and abroad.[13]

Throughout the period 1918–1964, numerous observers—both Argentine and foreign—criticized various aspects of the Republic's system of higher education. During these decades, the universities suffered from certain pervasive faults which have been reflected in the Republic's twentieth-century educational history. Many of these defects were inherited from traditions dating from the colonial period, but quite a number have resulted from the rapid growth of both the university and the nation in the twentieth century. The remarks that follow will refer primarily to the contemporary situation, but it should be emphasized that these conditions have prevailed generally for most of the twentieth century.

One of the most repeated criticisms of Argentine higher education is of the great emphasis given to the study of law and medicine. The disproportionately high number of students in selected professions often has undesirable consequences. The emphasis on law and medicine, it is argued, produces a severe lack of men trained in technical and administrative skills—a glaring gap in a country which urgently requires this kind of personnel. Compounding this problem is the exodus of the few trained technical and scientific graduates from Argentina, where their pay is low and their social prestige is negligible, to the more fertile fields of North America and Europe.

The number of new physicians and lawyers who flood the labor market every year results in a serious problem of economic assimilation as these professions become overcrowded and geographically concentrated. Unemployed professional men, usually located in Buenos Aires and unwilling to move to the interior provinces where they are desperately needed, can easily constitute a politically discontented group.[14] Many professional men, unable to find positions in their own specialties, turn to business or industry. However, lacking basic administrative and management skills and training, they are not an efficient manpower group. While postgraduate discontent does not relate to university students per se, students do have contact with graduates, especially through joint participation in university government, and they are very aware of the social and economic situations they will face upon receiving their degrees. Therefore, one motive for student political activity is to bring about changes in the national economic structure which will assure students of satisfying professional employment after graduation.

Despite the traditional importance of education in Argentina, the amount of national funds allotted to higher learning often does not meet the nation's educational needs. In 1964 UBA officials declared that they would need twice the number of pesos allotted to them by the national government to attend to the bare necessities of administering the institution.[15] A writer investigating the nation's educational budget between 1950 and 1963 found that, while the number of students enrolled in the nation's schools doubled during these years, government expenditure on education had not been increased to keep pace with new conditions.[16] The universities must depend almost exclusively upon national funds for operating budgets and expansion. Alumni contributions are rare, and grants from private industry or foreign foundations often encounter severe political difficulties.

The most visible result of the insufficient amount of money spent on education is the poor condition of university buildings. The situation improved somewhat in the post-1940 period in Buenos Aires, when new edifices for the Faculties of Law, Medicine, and Engineering were constructed. But as one North American observer pointed out in 1958, outmoded buildings are still in use and classroom space is difficult to find.[17] There have been attempts to improve these conditions through the proposed construction of "university cities," and under Perón land was set aside and several buildings were raised for this purpose. But by 1964 the "cities" had not progressed appreciably, and many of the new structures were being used for non-educational purposes.

Not only on the surface but also within the buildings, facilities are inadequate. In a number of faculties common comforts such as adequate heating, lighting, and sanitary facilities are often not available. Materials for experimentation in the scientific and medical courses are difficult to acquire and often entail a significant expense for the financially beleaguered student. Most of the university libraries are inadequately staffed and managed and rarely meet the needs of the students enrolled in the various faculties.

The university professor in Argentina also suffers from the lack of funds allotted to higher education. The larger number of faculty members in Argentina are very poorly paid. The low salaries in turn create part-time professors. Most university teachers are engaged in outside careers and travel to the universities only a few times a week to give lectures. This situation leads to a lack of professorial dedication to educational duties, poor and repetitious lectures, and very little student-professor contact; the lawyer or engineer who must rush back to his office to meet a new client has little time to discuss the fine points of his lecture with his students. The 1958 UBA census showed that only 10,517 students regularly consulted with their professors; 47,875 replied that they met with their teachers only a few times or not at all. Occasionally an Argentine professor holds positions in two universities, this being most common in the Universities of Buenos Aires and La Plata. Students have remarked that these professors teach with a watch in one hand and a train schedule in the other.

A final characteristic of the Argentine professor is his political activism. Faculty members often have been among the most notable of political party leaders. Alfredo L. Palacios, for example, for more than half a century served as a representative of the Argentine Socialist party in the National Congress and also held important teaching and administrative positions in the Faculties of Law in Buenos Aires and La Plata. As will be seen in later chapters, the political involvement of their professors has had a direct effect upon the political activity of the Argentine university youth.

The actual situation within the classroom is another aspect of the Argentine university system which has received considerable critical attention. Since the 1918 Reform, attendance at lectures in theoretical subjects has not been obligatory. As a result, particularly because so many students have to work, not only is attendance at these classes irregular, but often the number of persons attending a lecture is only a small proportion of those enrolled. Referring once again to the UBA census of 1958, only 6,169 students claimed to attend the majority of their theoretical lectures. Critics point out that unregulated attendance leads to a lack of interest on the part of both students and professors and inhibits the development of consistent and meaningful intellectual interchange in the classroom. Furthermore, lectures often become mere monologues, with those students who attend furiously copying down every precious word in robot fashion. Ordinarily there are few questions and discussions are limited.[18]

A final criticism is the extremely high drop-out rate which has characterized the twentieth-century Argentine university. Argentina ranks among the world's leaders in the percentage of persons enrolled in institutions of higher learning, but there is a tremendous disparity between the number of persons who enter the university and those who eventually receive their degrees. Kalman H. Silvert has observed of the UBA: "With 58,684 enrolled students, the university granted only 3,324 degrees in 1958. . . . Drop-out rates for recent years vary as much as 80 per cent in Architecture to 64 per cent in Law and 44 per cent in Medicine." [19] In explaining this high drop-out rate, financial problems often play the most important role. Although the actual cost of education is not great, many families cannot afford to have a wage earner engaged in a non-income–producing activity for five or six years. Many families, which at first believe that they are capable of supporting a son or a daughter through a full university course, discover after a year or two the economic impossibility of their hopes and force their children to discontinue their studies. Equally important are the poor quality of secondary school training and preparation and the lack of vocational guidance and aptitude tests. A student often enters upon an academic career for reasons of social prestige and is soon disappointed when he finds himself completely uninterested in his subject or unprepared for the demands of his chosen profession.[20]

To sum up: The Argentine university system is large, extensive, and comprehensive. The university suffers, however, from many defects. Of particular concern to students have been the large numbers of part-time professors, the poor quality of the teaching, the insufficient national funds directed toward higher education, and the failure of university training to relate to reality and the solution of national problems. The following chapters will examine the reaction of the students to these conditions, describing how they have acted through their own organizations in attempts to improve not only their educational institutions but also the society at large with which their universities are intimately connected.

NOTES

Note: Among the most valuable works on the Argentine student movement for the years 1918 to 1940 are the documents and essays collected by Gabriel del Mazo in two editions, one of six volumes and one of three, and included under the general title *La reforma universitaria.* The first six-volume edition was published in 1926 and 1927 in Buenos Aires under the auspices of the Federación Universitaria de Buenos Aires (FUBA). The second edition, in three volumes, contains the material published in the 1926–1927 edition plus documents and essays that bring the work up to date as of 1940; it was published by the engineering students of the University of La Plata under the general editorship of del Mazo in 1941. Both editions are referred to in this book and are identified as follows: del Mazo, ed., *La reforma universitaria* (year–volume); for example, del Mazo, ed., *La reforma universitaria* (1941–Vol. III). Complete titles for all the volumes are listed in the bibliography.

1. In 1960 the enrollment of the University of Buenos Aires was 65,068 out of a national total of 155,004 university students. Enrollment in the other universities in 1960 was as follows: University of La Plata, 36,188; University of the Littoral, 19,361; University of Córdoba, 15,505; University of Tucumán, 6,228; University of Cuyo, 4,075; University of the Northeast, 2,892; University of the South, 552; and University of La Pampa, 31. See República Argentina, Ministerio de Educación y Justicia, *Estadística educativa,* "Establecimientos, alumnos y profesores" (cifras provisionales) (Buenos Aires, 1960).

2. For information on the history of Argentina's universities see Heloise Brainerd, "Higher Education in the Argentine Republic," *Bulletin of the Pan American Union,* LXIII (January 1929), 31–41; Tulio Halperin Donghi, *Historia de la Universidad de Buenos Aires* (Buenos Aires, 1962); Edmundo Lassalle, *The Universities in Argentina* (Washington, D.C., 1944); and Gabriel del Mazo, *Estudiantes y gobierno universitario* (2nd ed.; Buenos Aires, 1955), pp. 15–19.

3. Of a total 155,004 students enrolled in institutions of higher education in 1960, only 2,889 were listed as attending private universities. See República Argentina, Ministerio de Educación y Justicia, *Estadística educativa* for 1960.

4. The figure for 1918 is taken from República Argentina, Ministerio de Justicia e Instrucción Pública, *Estadística,* "Universidades nacionales-datos estadísticos relativos a los alumnos y profesores, correspondientes al año 1918" (Buenos Aires, 1919).

5. Ismael Rodríguez Bou, *La educación superior en América Latina* (Washington, D.C., 1963), p. 58.

6. For an extensive study of the Argentine university structure, including some of the differences among the nation's institutions, see Horacio J. Sanguinetti, *Régimen administrativo de la universidad* (Buenos Aires, 1963).

7. Luis Alberto Sánchez, *La universidad latinoamericana* (Guatemala City, Guatemala, 1949), p. 46.

8. Gino Germani, "Informe preliminar del Instituto de Sociología sobre las encuestas entre estudiantes universitarios," *Centro* (Revista del Centro de Estudiantes de Filosofía y Letras) (Buenos Aires, October 1956), p. 40.

9. Universidad de Buenos Aires, *Censo universitario* (Buenos Aires, 1959).

10. For comment on this practice see Tomás Roberto Fillol, *Social Factors in Economic Development: The Argentine Case* (Cambridge, Mass., 1961), pp. 17–18.

11. Horacio J. Sanguinetti, "Datos para una historia de la revista del centro de estudiantes de derecho (1906–1958)," *Revista de derecho y ciencias sociales* (Buenos Aires, Winter 1958), pp. 117–122.

12. Theoretically, all centers are members of the federation, but many of these groups disaffiliate from the larger organization for varying periods because of political or administrative disagreements.
13. "Acta de fundación de la Federación Universitaria Argentina (abril 11 de 1918)," del Mazo, ed., *La reforma universitaria* (1927–Vol. II), pp. 73–84.
14. For information on the role of unemployed intellectuals in the radical and Socialist movements in the emerging nations see Edward Shils, "The Intellectuals in the Political Development of the New States," in John H. Kautsky, ed., *Political Change in Underdeveloped Countries* (New York, 1962).
15. "Universidad: un polígono de tiroteo ideológico," *Primera plana* (Buenos Aires, June 30, 1964), p. 20.
16. See Francisco A. Mezzadri, "El gasto en educación en la Argentina," *La Nación* (Buenos Aires), December 6, 1964, Sec. 4, p. 6.
17. See Kalman H. Silvert's chapter on his teaching experience in the University of Buenos Aires (UBA), "Other People's Classrooms," in his *The Conflict Society: Reaction and Revolution in Latin America* (New Orleans, La., 1961), pp. 162–182.
18. Alberto Ciria y Horacio J. Sanguinetti, *Universidad y estudiantes: testimonio juvenil* (Buenos Aires, 1962), pp. 124–125.
19. Kalman H. Silvert, "The University Student," in John J. Johnson, ed., *Continuity and Change in Latin America* (Stanford, Calif., 1964), p. 214.
20. Roberto Mac-Lean y Estenós, *La crisis universitaria en Hispano-América* (Mexico, D.F., 1956), p. 70.

Antecedents to the University Reform

2

The University Reform movement which began in Córdoba in 1918 appeared against the background of various economic, political, and social developments which occurred in Argentina in the latter half of the nineteenth century and the first two decades of the twentieth. This chapter will summarize the internal changes and international events which profoundly affected the thinking of the young men who initiated the University Reform. The changes in education which occurred from 1900 to 1918 will also be examined, as will be the ideas of several Argentine intellectuals concerning the relationship between education and national development. Finally, the specific conditions present in Córdoba as an immediate backdrop to the student revolt of 1918 will be described.

Between the years marked by the fall of Juan Manuel de Rosas in 1852 and the outbreak of the Córdoba Reform in 1918, Argentina underwent a profound economic expansion based on the exploitation of its agricultural resources. In the last half of the nineteenth century wire fencing and improved breeds of cattle were introduced, regulating and stimulating the nation's beef production—the backbone of the Republic's economic growth in that era. During these years, Argentina's extensive railroad system was constructed to carry agricultural products from the interior to the port cities of Rosario and Buenos Aires for export. Along the coast, principally in Buenos Aires, meat-packing plants arose to process beef and mutton for transport across the Atlantic in refrigerator ships. By the end of the nineteenth century, Argentina was one of the world's leading producers of agricultural products and depended primarily upon the export of meat and grain for its foreign exchange and credits.

While techniques to make the rich land produce changed during these decades, patterns of land ownership did not. *Estancias* (large estates), containing thousands of acres of land and immense herds of cattle, dominated the nation's agricultural economy. The control of the *estancias* remained in the hands of a privileged few families. Realizing enormous profits during the agricultural boom of the late 1800's, the landowners joined with their economic partners—the merchants and bankers of Buenos Aires—to form a political oligarchy which controlled the national government from 1880 to 1916. This oligarchy based its political control on keeping the size of the electorate limited and relied on their financial power to insure that administrations remained sympathetic to their economic and social interests. Conservative politically, the oligarchy was liberal economically, favoring laissez-faire trade policies as long as the results were beneficial to their own ends.

During these decades the Republic experienced growths and shifts in its population which were to affect the Conservatives' political control of the nation. Between 1895 and 1914 the population of the Republic doubled, increasing from approximately four million as counted by the second national census to approximately eight million as determined by the third census. Despite Argentina's dependence upon agriculture, the Republic's population became more urban than rural by the first years of the twentieth century. In 1869, the first census had shown 25 per cent of the Republic's citizens living in cities, 75 per cent on farms. By 1914, the ratio was 53 per cent urban to 47 per cent rural.[1] The growth and shift of the Argentine population were greatly affected by the influx of European immigrants during these years. From 1881 to 1910, more than two million immigrants came to and remained in Argentina, the largest number arriving from Italy and Spain.[2] Nearly all these immigrants either remained in the cities or returned to them after unsuccessful attempts at farming in the interior. The majority of the newcomers settled in Buenos Aires, where they generally found work in factories or began small businesses. They were discouraged in farming, because small operations were too easily overshadowed and overwhelmed by the predominant pattern of large-scale ownership and operation.

The increased tempo of trade and immigration between Argentina and Europe in the late nineteenth century was paralleled by an importation of political ideas from the Continent, ideas which were applied to Argentine conditions. Faced with a Conservative political system based on Spencerianism and laissez-faire liberalism, the immigrants began to introduce some of the revolutionary political theories which had swept Europe after 1848. From Spain and Italy came Anarcho-Syndicalists. Socialism and Communism were also introduced, and Argentine intellectuals began to explore the writings of Karl Marx, Friedrich Engels, and Eduard Bernstein. The urban worker, native and immigrant, confronted with poor working and living conditions, began to organize into small unions and co-operative groups. By 1905 the largest and most influential of these, the *Federación Obrera Regional Argentina* or FORA (Argentine Regional Labor Federation), had come under Anarchist influence and began to agitate by means of strikes and violence for improved social and economic conditions.[3]

New political parties also appeared in these years. Representative of the nation's growing middle classes was the *Unión Cívica de la Juventud* (Civic Union of Youth), organized in 1889 with lawyer Leandro N. Alem as its chief spokesman. Three years later the original *Unión Cívica* split into two groups, the more important of which was the *Unión Cívica Radical* (Radical Civic Union, more commonly known as the Radical party). Under the leadership of Hipólito Irigoyen, the Radical party organized to gain support from the various sectors of the middle class and the working classes as a way of wresting political power from the Conservatives. In 1894 an intelligent and able physician, Juan B. Justo, broke with Irigoyen and the Radicals and established the Argentine Socialist party. Attracting intellectuals and immigrants, the Socialists gained strength among the nascent labor organizations. Also splitting with Irigoyen at this time was a political leader from Sante Fe Province, Lisandro de la Torre, who formed the *Partido Demócrata Progresista* (Democratic Progressive party) of middle-class orientation. Following this "schism" pattern of political party formation, a group from the Socialist party broke from the parent organization and established the Argentine Communist party in January, 1918. Claiming that the Justo Socialists had taken a "soft" stand with regard to World War I and the Russian October Revolution, this group adopted the rubric *Partido Socialista Internacionalista* (International Socialist party).[4]

By 1900, Argentina's growing middle classes began to bring heavy pressure to bear upon the Conservative national administrations to expand the electoral base by easing franchise requirements. This pressure was effective and in 1912, during the presidency of Conservative Roque Sáenz Peña, legislation was approved extending the secret and obligatory ballot to all males over eighteen years of age. Four years later, in 1916, the Radicals, behind their candidate for president, Hipólito Irigoyen, won a close victory in the national elections. In capturing control of the executive branch of the national administration, the Radicals terminated the long rule of the oligarchy.

The emergence of new groups to political power affected the thinking of many young Argentines attending the Republic's universities immediately prior to the Córdoba Reform. The triumph of Irigoyen and the Radicals in 1916 seemed to indicate the establishment of effective and honest democratic procedures after many decades of narrowly based Conservative dominance. Many students began to discuss the possibility of extending the processes of democracy from the national level to the university and started to argue that all sectors in the institutions of higher learning, including professors and students, should participate in university administration.

In addition to these domestic developments, international events began to influence the thinking of Argentina's university youth. The Mexican Revolution of 1910 and the resultant constitution of 1917 emphasized reforms which favored the workingman and the rural peasant and undermined the privileged position of the landed interests and the church hierarchy. Events in Mexico indicated to the Argentines that significant changes were taking place in other areas of Latin America.

World War I was particularly important for the young men who implemented the University Reform. For many intellectuals and students the war represented the culminating failure of nineteenth-century ideas and institutions. Looking to their own country, young Argentines sought to eliminate European influences to insure that Argentina would not be forced to suffer involvement in a similar holocaust and perhaps lose the cream of her manhood in the way of England, France, and Germany. Gabriel del Mazo, participant in the 1918 Reform, later wrote that, "Faced with European civilization in crisis, the intellectual leadership of Europe was broken and there arose for the youth the vital need to save our people from the fate of the European people." [5]

Against this background of the apparent failure of capitalism, established religion, and nineteenth-century political philosophies, the Bolshevik Revolution of 1917 had an exhilarating effect on many Argentine youths. During the Revolution the news from Russia was incomplete and limited. But the basic outlines of the story were known. The reactionary czarist regime had been overthrown by a group of young intellectuals. The Bolsheviks had combined theories of social redemption with swift, organized action in an effort to pull their country out of the war. For the young Argentine, unaware of the full implications of Marxist-Leninist theories, the Revolution seemed to announce a new era of democratic rule and social justice in the Western world. Julio V. González, an important figure in the University Reform, captured the spirit of how the Russian experience affected the youth of the Republic, when he wrote in an article devoted to Vladimir Ilyich Lenin: "We say that Bolshevism is an elevation of the human spirit toward peace and love, a creative idea, a new philosophy and morality." [6] Undoubtedly, the spirit of the Revolution, its idealistic goals, and its claimed emphasis on social justice had a tremendous attraction for a postwar generation which felt itself part of a new historical cycle.[7]

Against the new forces which seemed to be enveloping their nation, the Conservatives of Argentina attempted to maintain a hold upon those institutions which had been traditionally under their influence. One of these was the university. Dominating economically and politically, the oligarchy was also influential socially and culturally in the late nineteenth century. They controlled the Universities of Buenos Aires and Córdoba, using the faculties of these institutions to train their sons as their successors. However, by the first years of the twentieth century the universities were also starting to show signs of change, as representatives of the emerging middle class began to enter the institutions.

Many of the educational modifications which took place in the early twentieth century were directed by professors and students, who sought to make Argentina's universities leaders rather than followers in the progressive development of the nation. In 1903, the students in the Faculty of Law of the University of Buenos Aires (UBA) went on strike to protest what they believed were injustices in the examination system. Discontent and demonstrations continued in the following years, and the law students were joined by their comrades from the Faculty of Medicine, who struck against favoritism in the administration of the Faculty. Too often the medical professors were selected for personal or political reasons rather than for intellectual and educational ability. By 1906, after considerable agitation, the UBA students' demands, which had expanded to include a more extensive reform, were finally met. Directive Councils with professorial representation were created. According to new regulations, members of the councils were to serve for specific periods and to be elected or re-elected by vote of the entire professorial body. As a model for future movements and as proof that student action could bring about significant changes within the university, this early campaign was an important antecedent to the Córdoba Reform of 1918.[8]

With the growth in size of the Argentine universities and the desire of the youth to play a more active role within them, students began to organize so as to co-ordinate their actions and to provide social and cultural services. Between 1900 and 1905 student centers were established in the Faculties of Law, Medicine, and Engineering in the University of Buenos Aires. In 1908 the felt need for a university-wide student organization was met with the foundation of the *Federación Universitaria de Buenos Aires* (FUBA). Following the example of Buenos Aires, students formed centers and federations in the Universities of La Plata and Santa Fe. In 1914 and 1915 a group from the UBA, under the leadership of Osvaldo Loudet, who was president of both the center of the Faculty of Medicine and the FUBA, tried to establish a national student federation. The project was greeted with initial enthusiasm, but at that time failed to arouse sufficient interest to permit its organization.[9]

There were other evident changes in the spirit and structure of the nation's universities in these years. An influential factor in changing the concepts of higher education in Argentina was the organization and administration of the new University of La Plata (ULP). Under the far-sighted direction of Joaquín V. González, this institution adopted many modern educational concepts from the United States and Europe. The ULP opened its doors to a broad range of students and to a wide variety of ideas, attempted to deal with community problems, and worked to establish closer contacts between professors and students. The University attracted liberal scholars and acquired a nationwide reputation and influence for its modern outlook. The UBA, located in the port city, was constantly under the impact of new ideas and currents and gradually began to modernize its structure and its professorial body. In 1910 it accepted as professor in the Faculty of Law the brilliant young Socialist politician and intellectual, Alfredo L. Palacios. Despite the resignation of several faculty members, who protested the first appointment of a Socialist to such a position, Palacios remained and established himself as a competent and influential scholar.[10]

A most important factor influencing the thought and action of the Reform generation was the intense intellectual activity which characterized Argentina between 1900 and 1920. During this period writers of the caliber of José Ingenieros, Ricardo Rojas, Leopoldo Lugones, and Alejandro Korn gave the Republic unquestioned leadership in Latin America in serious scholarship and the development of social, economic, and political thought. Generally, these men concerned themselves—often in an introspective and critical manner—with the origins, history, social composition, and future of their nation. Carlos Octavio Bunge, professor in the Faculty of Law and Social Sciences of the UBA, carefully analyzed and criticized the traditions and conditions in Latin America which led to political anarchy and caudillismo. Another university professor and prominent critic was Alejandro Korn, leader of the

Argentine anti-positivists and a staunch supporter of the University Reform. Leopoldo Lugones, Manuel Gálvez, and Ricardo Rojas emphasized the importance of a sense of nationalism for the country's future. Influential for the university youth was Rojas, who called for changes within the educational system which would produce a comprehensive, cohesive, and native national spirit.[11]

The Argentine intellectual who had the greatest impact upon the Reform generation was the young and versatile José Ingenieros. Author of impressive works on sociology, history, and philosophy, Ingenieros delineated the problems confronting the new generation and then offered suggestions as to how these might be solved. In 1915 he took a teaching position in the Faculty of Philosophy and Letters of the UBA and in the same year established the important periodical *Revista de filosofía*. The pages of this publication were filled with new social and political theories and included articles favoring university reform.

World War I, Wilsonian democracy, and the Bolshevik Revolution greatly stimulated Ingenieros. Like many of his generation, he saw a decadent Europe crumbling from within and a new Russia beginning a bold, progressive experiment. In his writings, which were widely read in Latin America, Ingenieros began to emphasize the need to accept social responsibility, the importance of a sense of nationalism, and the necessity of combating dogma with truth. He saw his own country and continent beginning a new era—one marked by social progress and democratic equality and led by men of a new generation. He argued that the motive forces in history were small groups of young men who brought about change through the power of their intellects and the completeness of their actions. Ingenieros foresaw a bright future for Latin America in the postwar years, when the leadership in the area would fall to the youth graduating from institutions of higher learning.

Ingenieros dealt directly with the problem of the university in a changing society in a speech presented at the Second Pan-

American Scientific Congress held in Washington, D.C., in 1916. In this brief essay, entitled *La universidad del porvenir* ("The University of the Future"), he outlined the basic themes which the Argentine youth adopted and put into action two years later. Ingenieros began by stating that "the university ought to be a school of social action adapted to its surroundings and its time." He argued that the universities of Latin America, traditionally characterized by medieval dogmatism and intellectual isolationism, should adjust to new conditions and necessities and become "American" institutions, dealing with national problems and producing insightful and responsible men capable of providing progressive leadership in the promising postwar years. In addition, he urged a democratization of the university, to wrest it from oligarchical control and to make higher education available to all who were capable of it, regardless of their social or economic condition. In sum, Ingenieros expressed concisely and forcefully the opinions and desires of many intellectuals who hoped to make the Latin American university a forward-looking and socially active institution.[12]

One result of the intellectual activity of Ingenieros and his colleagues in these years was the appearance of small cultural groups, many having close contact with the Argentine universities. In these organizations new ideas and philosophies were discussed in lectures, round tables, and informal talks. One of the most important of these groups was the *Ateneo Universitario*, formed under the leadership of José María Monner Sans in 1914. Composed of students from various faculties of the UBA, it listed among its initial membership several youths who were active in the 1918 Reform. In 1915 the *Ateneo* began to publish a periodical concerned with social, cultural, political, and philosophical themes, listing among its contributors such men as Ricardo Rojas, Leopoldo Lugones, and José Ingenieros, as well as many student authors. Until its demise in 1920 the *Ateneo* remained a strong advocate of university reform.[13]

In the period 1900–1918 the influence of new intellectual currents and the various changes made in higher education were restricted by and large to the Buenos Aires–La Plata area. The
University of Córdoba, located in a city geographically and economically remote from the national capital and possessing a strong
colonial, Catholic, and Conservative tradition, remained relatively
unaffected by the new forces evident in the port city. This school
was a perfect example of the socially remote university which
young liberals such as Ingenieros were seeking to reform. The
University of Córdoba suffered from Conservative control of the
administration, nepotism and part-time professorship, and a heavy
religious influence in the content of textbooks and lectures. The
institution appeared incapable of meeting the needs of a modern
and fast-moving society; in fact, it seemed to be resisting any
attempts to bring it into the twentieth century. A trip by Socialist
party Deputy Juan B. Justo to Córdoba just prior to the 1918
Reform revealed that the University's libraries did not contain a
single volume by Karl Marx, Friedrich Engels, or Charles Darwin.
In a speech to the National Chamber of Deputies, Justo also reported that the University did not respect the right of students or
professors to hold dissenting ideas or opinions.[14]

Despite Córdoba's isolation, the city did not remain completely
untouched by the developments occurring in the nation. By
1915, liberal ideas were beginning to leave their mark on several
young intellectuals. One of the first signs of this influence was a
speech given by Deodoro Roca, a young graduate of the local
university. Delivered in December, 1915, during the presentation
of diplomas in the University of Córdoba, the address was a fiery
call to action. In many respects echoing the ideas of Ingenieros,
Roca criticized the sterile scientism and worship of facts which
dominated the school. He pleaded for a university which would
initiate and direct change and produce men capable of solving the
problems Argentina would face in the future. As a means of

implementing this reform, Roca urged the students of Córdoba to make the present reality coincide with the future ideal through collective effort and action.[15]

In the wake of this talk, there was a significant growth of liberal influence in Córdoba and a small, talented, and dedicated group of university students and graduates began to discuss and promote the ideas of university reform. In 1916 *Ideas,* the magazine of the *Ateneo Universitario,* was introduced into Córdoba. At the same time these young rebels began to hold conferences on controversial subjects. Author Arturo Capdevila gave the first lecture in this series, which was attended by the men leading this intellectual activity in Córdoba, most notably the recent university graduates Deodoro Roca, Arturo Orgaz, and Saúl Alejandro Taborda. In his talk, Capdevila made a comparison between the tenets of the Buddhist and Catholic religions, representative of the themes which interested the liberals at that time. Later in the year, while introducing Alfredo L. Palacios to a Córdoba gathering, Arturo Orgaz openly criticized the University and the forces which controlled it. In 1917, more organizations and groups professing progressive ideas were formed. From a nucleus of students in the Faculty of Law of the University of Córdoba came a new periodical, *Cultura.* This publication served as an additional sounding board for Córdoba's young and active intellectuals.[16]

The strong Catholic and Conservative elements in Córdoba reacted with vigor against these developments. To combat the spreading influence of the liberal groups, the clerical and proclerical forces organized to battle for the minds and sympathies of the young people of the nation. In Córdoba an influential Catholic group, the *Corda Frates,* played an important role in the struggle against the new liberalism. A semi-secret organization, it included among its membership representatives from the church hierarchy, the local government, and the University. In 1917 these elements attempted to establish a *Federación de Estudiantes Católicos*

(Federation of Catholic Students) as an alternative to the reform-minded student groups appearing in Argentina's universities. The program of this new *Federación,* which never became a really effective organization, advocated full support for Catholic and "patriotic" professors, urged the use of textbooks which glorified the Argentine tradition, opposed the new scientific and philosophical works being introduced into the country's educational system, and criticized Joaquín V. González and the University of La Plata for their supposed ultra-liberalism and anti-clericalism.[17]

By the end of 1917 Córdoba appeared a divided city. A number of young men, acutely aware of the profound changes which had occurred in the Republic and inspired by the revolutionary and messianic hopes of the postwar period, prepared to grapple with the primary obstacle, as they saw it, to twentieth-century progress and development—the nineteenth-century University of Córdoba. The Conservatives, shaken by the political and economic changes which had undermined their control of the nation and its institutions, fearful of the new theoretical currents which seemed to bode a further deterioration of their position, and respectful of the traditions which had served them so long and so well, prepared to defend their university against all attempts at reform.

In 1918 the Conservatives lost the first battle in the confrontation, but they knew other victories as the clash between the two elements continued down through the twentieth century. In many ways this liberal-conservative, or pro-Reform–anti-Reform, confrontation, as developed in the years preceding the 1918 University Reform, served as an important background for subsequent student political action. Indeed, student and university political events were often a reflection on a smaller scale of a similar clash on the national scene.

NOTES

1. Figures from James R. Scobie, *Argentina: A City and a Nation* (New York, 1964), p. 276.
2. Thomas F. McGann, *Argentina, the United States and the Inter-American System, 1880–1914* (Cambridge, Mass., 1957), pp. 10–11.
3. S. Fanny Simon, "Anarchism and Anarcho-Syndicalism in South America," *Hispanic American Historical Review*, XXVI (February 1946), 40.
4. According to Robert J. Alexander, the new Communist party, although active in trade unions, could claim only 1,400 members in 1919. See his *Communism in Latin America* (New Brunswick, N.J., 1957), p. 156. The relative strength of the Republic's major political parties as revealed by popular votes in the 1916 presidential election was as follows: Radical party, 339,332; Conservatives, 153,406; Democratic Progressives, 123,637; and Socialists, 52,895. See Alfredo Galletti, *La política y los partidos* (Buenos Aires, 1961), p. 47.
5. Gabriel del Mazo, *La reforma universitaria y la universidad latino-americana* (Buenos Aires, 1957), p. 11. All translations from the Spanish are mine.
6. Julio V. González, *La reforma universitaria* (Buenos Aires, 1927), Vol. II, p. 174. This work should be distinguished from those with the same title edited by del Mazo.
7. For further information concerning the effects of World War I and the Bolshevik Revolution on Argentine intellectuals see José Ingenieros, *Los tiempos nuevos: reflexiones optimistas sobre la guerra y la revolución* (Madrid, 1921).
8. Partido Socialista, *La reforma universitaria y el partido socialista* (Buenos Aires, 1945), pp. 5–8; "Petitorio de reforma a la ley de universidades presentado al congreso por los estudiantes, durante el movimiento en la facultad de medicina de Buenos Aires (1905–1907)," del Mazo, ed., *La reforma universitaria* (1927–Vol. II), pp. 191–197; and Nicolás Repetto, *Hombres y problemas argentinos* (Buenos Aires, 1945), pp. 71–79.
9. Osvaldo Loudet, "Los orígenes de la Federación Universitaria Argentina," *Revista de psiquiatría y criminología* (Buenos Aires, May–June 1946), pp. 173–184.
10. Antonio Herrero, "Acción universitaria de Alfredo L. Palacios," *Nosotros* (Buenos Aires), XLVII (1924), 372–387.
11. Representative works by these authors include Carlos Octavio Bunge, *Nuestra América* (Barcelona, 1903); Alejandro Korn, *Influencias filosóficas en la evolución nacional* (Buenos Aires, 1936); and Ricardo Rojas, *La restauración nacionalista* (Buenos Aires, 1909).

12. José Ingenieros, "La universidad del porvenir," in *La universidad del porvenir y otros escritos sobre filosofía, educación y cultura* (Buenos Aires, 1956), pp. 15–37.

13. José María Monner Sans, *Historia del "Ateneo Universitario" (1914–1920)* (Buenos Aires, 1930).

14. Juan B. Justo, *El conflicto universitario de Córdoba* (Buenos Aires, 1918), p. 12.

15. See the speech entitled "Ciencias, maestros y universidades" in Deodoro Roca, *Ciencias, maestros y universidades* (Buenos Aires, 1959), pp. 13–21.

16. Julio V. González, *La universidad: teoría y acción de la reforma* (Buenos Aires, 1945), pp. 25–27; and "Los años 1916 y 1917 en Córdoba (crónica sumaria)," del Mazo, ed., *La reforma universitaria* (1927–Vol. II), pp. 208–214.

17. "Antecedentes sobre los sucesos de la Universidad de Córdoba," *Revista de filosofía* (Buenos Aires, 1918), pp. 135–145; and Sergio Bagú, "La pre-reforma," *Revista de la facultad de ciencias médicas y del centro de estudiantes de medicina* (La Plata, May–June 1938), p. 135.

The University Reform of 1918

―――――――――――― 3 ――――――――――――

The most significant result of the 1918 University Reform in Córdoba was the introduction of profound changes in the organization and orientation of higher education in Argentina, and later in all of Latin America. The reforms which the youth of Córdoba demanded and achieved continue, with modifications, as apparently permanent characteristics of Latin American university education. This chapter will discuss the educational changes initiated in 1918, underscoring the important fact that student political activity has been intimately connected with the achievement and maintenance of these reforms. Moreover, the actions and declarations of student organizations in the events of 1918 will be described in some detail. The Córdoba Reform awakened and sustained an active political interest among the university youth and also established patterns of action, methods of organization, and means of expression which have been followed by Argentine students down to the mid-1960's. Finally, attention will be given to those students, recent graduates, professors, and politicians who participated in the Córdoba Reform. Many of the "men of '18" continued in subsequent decades to participate in university politics and national affairs. They also authored many books and articles dealing with the Córdoba movement and later aspects of student action.

The initial issue which touched off the Córdoba Reform movement was of relatively minor importance. In late 1917, against the backdrop of the developing liberal-conservative confrontation in Córdoba, a group of students from the Faculties of Medicine and Engineering protested the closing of a boardinghouse which had served as a dormitory for medical students in the local university. In December, 1917, the medical students sent an extensive report to National Minister of Education José S. Salinas, in which they complained of the closing of the dormitory and also took the opportunity to plead for a larger reform which would eliminate nepotism and incompetence among the faculty members of the University. The youth suggested as a first step toward reform the renovation of the administrative councils, appointments to which up to that time had been regarded as almost self-perpetuating posts by Córdoba's Conservative professors.[1]

The movement for reform began as a co-ordinated effort on March 14, 1918, when the *Comité pro-Reforma* (Committee for Reform), representing the students of the University of Córdoba, called a general strike and boycott of classes until their demands for change were recognized. In their first manifesto, the youths attacked what they believed were the intellectual immorality and lack of an objective, scientific spirit within the University, and called for changes in method and orientation which would replace backwardness and decay with progress and growth. The students also criticized the religious influences and oligarchical control of the institution. They argued that all peaceful means of reform had been exhausted and that a general strike was their only remaining alternative.[2]

Despite the student strike and the threat of increased agitation, the officials of the University of Córdoba refused to accede to the Reformistas' demands. In response, the students determined to press forward with their activities and to arouse public sympathy and support for their cause. On March 31, the Committee for Reform held a large public rally in Córdoba.[3] The principal speakers were Arturo Capdevila and Arturo Orgaz, men who had been influential in the pre-1918 liberal activities in Córdoba; Gregorio Bermann, who was the representative of the *Federación Universitaria de Buenos Aires* (FUBA) to Córdoba; and three leaders of the student committee, Horacio Valdés (law), Gumersindo Sayago (medicine), and Ismael Bordabehere (engineering). The manifesto issued from this meeting reiterated the reasons for the strike and emphasized the need to form a university organized in such a way as to produce men capable of "struggling for the nation's progress, quick to realize the country's destiny in the consortium of modern societies." [4]

The strike was a notable success and the Córdoba professors faced almost completely empty classrooms on April 1, the day scheduled for the opening of the school year. In reaction to the student rebellion, the university officials decided to close the school until the agitation ceased. From this date the conflict began to change from a local educational dispute to an issue of national importance. In the first weeks of April, the two contending groups within the University of Córdoba sent delegations to Buenos Aires to seek the intervention of President Hipólito Irigoyen on their behalf. The authorities of the University sent to the capital two professors who, in interviews with the press, agreed that reforms in Córdoba were necessary, but who also added that the students seemed excessive and unreasonable in their demands. The two delegates from the Committee for Reform, Gumersindo Sayago and Horacio Valdés, carried with them extensive reports which outlined in detail the student arguments for reform.

Both delegations held lengthy meetings with Minister of Education Salinas and President Irigoyen. On April 11, Irigoyen decided to intervene in the conflict and assigned to his attorney general, José Nicolás Matienzo, the role of intervenor. Matienzo was instructed to investigate thoroughly the causes of the student revolt and to adopt measures for resolving the situation and reopening the University.

One of the most important results of the Córdoba campaign at this time was to stimulate new interest in forming a national student federation. The actions of the Córdoba students had aroused the concern and received the support of the majority of Argentina's university youth. While in Buenos Aires, for example, the Córdoba delegates were accompanied and encouraged in their meetings by officials and representatives of the FUBA. On April 11, the same day as the announced Matienzo intervention, a meeting was held in the University of Buenos Aires to organize the *Federación Universitaria Argentina* (FUA). Among the initial founders and primary leaders of the new federation were Osvaldo Loudet, chosen as first president of the nationwide organization, and other such Reform figures as Gregorio Bermann (FUBA), Gabriel del Mazo (FUBA), Guillermo Watson (FUBA), and Sayago and Valdés of Córdoba.

At this first meeting, the statutes of the FUA were approved and the organization's purposes were stated. The federation was to promote a spirit of solidarity among all the nation's students, protect student interests, advocate educational improvements, make known cultural achievements both within and outside the Republic, and represent the Argentine university youth in international student meetings. In the addresses which followed the discussion of organizational matters, the various founders emphasized the need to reform the nation's universities. The audience of some 500 youths listened with interest to Horacio Valdés' reports on the situation in Córdoba. Finally, the FUA pledged its full support to the Córdoba delegation and called for a nationwide student congress to discuss the general needs of Argentine higher education.[5]

When presidential intervenor Matienzo arrived in Córdoba on April 16, he initiated his intervention by urging that the normal functioning of the University be resumed. In co-operative response the students terminated their strike and returned to their classrooms. Matienzo then undertook his investigation of the situation in Córdoba and prepared a report which contained recommendations for change in the University which were to be submitted for presidential consideration. In his message the intervenor suggested that the faults of the institution could be traced, in part, to the lack of change among the members of the academic councils. He therefore urged that the chief executive approve student demands for periodic elections to council positions, the prohibition of representatives serving on both the Superior and Directive Councils, and university elections with the participation of the full professorial body. On May 7 President Irigoyen decreed that these suggested changes in the university statutes be made effective. As a result of the Matienzo intervention and the Irigoyen decree, all administrative posts in the University of Córdoba were declared vacant and elections to choose new officials were scheduled for the end of May.

Although the Matienzo reforms did not satisfy all the demands of the Reformistas, the young men of Córdoba were filled with optimism because of their initial success and continued to campaign for reform. On May 16 the student leaders replaced the Committee for Reform with the *Federación Universitaria de Córdoba* (FUC) (University Federation of Córdoba). This organization affiliated with the FUA and assumed the leadership of the Reform struggle in Córdoba. The FUC began the publication of a periodical devoted to student issues and on May 21 sent a telegram of congratulations to President Irigoyen, praising his attitude and actions with respect to the Matienzo intervention.

When new officials were selected to fill administrative posts at the end of May, the pro-Reform students were encouraged by the choice of one of their favorites—engineering professor Belisario Caraffa—to take the position of vice-rector. The election of the rector of the University, to be chosen by vote of the entire professorial body, was scheduled for June 15. As its candidate for this all-important office, the FUC announced Professor Enrique Martínez Paz of the Faculty of Law. Martínez Paz, young, not connected with the traditional groups within the University, and of a moderately liberal orientation, represented student aspirations for a more thoroughgoing reform.

The voting for the new rector took place, as planned, on the afternoon of June 15 in the main hall of the University of Córdoba. Fresh from a rally the night before in support of their candidate, the pro-Reform students jammed the room where the professors were met to choose the new executive. There were three principal candidates: the FUC-favored Martínez Paz and Conservative professors Alejandro Centeno and Antonio Nores. On the first two votes no candidate was able to gain a majority. However, on the third ballot Nores was elected. The students, who had fully expected the triumph of their candidate, reacted violently against the choice of Nores, a known Conservative connected with the Córdoba Catholic society *Corda Frates*. Even before the final results could be announced the students began a large-scale riot, breaking windows, shouting anti-clerical and anti-Conservative slogans, and attacking a Jesuit chapel connected with the University.

General disorder continued for several hours. The rioting students drove police and professors from the University and took control of the school buildings. During the tumult they were addressed and encouraged by FUC leaders Enrique F. Barros and Ismael Bordabehere and by graduates Deodoro Roca and Saúl Alejandro Taborda. Finally, the students left the University and paraded through the city in search of popular support. During their march the youth vowed to boycott classes until Nores offered his resignation. The next day the FUC sent a telegram to Minister of Education Salinas requesting a new intervention by the executive. The federation also directed a message to José Nicolás Matienzo, in which it claimed that his reform had been betrayed: "In place of a democracy a new despotism would have been inaugurated today." [6]

On the basis of newspaper accounts and the large number of signatures affixed to the FUC declarations, a large majority of Córdoba's students seems to have supported the strike of June 15. Nevertheless, there was a small but influential group of students and professors who opposed the actions of the Reformistas. These elements, after the tumultuous election riot, formed an anti-Reform organization, the *Comité por Defensa de la Universidad* (Committee for the Defense of the University). Conservative and Catholic in its composition, the *Comité* refused to join the general strike and supported the election of Nores. In the days that immediately followed the June 15 outbreak, the Defense Committee sent telegrams to various newspapers in which they criticized the violence which had occurred in the University as a result of the Reform movement. The anti-Reform organization also sent a delegation to interview President Irigoyen and to seek his intervention in the University on their behalf. A declaration issued by the *Comité,* signed by 300 members, stated the goal of the group at this time: "We proclaim once more, and in loud voice, that the committee has no other purpose than the defense of the University for the culture and liberty of everyone." [7]

Another result of the new outburst of agitation in Córdoba was to stimulate further the political consciousness and organizational activity of the pro-Reform university youth throughout the nation. Immediately upon receiving word of the June 15 disturbances, the federations in each of the Republic's universities sent the FUC telegrams offering complete support, and the FUA, under the direction of its original founders, called a four-day nationwide student strike (June 19–22). The headquarters of the national organization in Buenos Aires maintained telegraphic contact with the FUC, sent delegates to Córdoba as observers, and directed a message to Nores asking him to resign in the best interests of the University of Córdoba and the nation.

In addition to sympathetic responses from Argentine student federations, the Córdoba revolt also gained the support of national liberal groups and political parties. The most significant and wholeheartedly open backing that the students won from any political organization came from the Argentine Socialist party. Throughout the campaign for reform *La Vanguardia,* the Socialist party newspaper, filled its pages with reports and interpretations of the Córdoba events and gave full editorial backing to the student cause. When the youth rioted in the University of Córdoba in June, the editors of *La Vanguardia* stated that, "Save certain excesses, which are very justifiable in these moments of passion, the attitude of the Córdoba university youth deserves our warmest applause." [8] Several Socialist politicians, notably Alfredo L. Palacios and Mario Bravo, joined the students in public parades and rallies, thereby lending their personal prestige to the efforts to reform the nation's universities.

In the last weeks of June the Córdoba students began to receive support from other sources. Messages of encouragement arrived from student groups in neighboring Latin American countries, where the youth were vitally interested in the Córdoba movement and also dedicated to the idea of university reform. In Córdoba and other urban centers of the Republic, labor organizations, usually connected with the Socialist party, also gave full backing to the Reform movement. Their sympathy was evident in manifestoes encouraging the University Reform movement and in their enthusiastic and often turbulent participation in youth-led public demonstrations and street parades.[9]

By and large, the press of the nation gave support to the student actions. *La Vanguardia* of Buenos Aires and *La Voz del Interior*

of Córdoba were strongly sympathetic toward the Reform movement. But Catholic and Conservative journals were critical and in
frank opposition. The more staid but also more influential and
more widely distributed papers of the capital city attempted to take
a more objective view of the situation. The editorials of *La Prensa,*
for example, agreed with the need for educational reform and
showed sympathy for the motives behind the student movement.
Nonetheless, *La Prensa* deplored the use of violence by the students and expressed the fear that unscrupulous and partisan political groups would infiltrate and capture the movement for their own
ends.[10]

Regardless of editorial opinion, the Reformistas had no difficulty in keeping the public well informed about their aims and
actions. Almost all of the nation's leading newspapers received
students in their offices, published in full student manifestoes, and
devoted ample space to detailed reports of the entire movement. In
addition, liberal periodicals such as *Ideas, Revista de filosofía,*
and *Nosotros* filled their pages with news of the Reform and
offered their editorial influence to the student cause.

During this period, the anti-Reform elements also acquired the
backing of various organizations and individuals sympathetic to
their position. Several Córdoba congressmen adhered to the stand
of the Committee for the Defense of the University and criticized
what they considered the excesses committed by the striking
Reformistas. The Defense Committee also received support from
Catholic student centers and Catholic-oriented civic groups. On
June 25, a declaration signed by 170 prominent Córdoba professors, lawyers, politicians, and businessmen was sent to President
Irigoyen, deploring the actions of the Reformistas and asking for a
government intervention on behalf of the pro-Nores elements. A
Catholic women's group in Córdoba sent a similar message to
Irigoyen and made public their congratulations to the local legis-
lators who had championed the Defense Committee stand.

Against the background of an increasing national interest in and agitation over university reform, the Reformistas of Córdoba carried on a spirited campaign of political pressure and propaganda during the months of June and July, 1918. Public demonstrations, pro-Reform speeches by political and labor leaders, passionate manifestoes and declarations followed one another in rapid succession. The FUC continued to lobby in the halls of government, sending telegrams and reports explaining their position to the chief executive, and delegating federation leader Enrique F. Barros as their personal representative to National Minister of Education Salinas and President Irigoyen. Members of the Córdoba student federation also were sent to Buenos Aires and provincial cities to speak at student rallies in an effort to maintain the support of other university groups.

As the pace and scope of the Reform movement quickened and spread, the youth of Córdoba began to develop a broader conception of the need for university reform and of their own role in this movement. Nowhere was this development more evident than in the famous "Córdoba Manifesto" of June 21, 1918, which was directed by the Córdoba Reformistas to the "free men of South America." In this document the students claimed that the Reform movement implied the breaking of the final link which connected the twentieth-century University of Córdoba with the domination of the Spanish colonial tradition. The key element in severing this tie, they argued, was for student representatives to participate in university administration. This "democratization" of the University of Córdoba, the Reformistas concluded, would make the institution a "free republic," and as such the students could bring the University up to date by revising the curriculum, eliminating religious influences, and insuring that professors would be "the creators of truth, beauty, and good." [11]

In July, 1918, a more comprehensive statement with regard to the goals of the Reform emerged from the First National Congress of University Students, held in Córdoba. This nationwide student meeting had been proposed originally during the founding of the *Federación Universitaria Argentina* (FUA) in April. Inaugurated on July 21, the Congress was attended by twelve delegates from each of the five university federations and a dozen additional students representing the FUA. The purpose of the Congress was to give cohesion and impetus to the Reform campaign and also to discuss and co-ordinate the Reform program. The principles outlined at this meeting were later adopted as national educational policy by the Argentine government and served as the foundation for the Reform which spread throughout the Republic and eventually throughout Latin America.

The First Student Congress began with a series of speeches and reports which dealt with what the students believed were the measures needed to reform Argentina's institutions of higher learning. The most important of these was presented by the FUBA president, Guillermo Watson, who argued that the Argentine students should be allowed to participate in the election and administration of the university councils. The idea of student participation and "democratization" of the university was influenced by the new democratic currents introduced in the Sáenz Peña electoral reform law of 1912 and the election victory of the Radicals in 1916. The Reformistas pointed out that this concept was hardly shockingly new, since student participation had been a characteristic of the Spanish American colonial university. Moreover, a larger voice for the students in the administration of the university had been proposed and approved by student representatives of various Latin American countries gathered in meetings at Montevideo (1908), Buenos Aires (1910), and Lima (1912). Actual student representation on the administrative councils of the Uruguayan universities dated from 1909.[12]

Besides the report on student participation in university administration, the following proposals were also made at the First Student Congress: (1) Classroom attendance should be optional. (2)

Professorial positions should be competitive and should be reviewed periodically. (3) The principle of university autonomy should be constantly respected. (4) University education should be without cost and available to all who were academically qualified, regardless of their social or economic situation. (5) Student-professor contacts should be improved. (6) University extension courses for members of the working class should be encouraged. (7) University education should be directed more toward the consideration and solution of national social, economic, and political problems.[13]

The heart of the Reform program was—and continues to be—the principle of student participation in university government. The youth of 1918 believed that, by being allowed to voice their opinions in the academic councils, they would be able to renovate and reorient their institutions and bring them more into line with twentieth-century needs and developments. Other planks in the Reform program were intended to improve the quality of the faculty, to expand the scope and content of the curriculum, and to open the university to more members of the middle and lower classes. The principle of unregulated attendance at classes, for example, was designed to motivate professors to improve their teaching or face empty classrooms. It was also hoped that unregulated attendance would permit greater flexibility in class scheduling. This flexibility, in turn, would allow youths obliged to work at part-time or full-time jobs while studying to arrange their university schedules in a way that would not interfere with their need to earn a livelihood.

In sum, the Reformistas of 1918 were seeking to modernize the Argentine university, to update the Republic's institutions of higher learning in correspondence with the larger national developments which had occurred in the past few decades. The Reformistas hoped to make the Argentine university an agent of, rather than an obstacle to, change. If the university were modernized, they concluded, it could produce a national leadership capable of directing the development and modernization of the entire Republic.[14]

The First National Congress of University Students was significant not only for the program it produced, but also because it served as an example of the political sophistication and mental maturity of the Argentine students. The organization and administration of the meeting were smooth and efficient; the speeches and reports that were made were well written, effectively delivered, and tightly argued; and the papers and lectures that were presented displayed a comprehensive and profound awareness of educational and social issues. Moreover, the students showed themselves well informed on the advances made in the university systems of other nations. In fine, the conference provided a base for the development of ideas and forces which would continue to grow and expand after the July meeting terminated. The First National Congress of University Students also afforded an opportunity for the Reform leaders to meet in one place to exchange opinions, to stimulate one another intellectually, and to gain a sense of solidarity in their actions and a feeling of confidence in the ultimate triumph of their cause.

During the eight days the Reform leaders were meeting in Córdoba, activities in favor of the movement continued in other quarters. Socialist Congressman Juan B. Justo spoke out in the National Congress, supporting the Córdoba student federation (FUC), reiterating the need for drastic modifications in the University, and criticizing the Radical government for what he termed mismanagement of the entire situation. The FUC delegate to Buenos Aires, Enrique F. Barros, held several interviews with Minister of Education Salinas in attempts to speed the process of intervention.

These activities began to bear fruit when, shortly after the close of the First National Congress of University Students, President

Irigoyen named Telémaco Susini as the new intervenor in the University of Córdoba. This appointment was well received by the rebellious youth of the nation. Susini, a well-known liberal intellectual, previously had given full backing to the Reform cause. In a speech presented several days after the June 15 revolt, Susini had praised the Reformistas of Córdoba for their rebellion against Jesuit influence and their incorporation into the ranks of those who struggle on behalf of "the high spiritual conquests for which independent men clamor." [15]

As was to be expected, the Conservative reaction to this appointment was less than enthusiastic. The Committee for the Defense of the University directed a telegram to the President of the Republic asking that he reconsider his choice, and among the Catholic elements a vociferous clamor arose against the sending of the anti-clerical Susini to Córdoba. The announcement of the appointment of the new intervenor led several Conservative faculty members in Córdoba to resign. On August 7 one of the primary aims of the FUC was achieved when Rector-elect Nores sent a message of resignation to President Irigoyen. Whereas the Reformista elements received this surrender with delight, the Defense Committee continued to back Nores.

The initial enthusiasm of the university youth began to dim, however, when President Irigoyen—apparently under heavy pressure from influential Conservative elements—continued to procrastinate in his decision to send Susini to Córdoba. In the days that followed the Nores resignation, student groups throughout the Republic began to barrage the Casa Rosada (the Argentine executive headquarters in Buenos Aires) with telegrams which urged a speedy intervention. Córdoba students sent delegates to other cities to speak at public rallies designed to force government action. Irigoyen, caught between the crossfire of Conservative reaction and a growing liberal discontent, sought the road to compromise by replacing Susini as intervenor with his minister of education, José S. Salinas. This move pleased both contending factions. The Conservatives were now in position to deal with an intervenor of a more official and less openly liberal character. For the Reformistas, increasingly concerned because of the loss of time and academic credit in the pursuit of their scholastic careers, the new intervention promised a rapid solution to the crisis.

By the second week in September, however, student hopes for a speedy intervention in the University once again dimmed. National Minister of Education Salinas still had not begun his journey to Córdoba. Faced with a further extension of the university shutdown, now already nearly three months old, the youth of Córdoba decided to take direct action. On the morning of September 9, eighty-three members of the *Federación Universitaria de Córdoba* entered the buildings of the University of Córdoba by force, barricaded the doors, and proclaimed themselves in charge of a new administration. In a message directed to intervenor Salinas, the students advised the Minister of their actions and requested that he arrive on the scene as quickly as possible. A body of troops, dispatched by the local government, soon entered the University and placed the rebellious students under arrest. Nonetheless, the principal goal of the Reformistas had been attained: Two days after the taking of the University, Minister Salinas left Buenos Aires to assume his duties as intervenor.

Salinas arrived in Córdoba on September 12, where he was greeted by a large and sympathetic crowd of students. The Minister began his activities by taking over direction of the University and interviewing administrative officials and student leaders. After two weeks in Córdoba, Salinas returned to Buenos Aires to confer with the chief executive. As a result of this intervention, President Irigoyen issued on October 7, 1918, a decree which included in its provisions nearly all of the reforms the rebellious youth of Córdoba were requesting. The basic articles of the presidential declaration sanctioned student participation in university government through representatives on the administrative councils, approved electoral procedures which would permit periodic renewal and infusion of new blood among the members of these same councils, introduced the principle of free attendance at classes, granted professors more freedom in their choice of lecture materials, and permitted greater flexibility in examination procedures.[16]

Certain changes were also made in the personnel of the University of Córdoba. The intervenor selected a new Superior Council, which included student favorites Enrique Martínez Paz as vice-rector and Belisario Carrafa as dean of the Faculty of Engineering. Salinas accepted the resignations of two professors prominent in the Conservative opposition to the Reform, former Rector Nores and Arturo N. Bas, the latter a frequent speaker at Defense Committee rallies. On the other hand, Deodoro Roca and Arturo Capdevila, two leading members of the pro-Reform forces, were appointed to fill professorial chairs.

When it became apparent that their aims had been achieved, the leaders of the FUC applauded the actions of Susini and Irigoyen and ended the student strike begun on June 15. The triumph of the Reformistas was complete, but the rancor of the long struggle remained. Late in October two students affiliated with the Defense Committee attacked FUC president Enrique F. Barros, rendering him unconscious and near death. The incident aroused passions on both sides. However, when Barros recovered and pardoned his assailants, the furor subsided. This final outburst of the year 1918 underscored the often violent nature of the struggle to reform the University of Córdoba.

The educational changes initiated in 1918 by the Córdoba youth stand out as the primary accomplishments in this first period of Argentine student political activity on a national scale. Particularly significant was the establishment of student representation in university government. This key aspect of the Reform program served to give the youth a prominent position in university administration and to stimulate among the students a lasting interest in problems of higher education. When the Reform spread to other Latin American republics, this feature of student participation gave a special character to the Latin American university in comparison with like institutions in other parts of the world. The execution of the articles of President Irigoyen's decree, such as unregulated attendance at classes, periodic changes in appointments to professorial chairs, and periodic renewal of the membership of the administrative councils, marked other profound changes in the character of Argentina's university system. Finally, the action of the youth highlighted the need for the university to consider national social, economic, and political problems. No longer, the Reformistas argued, could Argentina's institutions of higher learning remain "ivory towers" of classical learning. The Córdoba movement indicated clearly that the students of the Republic planned to reorient the universities toward the examination and solution of pressing national issues.

On the political level, the characteristics of student activity were clearly defined and models of action were definitely marked by the events of 1918. Most significant was the establishment of a national organization, the *Federación Universitaria Argentina* (FUA), to co-ordinate all of the Republic's student groups. The leadership of the FUA, mobilization of support from all of Argentina's universities, sympathetic reactions from student federations in other nations, and the active co-operation of liberal elements were aspects of Argentine student politics which were repeated constantly in the years that followed the Córdoba Reform. So too were the techniques of student action: that is, the use of manifestoes and meetings to attract public attention and to gain public support, the holding of interviews with government officials, and the tendency to take direct and sometimes violent measures when these seemed necessary.

The Reform of 1918 was also significant in that it introduced a number of characteristic student attitudes and ways of thinking, attitudes and ways which eventually developed into a kind of Reformista philosophy. One of the dominant themes of the Córdoba movement was the emphasis upon nationalism. Throughout the student speeches and declarations, the idea was repeated that the Reform was to change the Argentine university to serve the *national* interest and to produce *national* leaders. Showing the influence of new intellectual currents, the men of the Reform espoused, moreover, what might be called an integrating and inclusive nationalism. Inherent in their principles of free education and unregulated attendance was the belief that all Argentines as individuals had a right to enter the university and to participate in the formation of the national conscience and culture. Rejecting the colonial tradition of an elite institution solely for the education of the privileged classes, the Reformistas sought to introduce changes which would make their schools more truly representative in character and orientation of all Argentines.[17]

In addition to a sense of nationalism, other features of Reform thought included a predilection for idealism as opposed to materialism, a faith in democracy and democratic procedures, and a rejection of the past and an orientation toward the future. Clearly evident were the students' anti-Conservative sympathies. These were the forces the Reformistas saw as hindering the progressive growth of the university and the nation.

Anti-clericalism was another important theme for the youth of 1918. From careful reading of student documents it appears that this aspect of Reformista thought was more a reaction against the conservatism of the church than opposition to religious principles per se. The students objected to the clergy's tie with Conservative politics, the religious influences within the University of Córdoba, and the resistance of Catholic elements to educational change.

One of the most interesting aspects of the Reform was the solidarity the students sought with the urban workers. The leaders of the Reform and the labor leaders in 1918 came from different class backgrounds and had different goals, but for the moment the interests of the two groups coincided. The labor forces had little concern with the problems of the university, from which they were excluded, but they were stimulated by the new ideas which young intellectuals presented to them and found common ground in the progressive and democratic principles of the Reformistas. The students, for their part, welcomed the political support of the working class and imitated labor techniques of organization and agitation. Idealistically, the youth turned much of their attention toward the proletariat, endeavoring to put their theories of social concern and inclusive nationalism into practice. The incorporation of plans for university extension courses and night classes for workers within the movement's program underlined the Reformistas' hopes in this regard.

The crystallization of these attitudes apart, other aspects related to subsequent student politics were found in the Córdoba movement. First, not all of the Argentine university youth favored the Reform. Although a large majority of them did support the renovating ideas of the Reformistas, there were significant minority groups, such as the Committee for the Defense of the University, which bitterly opposed the actions of the newly formed student federations. Second, at this time the students received little aid from professors. The Córdoba movement, conceived, initiated, and carried out by the youth themselves, was in opposition to the professorial body, which the students were seeking to change and infuse with fresh blood. In addition to the faculty members who objected to the Reform for sound educational and procedural reasons, there were many professors who, treasuring their privileged positions, were not anxious to lose those privileges by backing the Reformistas. Third, although the youth did not have professorial support, they did enjoy the advice, encouragement, and guidance of various young alumni. Particularly important in the

Córdoba Reform were twenty-seven-year-old Deodoro Roca and thirty-three-year-old Saúl Alejandro Taborda. Both of these men were beginning prominent careers as liberal intellectuals and in the years to come provided further leadership for the university youth.[18]

Other important aspects of the 1918 Reform were the social and economic backgrounds and ages of the student leaders. According to observations made by such participants in the Reform as Gabriel del Mazo, Gregorio Bermann, and Julio V. González, all of whom later became historians of the movement, the leadership of the student revolt came from the various sectors of the middle class. On the basis of the evidence available this seems a valid assumption. For one thing, the thinking of the Reformistas was quite close to that which has characterized middle-class activities in Latin America during the twentieth century.[19] Moreover, most students from the upper class would have been opposed to the Reform, and the working class in 1918 was not represented in the Argentine university. With regard to age, the outstanding leaders of the movement were young men: In 1918 Enrique F. Barros was twenty-four as were Gregorio Bermann and Ismael Bordabehere; Julio V. González was nineteen; Gabriel del Mazo, twenty; Gumersindo Sayago, twenty-five; and Guillermo Watson, twenty-two. The oldest leader of importance was twenty-nine-year-old Osvaldo Loudet, already a graduate and called in by the more active younger students to lend his prestige to the FUA.[20]

Still another important characteristic of the Reform movement in 1918 was its relationship to Argentina's political parties. Although the Reformistas were "liberal," they were not of any defined political affiliation. Throughout the months of agitation they were careful to deny any specific political tendency. For example, a FUC declaration of October, 1918, disclaimed the connection of the Reform with any national political movement, stating that "the conduct observed by it [the FUC], places it above all political struggle, pursuing solely the noble purpose of improving the university." [21] Despite the support of the Socialists and Radicals, none of the principal directors of the movement were members of those parties in 1918. Some of the Reformistas did enter into politics soon after the events of 1918, but the majority of the students preferred to keep the university movement itself independent of partisan politics.

There can be no doubt of the clear and sympathetic support the Reformistas received from the Socialists and Radicals. The government of Irigoyen had been favorably disposed toward the Reform from the first signs of revolt. However, the Radical president was aware of the Conservatives' power in the universities and was cautious in dealing with the Córdoba movement. Although his sympathies lay with the striking students, Irigoyen was not a leader of the University Reform. As in his procrastination over the Salinas intervention, Irigoyen's political caution prevented him from taking any bold measures which would have given him a more prominent role among the initiators of the movement.

It often has been argued, especially by anti-Reformistas, that Communists and Anarchists greatly influenced the Córdoba movement. Yet the facts do not seem to support this contention. Historical documents of the Reform do not reveal any significant participation by Anarchists or Communists in the events of 1918. Few of the Reformistas ever entered the Communist party, the majority eventually joining the ranks of the Socialists or Radicals (see Chapter 5). Nor were the ideas of the "men of '18" in line with Communist or Anarchist thought. The Reformistas wanted to change the university through democratic procedures and active participation in university government. They did not seek to abolish structural lines, nor to remake the institution by a radically different pattern.

The accomplishments of Argentina's university youth in the year 1918 were significant and lasting. Through effective use of organizational techniques and direct action, they succeeded in forcing the national government to accept their demands for profound change. They could look with pride to the administrative modifications they achieved and be content with the power they had shown in ridding the University of Córdoba of various professors whom they opposed. Moreover, student organizations had entered into national affairs. Students had met with the President of the Republic, had occupied much of the time and concern of executive and legislative officials, had attracted large numbers of people to their cause, and had pre-empted a substantial share of Argentina's newspaper space. Student political activity, with its corresponding educational and social interests, had become a permanent and important part of Argentine life—and the rallying point of this new political force was the University Reform.

NOTES

1. "Memorial del centro de estudiantes de ciencias médicas referente a la organización y funcionamiento de la escuela de medicina (Córdoba, 21 de diciembre de 1917)," *La reforma universitaria: en la Universidad de Córdoba; en la Universidad de Buenos Aires, año 1918* (Buenos Aires, 1919), pp. 17–46.
2. "Manifiesto a la juventud argentina (marzo 15 de 1918)," and "Resolución correspondiente (marzo 13 de 1918)," del Mazo, ed., *La reforma universitaria* (1927–Vol. II), pp. 16–18.
3. Such meetings, usually held in large auditoriums or in public squares, were employed frequently by the Argentine students during the 1918 Reform and in later years.
4. "Nuevo manifiesto (marzo 31 de 1918)," del Mazo, ed., *La reforma universitaria* (1927–Vol. II), pp. 19–21.
5. *Boletín de la federación universitaria* (Buenos Aires), April 1918, pp. 50–64.
6. "La federación universitaria pide al poder ejecutivo nueva intervención después de los sucesos del día 15 de junio," del Mazo, ed., *La reforma universitaria* (1927–Vol. II), pp. 46–47.
7. *La Prensa* (Buenos Aires), June 20, 1918, p. 9.
8. *La Vanguardia* (Buenos Aires), June 17, 1918, p. 2.

9. In September, 1918, the Córdoba Reformistas returned this working-class support by providing encouragement and leadership for a labor union strike called in that city. *La Prensa,* September 6, 1918, p. 10.

10. For excerpts from various of the nation's newspapers concerning the Córdoba events see *La reforma universitaria: en la Universidad de Córdoba,* pp. 467–693.

11. "Córdoba manifesto," del Mazo, ed., *La reforma universitaria* (1927–Vol. II), pp. 7–15.

12. Gabriel del Mazo, *Estudiantes y gobierno universitario* (2nd ed.; Buenos Aires, 1955), pp. 25–27; and Guillermo Watson, "Teoría del gobierno republicano de la universidad," del Mazo, ed., *La reforma universitaria* (1927–Vol. I), pp. 23–30.

13. For a complete review of the actions and resolutions of the First National Congress of University Students see del Mazo, ed., *La reforma universitaria* (1927–Vol. III). It is interesting to observe that these Córdoba principles of 1918 correspond closely to student programs which have appeared since the end of World War II in other nations. The charter of the French Student Union, published in 1946, follows almost point for point the articles of the 1918 Argentine resolutions. See Frank A. Pinner, "Student Trade-Unionism in France, Belgium and Holland: Anticipatory Socialization and Role-Seeking," *Sociology of Education,* XXXVII (Spring 1964), 179–180.

14. In a more contemporary context, Seymour Martin Lipset has written: "In the underdeveloped or emerging countries, the critical attitude of the educated stratum resembles the reactions of intellectuals in pre-communist Russia and China. Their concern is, from a nationalist standpoint, with the modernization of their country, which would permit it to take its place with the leading countries of the modern world. . . . Awareness or concern with the inferior position of the nation is most acute among those who have received or are receiving a university education, since the culture which that conveys is so obviously part of a universal culture and the university community has such close ties with the international community of scholars and universities." Lipset, "University Students and Politics in Underdeveloped Countries," in Seymour Martin Lipset, ed., *Student Politics* (New York: Basic Books, 1967), pp. 13–14. With some slight changes these remarks can also be applied to the Argentine Reformistas of 1918.

15. *La Vanguardia,* June 21, 1918, p. 2.

16. *La Prensa,* October 11, 1918, p. 11.

17. For additional comments on the nationalism of the Reformistas see Angel S. Caballero Martín, *La Universidad en Santa Fe* (Santa Fe, 1931), p. 226; and the essays in Gabriel del Mazo, *Reforma universitaria y cultura nacional* (Buenos Aires, 1955).

18. For information on and examples of the works and ideas of Roca and Taborda see Deodoro Roca, *Ciencias, maestros y universidades* (Buenos Aires, 1959); Deodoro Roca, *El difícil tiempo nuevo* (Buenos Aires, 1956); and Saúl Alejandro Taborda, *Facundo* (Buenos Aires, 1959).
19. A description of the characteristics of Latin America's middle sectors can be found in John J. Johnson, *Political Change in Latin America: The Emergence of the Middle Sectors* (Stanford, Calif., 1958), pp. 1–14.
20. Some biographical information on prominent Reformistas is included in "Quién es quién en la reforma argentina," Federación Universitaria de Buenos Aires, *La reforma universitaria, 1918–1958* (Buenos Aires, 1959), pp. 367–375.
21. "El momento universitario," *La reforma universitaria: en la Universidad de Córboda,* p. 647.

Reform and Counterreform, 1918–1930

4

Between 1918 and 1930, Radical party administrations governed Argentina. Hipólito Irigoyen's first presidential term ended in 1922. During his six years in office, the Radical President allowed labor unions more freedom of action than they had previously enjoyed and passed some social legislation. In international affairs, he maintained a strict neutrality in World War I and withdrew from the League of Nations in 1920 when the world organization refused to admit the Central Powers to membership. The most prominent feature of Irigoyen's first administration, and probably the greatest weakness, was its personalistic nature. Irigoyen interviewed almost anyone who wished to see him, regardless of the importance of the visit. He refused to delegate responsibility, and affairs of state often remained neglected for months until the chief executive personally attended to them. Hoping to cure the country of the vices of bureaucratic corruption and rigid political control which had marked Conservative administrations, Irigoyen only managed to perpetuate these defects by allowing Radical party followers to take government positions as personal sinecures and by intervening in provincial political affairs more than any Argentine leader since the mid-nineteenth century.

Despite his administrative inefficiency, strange manners, and enigmatic personality, Irigoyen became a popular figure among Argentina's middle and lower classes. The Conservatives, on the other hand, who still maintained many positions of national influence, detested the eccentric Radical leader. In 1922 the privileged classes in the nation were pleased when Marcelo T. de Alvear was chosen as Irigoyen's successor. Although a Radical, Alvear was from a traditional, wealthy family and his accession to the presidency permitted the Conservatives to regain much of the political ground they had lost in 1916. Under Alvear, whose term extended from 1922 to 1928, governmental efficiency improved and the nation's economy expanded. Political corruption, however, continued to increase. In 1924 Irigoyen, who had picked Alvear as his successor, broke with the President and split the Radical party. The two factions which emerged were the anti-personalistas, headed by the presidential incumbent, and the personalistas, led by Irigoyen. In the national elections of 1928 Alvear joined with the Conservatives against the personalista candidate. However, the seventy-six-year-old Irigoyen swept to a smashing victory and began his second term as chief executive of the nation.

During the years of Radical rule immediately after the Córdoba Reform of 1918, Argentina's university youth continued to etch a record of considerable achievement. Between 1918 and 1922, they spread their Reform movement to the other universities in the Republic. The Argentine students were also influential at this time in extending the Córdoba principles to other Latin American countries, particularly to Peru and Chile. In the 1920's certain themes characteristic of the student movement continued to be developed, and new aspects of student thought began to appear as the Reformistas reacted to the social, economic, and political conditions of their nation and continent.

The concrete and positive achievements of the Reformistas ended, however, near the end of 1922. During the Alvear administration the Argentine Conservatives regained their strength both in the government and in the universities and mounted a counter-Reform movement, which between 1922 and 1928 nullified or neutralized many of the Reformistas' advances in the field of higher education. The Conservative cause was aided in these years by student apathy and differences of opinion as to what direction the Reform should take, differences which split some formerly cohesive university groups and caused the complete demise of others.

In the first four years after the Córdoba Reform, all of Argentina's institutions of higher learning underwent significant changes. In the University of Buenos Aires (UBA) the reform of the administrative statutes took place much more smoothly than in Córdoba. This was due largely to the more liberal atmosphere of that port city, the greater percentage of progressive-minded professors in the UBA, and that institution's precedent of having accepted structural reforms in 1906. In mid-1918 the *Federación Universitaria Argentina* (FUA) and the *Federación Universitaria de Buenos Aires* (FUBA) directed a message to the rector of the UBA urging that reforms similar to those considered in Córdoba be introduced. Because of student pressure, the administrative councils of the UBA began to consider various changes in the institution's organization. On September 11, 1918, President Irigoyen approved a list of administrative reforms presented to him by UBA officials and thereby introduced at that university student participation in university government, unregulated attendance at classes, and periodic changes in administrative and professorial appointments.[1]

The movement for university reform in La Plata was initiated by a group of students who opposed the control of the ULP's administrative councils by professors who were under the influence of positivism. According to the Reformistas, these "positivist" professors had seriously delayed the progressive development of the University by monopolizing administrative posts for long periods. As early as 1917, students in the Faculty of Agronomy began to campaign for reforms in their school's statutes and for changes in the professorial body. In July, 1919, members of the Agronomy student center presented to the president of the ULP a report which outlined their demands for reform. When the administration failed to consider their proposals, the Reformistas replied by boycotting classes. Under the leadership of the *Federación Universitaria de La Plata* (FULP), other centers quickly came to the support of the agronomy students, and a general university strike was called on October 17, 1919.

The student campaign for university reform which followed the October strike in the ULP was similar in many respects to the actions of the Córdoba students in 1918. There were manifestoes which criticized the professors of the ULP; telegrams to the national executive seeking intervention and reform; declarations of support from liberal groups, political parties, and other student federations; and finally, direct action through demonstrations and strikes. After eight months of activity the student aspirations were realized through the support of President Irigoyen who, in June, 1920, approved the introduction of Reform statutes into the ULP.[2]

The Reformistas of La Plata received much of their intellectual leadership from anti-positivist philosopher Alejandro Korn. During the 1919–1920 student activities Korn, himself a professor in the ULP, criticized the universities of Argentina for their failure to provide intellectual and moral leadership and called for a rejection of the scientism and utilitarianism which he believed had heretofore characterized the Republic's institutions of higher learning. In place of positivism, Korn urged the nation's youth to seek "the light of new ideals." Héctor Ripa Alberdi, one of Korn's students and an important figure in the La Plata Reform, castigated Argentina's past leaders, "men of the last century, formed by the harsh hand of the positivist philosophy." Ripa Alberdi predicted a great future for Argentina in the twentieth century, when the nation would be directed by men with an "idealistic generosity of new ideas." [3]

One of the planks of the Reformista program, as stated in the resolutions of the First National Congress of University Students in 1918, was to campaign for the nationalization of the provincial Universities of the Littoral and Tucumán. The movement to place the University of the Littoral under national control had begun in 1912 among small groups of law students in the cities of Santa Fe and Paraná. In May, 1919, the agitation of these youths culminated in a university-wide strike protesting the existing statutes, demanding student participation in university administration, and asking for the removal of incompetent professors. As a result of the strike the provincial government intervened in the University.

The Reform movement in the University of the Littoral was led by the *Federación Universitaria de Santa Fe* (FUSF) and followed the pattern of the Córdoba revolt. The students held public rallies, lobbied in government offices, and received support from other student federations. Julio V. González, president of the FUA, visited the University of the Littoral during the student agitation, and prominent Reformista intellectuals such as Deodoro Roca and Arturo Capdevila provided verbal and written inspiration for the members of the FUSF. As had happened in other university movements, a small group of students opposed the Reform. In Santa Fe the *Unión Universitaria* (University Union) attempted to perpetuate the existing rules and administration of the institution. But lacking support and outnumbered, the *Unión* failed to halt the Reformistas' efforts to renovate the University during this period.

In October, 1919, the Argentine students marked another success when President Irigoyen decreed the nationalization of the University of the Littoral and extended to it the statutes of the Reform. In April, 1921, after another lively student campaign, the

University of Tucumán also was nationalized and given Reform statutes.[4]

Within the space of four years, then, the principles enunciated by the First National Congress of University Students of 1918 were written into the regulations of Argentina's five established universities. Initiated and conducted by the students themselves, the extension of the Reform to Buenos Aires, La Plata, Tucumán, and the cities of the littoral benefited greatly from the initial success and resulting enthusiasm of the Córdoba movement. Campaigns subsequent to the 1918 revolt were able to borrow agitational techniques and enjoy the advice and support of participants who had been active in the initial movement. The extension of the Reform also was aided by the friendly reception it received from the Irigoyen government. The signatures of the Radical President and his Minister of Education Salinas were found at the bottom of every Reform decree issued in these years. If the Irigoyen administration did not initiate the movement, it at least approved the end results of the student activity.

The need for university reform was not unique to Argentina, and in the 1920's the Córdoba movement affected almost all of Latin America. Argentina, because it had taken the first step, served as the inspirational leader of the Reform, and prominent Reformistas began to carry the ideas of the 1918 revolt to universities in neighboring countries. In May, 1919, for example, Alfredo L. Palacios, Socialist politician and university professor, traveled to Bolivia and Peru, where he outlined the Reform principles and described the Argentine experience to various student groups. As the Reform spread throughout the continent, the Argentine student federations returned the support shown by students of other nations in 1918 by sending telegrams and letters of encouragement to fledgling movements. Verbal and written contact between student leaders began to create a bond of solidarity among the young Reformistas, who found themselves on a common ground formed by similar ideas, aspirations, and actions.

In Chile, the movement for university reform had early Argentine support. The student federations of both countries maintained close contact, and declarations and ideas were frequently exchanged between the two youth movements. Late in 1918, the FUA directed a note to the Chilean student federation suggesting that Chile's northern boundary dispute with Peru be settled through the establishment of a binational youth arbitration commission. In December, 1920, the *Federación Universitaria Argentina* and the *Federación de Estudiantes de Chile* (FECH, Federation of Students of Chile) signed an accord outlining common points of view and including articles which provided for the joint study of social issues, university extension courses, and student exchanges between the two countries.

The *Federación de Estudiantes del Peru* (FEP, Federation of Students of Peru), which led the movement for university renovation in that country, enjoyed a firm and friendly relationship with Argentine student organizations. In August, 1920, Victor Raúl Haya de la Torre, then president of the FEP, and FUA president Gabriel del Mazo, signed an accord of solidarity between the two federations similar to the aforementioned Chile-Argentine declaration. Contacts between the youth groups of the two countries were further strengthened in 1922 when Haya de la Torre, at the invitation of Minister of Education José S. Salinas, made a speaking tour of Argentina's universities.

The University Reform in Peru, greatly stimulated by the Córdoba example, was one of the most significant in Latin America. From the campaign for educational renovation in that country emerged a political party, the APRA or *Alianza Popular Revolucionaria Americana* (Popular Revolutionary Alliance for America), which in later years became one of the most influential political groups in Peru. Founded by Haya de la Torre in 1924, the *Aprista* party included among its principal leaders men who as students had been active in the 1919–1923 Peruvian University Reform movement. Haya de la Torre, in attempting to spread the ideas of the *Aprista* group throughout Latin America, often emphasized the connections between his philosophy and the program of the Reform.[5]

Diffusion of the Córdoba principles and the increasing excitement generated among the Latin American university youth by the Reform inspired the International Student Congress, which convened in Mexico in 1921. This Congress was called to consider the implications of the Reform movement and to issue declarations related to a broad range of issues. Attended by university students from twenty-three nations, the conference included delegations from Europe, the United States, and Asia. Presided over by Daniel Cosío Villegas, later one of Mexico's foremost historians, the Congress urged all Latin American universities to adopt Reform statutes such as student participation in university government and unregulated attendance at classes. Moving from educational concerns, the youth proclaimed themselves in favor of closer ties with the proletariat through university extension courses and voiced their firm opposition to the presence and growth of militarism, dictatorship, and imperialism in Latin America.[6]

Argentina was represented in Mexico City by several student leaders, the most prominent being Héctor Ripa Alberdi of the University of La Plata. One of the most influential figures in the spread of the Reform, Ripa Alberdi presented at the inaugural session of the Congress an address in which he emphasized the important changes he believed were occurring in the cultural institutions of Latin America because of the "vigorous rebirth of the idealist philosophy and the healthy rebelliousness of the youth." On his return journey from the meeting, the young Argentine stopped in Peru to give a lecture at the Popular University of Lima, an educational institution for workers established through the efforts of the Peruvian Reformistas. In his talk there Ripa

Alberdi discussed his idealist and anti-positivist ideas and helped to spread further the theories of the Córdoba movement.[7]

Attempts to maintain contacts and to form a sense of solidarity with Reformista groups in other Latin American nations, characteristic of the early period of the Reform, continued as an important feature of Argentine student political activity throughout the 1920's. When Chilean students criticized a belligerent anti-Argentine speech presented in Santiago in 1924, youths from the UBA Faculty of Law sent them a message of congratulation. In 1928, when Venezuelan dictator Juan Vicente Gómez imprisoned students and workers who had led a revolt against his regime, youths from the UBA Faculty of Economic Sciences protested the incarcerations. A note to the Venezuelan government from the Argentine students demanded the release of the prisoners and announced support for the actions of the university youth in the sister republic.[8]

Coincident with the national and international extension of the University Reform were the expansion and application of the social, political, and economic themes which had marked Argentine student opinion in the movement of 1918. Moreover, new attitudes began to appear, attitudes which were the result of the application of liberal Reformista ideas to post-World War I situations.

The meaning of nationalism, which had been an important element in the 1918 program, was amplified by the Reformistas in the 1920's to include opposition to imperialist influences in Latin America. This anti-imperialism, which has had great transcendence in the history of Argentine university politics, was most often directed against what the students believed were the expansionist and exploitative policies of the United States. The first student statement on imperialism was issued by the *Federación Universitaria Argentina* in October, 1920. In this document the youth condemned colonialism and imperialism as the causes of

World War I and criticized the ineffectiveness of the Versailles Treaty. To prevent the recurrence of another world conflict, the Reformista document urged self-determination for all peoples, emphasized the need for an effective organization to solve international disputes, and denounced categorically the "maneuvers of world imperialism." [9]

Two intellectuals closely connected with the Reform, José Ingenieros and Alfredo L. Palacios, were prominent in forming the ideological basis for the anti-imperialism of the students. The ideas of both these men with regard to imperialism, in many respects founded more on emotion than on fact, continue to appear in various forms in contemporary Argentine student documents. Both Ingenieros and Palacios were deeply concerned with what they believed was the failure of European civilization, as reflected by World War I, and the need for Latin America to avoid a similar disaster. The United States, in their minds, was a mere extension of Europe, dominated by materialism, controlled by reactionaries, and posing a definite expansionist threat to the nations south of the Río Grande. Ingenieros, for his part, attacked the Monroe Doctrine, the idea of Pan-American Union, and "dollar diplomacy" as mere masks covering the face of an aggressive North American imperialism. Palacios echoed these sentiments, arguing that the United States was dominated by a capitalistic-monopolistic oligarchy which sent soldiers to protect invested dollars. He called upon the workers and students of North America to remember their democratic and liberal past and repudiate the actions of the elite which—so he believed—was controlling the nation's destiny. Both men placed their faith in the "new generation" of the University Reform to organize and to lead the resistance against the invasion from the north.[10]

In March, 1925, Ingenieros and Palacios began to put their thoughts into action by promoting the formation of the *Unión Latino Americana* (Latin American Union), an organization which included many prominent Reformistas. The purpose of the *Unión,* which shared many of the ideas and received encouragement from Haya de la Torre's *Aprista* movement, was to stimulate among all Latin American intellectual elements a continent-wide solidarity against imperialism. The *Unión's* program, written by Ingenieros, promoted social justice, national sovereignty, democracy, and nationalization of natural resources. It opposed militarism, Pan-Americanism, dictatorship, and imperialism. Significantly, the final article of the *Unión's* statutes called for "extension of secular, obligatory and free education and complete university reform." [11]

Argentina's student groups in the 1920's supported the *Unión Latino Americana* and shared the attitudes of its founders. These sympathies were evident between 1927 and 1928, when the U.S. Marines invaded the Central American nation of Nicaragua to protect North American interests there. Student federations throughout Argentina protested the Marine invasion. Reformista declarations emphasized student belief that the aggressive nature of United States policies in the Caribbean represented a real threat to the sovereignty of Argentina, and that it was the duty of the university youth to resist these "imperialistic" advances. Many Reformistas, among them Gabriel del Mazo, Deodoro Roca, Gregorio Bermann, and Enrique F. Barros, signed a message of sympathy directed by the *Unión Latino Americana* to Augusto César Sandino, leader of the forces in opposition to the U.S. Marines.[12]

In considering the anti-imperialist attitudes of the Argentine students, as they developed in the 1920's, it is interesting to note the emphasis on the United States as the principal threat to national sovereignty. For Argentina, Great Britain was in fact the foreign country which historically had the largest economic and political influence in the Republic. However, little can be found in student manifestoes of the years 1918–1930 relative to British imperialism. The subtlety of British investment, the lack of intellectual awareness of this control, the more spectacular actions of the "Yankees," and the feeling of solidarity with other youth movements which resisted actual invasions by the United States kept the North American republic in the foreground and Britain in the background of nationalist publications. It was not until the world depression of 1929 revealed the extent of Argentina's economic dependence on Great Britain that Argentine university groups began to attack British influence in the Republic.

During the 1920's, the Reformistas began to develop other attitudes which were closely related to their anti-imperialism. One of these was opposition to dictatorship in Latin America, a stance rooted in pre-1918 student activity and continued and expanded following the Reform. Because workers, students, and intellectuals were instrumental in introducing new theories of social justice and in advocating respect for individual rights in the years after World War I, these elements became prime targets for dictatorial repression throughout the area. For the university youth, the majority of Latin America's dictators were seen as the front men of a landed oligarchy which was living off the poverty of the masses and was supported by United States dollars. Opposition to authoritarian rule came to characterize and to solidify students in all Latin American republics during the 1920's. In addition, pacifism and opposition to militarism, often connected closely in the student mind with dictatorship and imperialism and based in part on reaction to World War I, began to emerge as dominant features of Reformista thought.

The connection between workers and students, which had been established during the 1918 revolt, continued to be an important aspect of the student program. In January, 1919, when a strike in Buenos Aires led to severe government repression and considerable violence in the so-called *Semana Trágica* (Tragic Week), the pens of the nation's student groups immediately came to the defense of the workers. The University Federation of Córdoba criticized the government's handling of the situation and offered full support to the proletariat. The FUC declaration demanded the improvement of social and economic conditions in the nation to raise the "material and moral level of the working people." [13]

One year after the *Semana Trágica,* in 1920, the Reformistas began to put into practice the principle of university extension which had been proposed during the First Student Congress of 1918. In the University of Buenos Aires (UBA) Faculty of Law, student leader and Reformista Florentino V. Sanguinetti organized courses for workers. The first classes for the labor groups had a definite political content. Liberal intellectuals spoke on such topics as the nature of governmental structures in the Soviet Union, various theories of Socialism and Anarcho-Syndicalism, and the need to reform society as well as the university.

Because of the initial enthusiasm first aroused by the idea, the university extension courses in the UBA enjoyed some preliminary successes and were favorably received by the workers. However, as time passed the classes for workers became less effective and less well attended. By the end of the decade the opposition of Conservative and anti-Reform administrative officials, both in the university and in the national government, combined with a growing apathy on the part of both the university youth and the labor groups, made university extension a dead letter in most faculties. The failure of the Reformistas to deal with practical concerns or to concentrate on issues, such as technical training, caused university extension to lose much of its appeal. As one student leader remarked in 1928, "University extension, anemically formulated as it has been up to now, will not be able to realize the vision of the Reform because it has weakened its character with academic dissertations in places where these are no longer necessary." [14]

The final important aspect of Reformista thought and action developed during the years of Radical rule was opposition to the reactionary ultra-nationalist groups which appeared in Argentina at this time. During the last days of the *Semana Trágica* of January, 1919, which occurred against the national background of increasing liberal influences and the international impact of the Bolshevik Revolution, various "super-patriot" groups, using violence and dedicated to the prevention of a "Communist" revolution, began to roam the streets of Buenos Aires. The principal organization of this kind was the *Liga Patriótica* (Patriotic League), "a proto-fascist organization of the period, which hated communists, labor and the Jews." [15] Under the direction of the *Liga,* many Jews, who were identified by the "super-patriots" with "Bolsheviks," were taken from their homes and shot to death during the *Semana Trágica.*

Subsequent to the events of January, 1919, the Argentine student federations issued many declarations attacking the extremist groups represented by the *Liga Patriótica.* The Reformistas considered themselves nationalists, but professing a nationalism quite removed from the concepts of the "super-patriots." The *Liga Patriótica* was essentially an elitist organization, reactionary, anti-Semitic, opposed to actions which would better the conditions of the working class, and distrustful of anything which seemed "foreign" or "revolutionary." In a declaration issued in May, 1919 the *Federación Universitaria de Córdoba* (FUC) attacked the concepts of the *Liga,* arguing that Argentina was not endangered by "foreign" elements. The manifesto criticized the narrowly defined, chauvinistic, and exclusive nationalism of the "super-patriots," stating that the "sentiment of patriotism is not the exclusive right of anyone, because the elevation of all nations should constitute the aspirations of all the men who inhabit nations." [16]

Perhaps the basic difference between the two organizations was that the ultra-nationalists wanted to exclude the lower classes and certain ethnic groups from participation in national affairs. The Reformistas, on the other hand, as they showed with their interest in the working classes through university extension, their emphasis on democracy and social justice, and their desire to open the universities to all academically qualified students regardless of social and economic status, were interested in allowing all Argentines to participate fully in national life. In the words of Gabriel del Mazo, "The nationalism of the Reform is that of the Nation with its people. The nationalism of the nationalistas is that of the Nation without its people." [17]

Following the Córdoba Reform of 1918, then, the Argentine university youth formulated attitudes on social, economic, and political issues which were to characterize the actions and thinking of the university groups up to the 1960's. The themes of opposition to imperialism, dictatorship, and ultra-nationalism and of support for social justice, solidarity with the working classes, and solidarity with youths in other Latin American republics became key points in a gradually emerging Reformista philosophy. It should be noted, however, that ideas on national issues often were drawn from sources which were outside the Reform movement. The Reformista philosophy, which represented the thinking of the liberal pro-Reform students, was a composite of principles espoused by political groups such as the Radical and Socialist parties and the thoughts of more independent figures such as those of José Ingenieros. This philosophy did not arise *sui generis* from the movement to reform Argentina's universities, although student thinking was undoubtedly stimulated by the youth's increased activism after 1918.

The attitudes of the Argentine Reformistas, moreover, were not unique in Latin America. Between 1918 and 1930, student movements throughout the area began to support similar causes and to express similar goals. From out of the continental movement for the reform of institutions of higher learning came a generation of young liberals who shared common viewpoints on many social, economic, and political issues. Victor Raúl Haya de la Torre of

Peru and Rómulo Betancourt of Venezuela, who were important student leaders during this period, later became two of the most significant political figures in Latin America. Betancourt, Haya de la Torre, and other student activists of the Reform years eventually formed the leadership of the so-called democratic, non-Communist left in Latin America, a movement whose program echoed many of the principal points of the Reformista philosophy.

Between 1918 and 1922, the *Federación Universitaria Argentina* gave its full support to the movement for continental solidarity among the university youth, the extension of the Reform to other nations, the development of characteristic student attitudes, and the spread of the Córdoba principles to all of Argentina's universities. In the years immediately after the 1918 Reform, the national federation was an active leader of the Argentine student movement. Besides completing its normal duties of co-ordinating all federations, publishing manifestoes and declarations on various issues, and acting as the directive voice of the Argentine university youth, the FUA also carried out several extensive campaigns related to specific educational and political problems.

Despite these activities, however, by late 1922 the national student federation began to decline in numbers and influence. This decline commenced as the enthusiasm generated by the Reform diminished and gave way to apathy, as the "men of '18" graduated from universities, and as the counter-Reform movement began to gather strength. By 1923 decay had reached the point where the Argentine federation ceased to exist as an effective organization. The decline of the national group was paralleled by a similar loss of influence and effectiveness on the part of the individual university federations.

An important factor in explaining the ineffectiveness of the formal university organizations was the general fragmentation of the Argentine student movement which took place in the 1920's.

The Reform depended on the leadership of intellectuals, who in Argentina have historically tended to follow very independent lines of thought, thereby making it difficult for any movement they control to remain monolithic for long. Reflecting this tendency, diverse university groups began to appear, each defining its own principles as to the direction they believed the Reform should take. In Buenos Aires a student center called *Insurrexit* was formed in 1920. *Insurrexit* proposed the complete destruction of the capitalist system, which was to be replaced by a new order based on the principles of the Communist International. The *Grupo Concordia,* established in 1923 also in Buenos Aires, attacked what it called the "Anarchist" and "Communist" influences evident in the Reform movement.

Neither *Insurrexit* nor the *Concordia,* which represented the left and right wings of the student political spectrum, exerted much influence on the university youth at this time. More important and more in the mainstream of Reformista thought was the *Agrupación de Izquierda del Partido Unión Reformista* (Leftist Group of the Reformista Union Party). Headed by former student leaders Julio V. González, Carlos Sánchez Viamonte, and Florentino V. Sanguinetti, all of whom in the mid-1920's were young professors in the Faculty of Law of the University of Buenos Aires, the *Agrupación* denied affiliation with any national political party. In its program it reiterated the Reformista themes of opposition to imperialism, dictatorship, and clerical-military interference in political affairs. Positively, the *Agrupación* supported respect for university autonomy and the implementation of effective Reform principles in all institutions of higher learning. The ideas of the *Agrupación* appeared throughout the pages of *Sagitario,* a periodical which Julio V. González and Carlos Sánchez Viamonte founded and edited in 1925.[18]

The decline of the *Federación Universitaria Argentina* and the splintering of the Argentine student movement in part resulted from the counter-Reform movement, which began with the inauguration of Radical President Marcelo T. de Alvear in October, 1922. The first concrete sign of the counter-Reform came in November, 1922, when, after a student disturbance, the national government took over the University of the Littoral. In May, 1923, the Alvear administration also intervened in the University of Córdoba. Subsequent to these interventions, the political Conservatives in the institutions, with the co-operation of the Alvear government, began to nullify the changes the Reformistas had introduced. Between 1922 and 1928, Córdoba principles of student participation in university government, unregulated attendance at classes, and the promotion of university extension courses were often rendered ineffective by Conservative-controlled administrations. Reformista attempts to oust Conservative professors, generally successful in the period 1918–1922, usually were stymied during the counter-Reform.

With the Conservative resurgence under Alvear, many Reformistas began to reanalyze the Reform. Anti-Reform criticisms of the Córdoba principles had centered on student participation in university administration and unregulated attendance at classes as features which detracted from the quality of education and led to a deplorable increase in political activism. Some liberal critics agreed. Many youths, it was argued, were so involved in university elections that they were becoming minor-league politicians, neglecting their studies and failing to live up to the high ideals of the Córdoba Reform. These defects could be remedied, the Reformistas reasoned, not by rolling back the advances of 1918, but only by a more thoroughgoing implementation of the Reform principles. Generally the aforementioned critics urged the Argentine students to move more actively into national political affairs to achieve this goal. They argued that the coincidence between the Alvear administration and the counter-Reform made it necessary that there be changes on the national level before profound and lasting improvements could be made within the Republic's institutions of higher learning.

The strongest proponent of a more active political role for the Reformistas in these years was Julio V. González, former president of the FUA. In 1927, González proposed the formation of a *Partido Nacional Reformista* (National Reformista party). González was encouraged to make this proposal largely because of his belief that the men of the Reform had been molded by a particular set of circumstances which had created a distinct generation. Looking to the common characteristics and themes developed by the student movement, he foresaw a party similar to the APRA of Peru emerging from the Argentine University Reform and wielding real political influence.[19] However, the fragmentation which had occurred among the student groups, the continued reluctance of the Reformistas to enter into national partisan politics, and the awareness that the introduction of a new political party at this time would only divide rather than unite liberal forces prevented González' idea from ever becoming reality.

The effects of the 1922–1928 counter-Reform were felt in every university in the Republic, but probably nowhere was the clash between pro-Reform and anti-Reform elements so dramatic as in the University of Buenos Aires (UBA) Faculty of Law. Within that Faculty a group of anti-Reform professors, representing some of the most Conservative political elements in the nation, were supported in their efforts to resist the Córdoba principles by a large segment of the student body, many of whom were from Argentina's wealthiest families. Opposing the Conservatives was a dedicated group of liberal and pro-Reform students. During the 1920's, the pro-Reform youth in the law school enjoyed the leadership and support of such young Reformista professors as Julio V. González, Carlos Sánchez Viamonte, and Florentino V. Sanguinetti, who represented the students' interest on the Faculty of Law Directive Council. Events in this Faculty serve as a graphic example of what was occurring throughout the Republic's universities during the counter-Reform.

In August, 1927, the struggle between the conflicting elements in the UBA Faculty of Law became an issue of general public concern when the Reformistas opposed a military officer's lecture delivered in the auditorium of the school. This dispute arose out of an arrangement made by the Conservative and anti-Reform dean of the Faculty, Ramón S. Castillo, with the *Escuela Superior de Guerra* (War College) to present a series of lectures on military topics in the UBA. Opposition to militarism was one of the principal points of the Reformista philosophy, and the announcement of the first talk in this series, scheduled for August 19, aroused the immediate protest of the liberal youths n the Faculty of Law. On August 16, seven law students issued a manifesto which objected to the proposed address. In their statement, the Reformistas declared themselves in favor of "universal peace and human harmony," and opposed to the introduction into the University of "concepts molded in a chauvinistic and aggressive sensibility." [20]

Despite the protests of the Reformistas, the War College lecture was given as scheduled on August 19. Moving from manifestoes to direct action, the rebellious youth of the Faculty demonstrated in the halls of the law school and successfully disturbed the process of the talk. These actions aroused many complaints from the military hierarchy of the Republic. Soon after the lecture, Agustín P. Justo, Alvear's minister of war, demanded that the authors of the student protest note, who in the Minister's opinion were responsible for the disturbances of August 19, be punished by university officials. On August 26, after a long and acrimonious debate, the Conservative-dominated Directive Council of the Faculty of Law voted to suspend for a period of two years the seven students the Minister of War had pointed out for punishment.

The decision of the Directive Council brought an immediate response from liberal elements. Student federations and centers, along with leftist intellectuals and politicians, quickly came to the support of the dismissed students. Several days after the expulsion, student representatives Florentino V. Sanguinetti and Carlos Sánchez Viamonte resigned from the Directive Council as an act of protest. During the dispute arising from the lecture series, liberal opinion focused its criticism on the evils of militarism, which it connected with super-patriotism and lack of respect for civilian authority.

As on previous occasions, the Conservatives again had factional support among university and other nonmilitary groups. In the lecture hall of the *Liga Patriótica,* a conference was presented which honored the Argentine military tradition and condemned the "unpatriotic" attitude of the Reformista students. Among the law students themselves, a group appeared to support Dean Castillo and the Council's decision. The *Círculo Argentino de Estudiantes de Derecho* (Argentine Circle of Students of Law) refused to join the Reformistas in protesting the expulsion of the anti-militarist students and promised to reaffirm "once more their nationalist sentiments . . . and to maintain order and discipline in the Faculty by all means in their power." [21] Despite Conservative support for the War College addresses, however, the Reformista campaign finally succeeded in having the military lecture series canceled.[22]

The significant developments in the Argentine student movement between 1918 and 1930 included the spread of the Reform to all of the Republic's universities, the diffusion of the Córdoba principles to other Latin American countries, the fragmentation of the university organizations in the early 1920's, and the student campaign against the counter-Reform. Moreover, during the 1920's many of the young men who had participated in the Reform campaigns began to take professorial chairs in the nation's universities. In the struggle against the counter-Reform, the Reformista students discovered that an increasing number of faculty members were sympathetic with the Córdoba principles. Indeed, in the University of Buenos Aires Faculty of Law, such young Reformista professors as Julio V. González, Florentino V. Sanguinetti, and Carlos Sánchez Viamonte played a more important role as Reform leaders than did the university youth themselves.

Perhaps the most important development for the Argentine university youth during this period was the formulation of attitudes which were identified with an emerging Reformista philosophy. In the 1920's, the students moved from the field of educational problems to consider broad social, economic, and political issues. The expansion of the scope of Reformista ideas led some to urge an even more extensive role for the university youth in national politics. But the Reform still carried with it an apolitical tradition, a sentiment that remained strong throughout the post-Córdoba decade.

The period that followed, beginning with the 1930 revolution and the return of the Conservatives to national power, created a profound crisis for the Reformistas and caused a serious reevaluation of the student position on partisan political activity.

NOTES

1. "Decreto aprobando la reforma de los estatutos," *La reforma universitaria: en la Universidad de Córdoba* (Buenos Aires, 1919), pp. 351–355.
2. For documents on the University Reform in La Plata see del Mazo, ed., *La reforma universitaria* (1927–Vol. IV).
3. Alejandro Korn, "La reforma universitaria," del Mazo, ed., *La reforma universitaria* (1927–Vol. IV), pp. 219–224; and Héctor Ripa Alberdi, "El renacimiento del espíritu argentino," del Mazo, ed., *La reforma universitaria* (1926–Vol. I), pp. 43–47.
4. For documents on the student campaigns in Santa Fe, Rosario, and Tucumán see del Mazo, ed., *La reforma universitaria* (1927–Vol. III), pp. 229–276; and del Mazo, ed., *La reforma universitaria* (1927–Vol. V), pp. 35–54.

5. For further information on this aspect of the University Reform see Victor Raúl Haya de la Torre, "En el XI aniversario de la reforma," *Revista de filosofía* (September–November 1928), pp. 121–133; and Harry Kantor, *The Ideology and Program of the Peruvian Aprista Movement* (Berkeley, Calif., 1953), pp. 7–21.

6. "Resoluciones del Congreso Internacional de Estudiantes reunido en Mexico," del Mazo, ed., *La reforma universitaria* (1927–Vol. VI), pp. 75–84.

7. Héctor Ripa Alberdi, "La Argentina naciente" and "Por la emancipación futura del brazo y de la inteligencia," del Mazo, ed., *La reforma universitaria* (1927–Vol. VI), pp. 386–396.

8. The youth of Venezuela who rebelled against Gómez, the "Generation of '28," included many of the future leaders of that country's democratic and leftist political parties. Rómulo Betancourt, later leader of the *Acción Democrática* and President of Venezuela between 1958 and 1964, was among the students imprisoned by Gómez in 1928. See John D. Martz, "Venezuela's 'Generation of '28': The Genesis of Political Democracy," *Journal of Inter-American Studies,* VI (January 1964), 17–32.

9. "La Federación Universitaria Argentina contra el imperialismo mundial," del Mazo, ed., *La reforma universitaria* (1927–Vol. VI), pp. 31–33.

10. Sergio Bagú, *Vida ejemplar de José Ingenieros: juventud y plenitud* (Buenos Aires, 1936), pp. 218–228; and Alfredo L. Palacios, *La Unión Latino-Americana y el imperialismo yanqui* (Buenos Aires, 1927).

11. Bagú, *op. cit.,* pp. 232–233.

12. "Mensaje a Sandino," del Mazo, ed., *La reforma universitaria* (1941–Vol. II), pp. 152–153.

13. "La Federación Universitaria de Córdoba se adhiere al paro obrero de protesta por los sucesos de Buenos Aires (enero 12 de 1919)," del Mazo, ed., *La reforma universitaria* (1927–Vol. V), pp. 55–56.

14. "Discurso del presidente del centro estudiantes de ciencias económicas Señor Armando M. Rocco," in Centro Estudiantes de Ciencias Económicas, *Conferencias* (Buenos Aires, 1929), p. 5.

15. Ysabel Fisk Rennie, *The Argentine Republic* (New York, 1945), p. 216n.

16. "La Federación Universitaria de Córdoba, al pueblo y a los estudiantes con motivo del aniversario patrio, a raíz de la aparición de un manifiesto de la 'Liga Patriótica Argentina' (25 de mayo de 1919)," del Mazo, ed., *La reforma universitaria* (1927–Vol. V), pp. 80–81.

17. From the answers to a series of written questions which I presented to Gabriel del Mazo in Buenos Aires in November, 1964.

18. "Definición social de la reforma universitaria; declaración de principios

de la agrupación de izquierda del partido unión reformista," *Sagitario* (La Plata, July–August 1925), pp. 262–264.

19. Julio V. González, "El partido nacional reformista," *Revista de ciencias económicas* (Buenos Aires, September 1927), pp. 1093–1098.
20. "Manifiesto de la junta provisoria de la unión reformista–centro izquierda," del Mazo, ed., *La reforma universitaria* (1941–Vol. I), p. 255.
21. *La Prensa,* August 31, 1927, p. 10.
22. For more information on this issue within the Buenos Aires law school see "Conflicto de los militares en la Facultad de Derecho," del Mazo, ed., *La reforma universitaria* (1941–Vol. I), pp. 255–268.

Students and Conservatives, 1930-1943

5

With the military-led revolution of September 6, 1930, the Argentine Conservatives regained the national political power they had lost with the Radical victory of 1916. From 1930 to 1943 the Republic was ruled by a so-called *Concordancia,* composed of military officers, *estancieros,* merchants, bankers, and members of the high clergy. These years of Conservative control were characterized by the repression of political opposition, widespread electoral corruption and fraud, and neglect of the social and economic needs of the nation's lower classes. During this period the democratic parties were splintered into diverse groups and failed to present any effective opposition to the *Concordancia.*

Once the 1930 revolution had succeeded, General José F. Uriburu served as the provisional president of the Republic. Under Uriburu Argentina suffered from the harshest political dictatorship it had experienced since the days of Juan Manuel de Rosas. Radical party members were removed from all governmental posts and replaced with Conservatives. Members of the political opposition were terrorized by the "special section" of the federal police, created by Uriburu to control public life. Radicals, Socialists, and Communists were persecuted, imprisoned, and exiled. The post-revolutionary government attempted to censor the press, dissolve the national Congress, and impose a corporate state system upon the nation. By late 1931, Uriburu's measures had lost him most of the popular support he had enjoyed immediately after the 1930 revolution, and he was forced to call presidential elections.

In November, 1931, Conservative Agustín P. Justo, an army general and minister of war under Alvear, was elected as Argentina's chief executive. Under Justo opposition groups were allowed to carry out their normal activities in relative freedom, and the repressive police actions which had characterized the Uriburu regime gradually disappeared. However, under Justo the Conservatives continued to control the political life of the nation through electoral fraud and a monopoly of the government bureaucracy. The outstanding achievement of the Justo administration, which governed Argentina from 1932 to 1938, was to protect the nation from the effects of the world depression of 1929. In so doing, however, the Conservatives permitted great concessions to foreign capital, particularly to Great Britain, and stimulated among the Argentine public a strong sentiment of economic nationalism.

When President Justo was succeeded by Conservative Roberto Ortiz in 1938, it was expected that the political corruption which had characterized the *Concordancia* would continue. But Ortiz, to the surprise of his own backers, permitted free and honest elections during his administration. When World War II began to unfold in the late 1930's, Ortiz indicated that he was sympathetic to the Allies—a position completely opposed to that of the many elements in the *Concordancia* who supported the Axis. However, this short period of political "liberalization" ended in 1940, when illness forced President Ortiz to turn control of the government over to his vice-president, Ramón S. Castillo. Under Castillo, who was a Conservative and pro-Axis, the Republic returned to the pattern of political corruption, electoral fraud, police repression of opposition elements, accompanied by attempts to restrict freedoms of the press, assembly, and speech.

During the years of *Concordancia* rule the Argentine student movement underwent significant modifications. In reaction to the repressive measures of the Uriburu regime and the political corruption of the Justo administration, the nation's university youth became important members of the political opposition. When the Conservatives, with the aid of Uriburu and Justo, initiated a second counter-Reform in the Republic's institutions of higher learning, many of the Reformistas abandoned their former independent stance and began to participate actively in national politics. By the early 1930's many students realized that the Republic's universities could not be reformed unless profound changes were made on the national level, changes which would produce governments that would respect democratic procedures, individual liberties, and university autonomy.

The basic concepts of the Reformista philosophy continued to be developed between 1930 and 1943. The principles of opposition to ultra-nationalism and foreign imperialism and of support for the continental solidarity of youth groups were applied and adapted to changing conditions. During these years, the Argentine youth continued to participate in international student conferences and to increase their interest in international affairs. By the end of the 1930's, the Reformistas were impelled to turn their attention to the beginnings of World War II and to consider their attitude with regard to the emerging world conflict.

The revolution of September, 1930, which put the Conservatives back into public office, was supported and in part initiated by Argentina's university youth. A description of these events provides a good example of the student role in a Latin American revolution.

Student dissatisfaction with Hipólito Irigoyen's second term in office, begun in 1928, reflected the general national discontent with the Radical government. By 1930 the seventy-eight-year-old Irigoyen seemed incapable of providing effective executive leadership to halt the increasing bureaucratic corruption and governmental inefficiency which characterized all levels of the administration. The President also faced a growing opposition from the press, the military, the Conservatives, the Socialist and Communist parties, and even from some elements of the badly splintered Radical party. Nor did the Irigoyen government in 1930 appear able to solve the national economic problems caused by the world depression, particularly the problem of widespread unemployment.

A student manifesto issued in Buenos Aires on August 31, 1930, marked the beginning of an intensive drive by the university groups to oust President Irigoyen—the man who a decade earlier had approved the University Reform. In its early stages, the campaign to overthrow the Radical government enjoyed both Reformista and anti-Reformista support, as the two groups momentarily joined in the common effort to force political change. Subsequent to the 1930 revolution, as will be seen, these two factions split over support for the post-revolutionary administration. The August 31 declaration, signed by several hundred university students, called for a drastic shift in Argentine government policy to meet the recent domestic crises in administration and the economy and warned that the youth would demonstrate in the streets to enforce this demand.[1]

Having signed this declaration, students in Buenos Aires, principally from the Faculties of Law and Medicine, sought to arouse public support for a governmental change. The most important events in the student campaign against the Radical government occurred on September 4, 1930. In the wake of an anti-government rally in the Faculty of Medicine, several thousand students began a march through the streets of Buenos Aires toward the Casa Rosada, shouting the cry that Irigoyen must resign. Their actions were warmly received by an enthusiastic public who crowded the sidewalks to view the student demonstration. Gaining confidence and popular support as they walked, the student parade reached the Plaza de Mayo, directly in front of the government house. There the youths were halted by police forces and members of the security guard. However, by taking various circuitous routes small groups began to filter into the plaza and to continue their advance upon the executive offices. After entering the Plaza de Mayo, a number of youths gathered around a statue in the middle of the square and attempted to raise a flag. As the police arrived with sabers to dislodge the demonstrators, shots rang out and several students and one member of the security forces fell to the ground seriously wounded. There was general confusion as the wounded were carried off to be treated, and although it could not be established who had fired the shots, the students immediately charged the government with police brutality. Agitation in the Plaza de Mayo continued for several hours before the government forces managed to disperse the demonstrators.[2]

This demonstration, occurring at a time of increasing popular discontent with the Irigoyen government, served greatly to generate public support for anti-government forces. The shooting of several students in the Plaza de Mayo aroused a general public indignation against the Radical government. When one of the youths involved in the demonstration died as a result of the riot, the anti-Irigoyen elements were provided with a young martyr. The city's newspapers, already opponents of Irigoyen, severely criticized the government's treatment of the students. On September 5, the day after the Plaza de Mayo demonstration, the editors of *La Prensa* praised the "beautiful expression of healthy youthful vigor" shown by the university youth, and attacked the government police for their alleged brutality.[3]

President Irigoyen, under pressure from all sides and by then a very ill man, surrendered control of the government to his vice-president on September 5. A meeting of the cabinet which followed this move declared a thirty-day "state of siege," granting the government broad powers to restrict public activity. Meanwhile, groups of students continued their agitation, fighting in all parts of the capital with pro-Irigoyen elements and repeating their demands that the chief executive resign. Within the University of Buenos Aires, classes were suspended as student speakers used the academic halls to arouse the youth to political action.

On September 6, 1930, the Argentine military, which had not interfered openly in politics since the nineteenth century, marched into Buenos Aires to oust Irigoyen's government. Led by Generals José F. Uriburu and Agustín P. Justo, the army's march into the city was practically a triumphal parade. The armed forces encountered great public approval and little physical resistance. Arriving at the Casa Rosada, the generals expelled the Radicals and replaced civilian leaders with military officers.[4]

Student activity was an important factor in the military's final decision to remove the Irigoyen government. Colonel J. Beresford Crawkes, a participant in the army's maneuverings in the fall of 1930, credited agitation among the university population with forcing the generals to show their hand. According to Crawkes, elements within the army had been plotting a move against the government for some time, but their plans for a military take-over had been repeatedly postponed for one reason or another. When independent student actions aroused public opinion to a clear anti-government position, the army elements ended their procrastination and took advantage of the situation to initiate their revolt.[5]

The part played by the Argentine university youth in the revolution of 1930 later came under strong criticism, particularly when the reactionary nature of the Uriburu administration became evident. However, student support for the Uriburu *revolt* should not be confused with support for the Uriburu *government*. A declaration issued by the *Federación Universitaria de Buenos Aires* (FUBA) several days after the army coup may be considered as representing student thinking at that time. Mentioning with pride their participation in the revolution, the youths declared that September 6 could be the beginning of a general national renovation. But the base for that renovation rested on the re-establishment of constitutional normality, the full exercise of political rights, observance of the Sáenz Peña electoral law, and the "jealous respect for university autonomy in all the nation." Throughout this statement the FUBA emphasized the importance of the civilian tradition in national political life and implied that the army should serve merely as a caretaker government until a democratically elected administration could replace military control.[6]

With the exception of Conservative anti-Reformista groups such as the *Círculo Argentino de Estudiantes de Derecho,* which supported the new government without qualification, most of the university students viewed the Uriburu coup in the terms outlined in the FUBA declaration. The youth backed the military as instruments of change to rid Argentina of the Irigoyen administration. But most students expected the armed forces to surrender control to civilians and to restore constitutional guarantees. When it became clear that the army planned to remain in power, the university youth quickly became leaders among those elements which opposed the Conservative government.

These remarks are not intended to absolve the students from all criticism with regard to their actions in 1930, but are meant only to clarify the nature of their position at the time. In the September revolution the Reformistas ignored their own principles of support for democratic procedures and opposition to militarism when they backed a military-sponsored move to oust a democratically elected president—a president who had sympathized with their aspirations and had approved their actions. Furthermore, they displayed a considerable political naïveté in believing that the military would return the government to civilian hands. The university youth had had little contact with the armed forces before the revolution, and it had no concrete evidence of the army's future plans. Their belief that the generals would step down after seizing power seems to have been based more on hope than logic. In September, 1930, the Argentine students sought a rapid political change, a change by any means, and they succumbed to their propensity to ignore institutional procedures in favor of direct action. This time the stakes were high, change on the national political level, and after their direct action the students were forced to pay a correspondingly high price for the results their own activities had helped to produce.

Provisional President Uriburu, in late 1930, followed the pattern of many Latin American dictators, at first welcoming and praising the student support which had placed him in power and then taking measures to insure that the university groups could not pose a threat to the stability of his own regime. Having promised to respect university autonomy after his coup, it took Uriburu only three months to reverse himself and to intervene and take control of the University of Buenos Aires. In December, 1930, the rector of the UBA was forced to turn his office over to an anti-Reform government intervenor appointed by the provisional President. This action marked the beginning of a second counter-Reform movement in the Republic. In the following months the military administration intervened in most of Argentina's universities and replaced administrative officials with government agents. Throughout the nation's institutions of higher learning Reform principles, many of which had been restored during Irigoyen's short second term, were once again rescinded or made ineffective through cumbersome rules and regulations. In many schools the military-dominated government assigned Conservative and anti-Reform professors to fill administrative and professorial posts. Some anti-Reform professors from the UBA Faculty of Law moved directly into the Uriburu government, strengthening the bond between the Conservative national leadership and the university's administrators.

On the national level the Uriburu administration began to use arrests, imprisonments, and repressions of public demonstrations to control growing opposition groups. The Reformista students, who began to organize their opposition to the Uriburu government during the university interventions, were among the principal targets of government action. Imprisonment was often the result of student political activity. The Conservative intervenor at the UBA, when faced with a university strike in December, 1930, ordered the police to arrest student leader Pablo Lejarraga. Another student prominent in university politics, Héctor P. Agosti of the University of Buenos Aires (UBA) Faculty of Philosophy and Letters, spent several years in prison because of his opposition to the government. When a delegation of the *Federación Universitaria Argentina* (FUA) attempted to present a petition protesting new anti-Reform statutes to President Uriburu in May, 1931, not only were they refused an interview but the president of the federation, Juan Manuel Villareal, was arrested upon leaving the Casa Rosada and placed in prison for several months. In the early 1930's, student journals began to publish lists naming dozens of youths incarcerated because of political activities.[7] Other students, escaping arrest, passed months in exile because of their political opinions and activities.

After the 1930 revolution, many pro-Reform professors in the universities were subjected to the same government repression as the Reformista students. A number of faculty members were separated from their university posts or resigned voluntarily in protest of government actions. Mario Sáenz, Reformista professor of law in the UBA, resigned in December, 1930, protesting against what he considered the illegalities of the Uriburu intervention in the University. José Peco, another pro-Reform professor in the

Buenos Aires law school, was forced to give up his position after being accused of "Communist" sympathies when he defended in court workers and students arrested by the government. Still other Reformista professors, among them Gabriel del Mazo, Julio V. González, Gregorio Bermann, and Jorge Orgaz, all of whom opposed the government intervention in the Republic's universities, also were dismissed from their university teaching positions.[8]

Despite the measures of the Conservative regime against students and professors, the university youth were able—under duress—to carry on a spirited campaign of agitation and opposition. In March, 1931, the *Federación Universitaria Argentina* (FUA) was reorganized under student leadership.

On April 11, 1931, the new FUA published a manifesto demanding an end to the university interventions, the reintegration into the faculties of dismissed professors, the liberation of arrested students, and the "immediate constitution of the normal and legal government of the University." Later FUA statements attacked the dictatorial aspects of the Uriburu administration and demanded the restoration of democratic procedures and constitutional guarantees.[9]

Following the lead of the national organization, individual university federations began to register their opposition to the government's educational and political policies. In Córdoba the youth demanded a return to Reform statutes and supported with meetings and manifestoes Reformista professors Gregorio Bermann and Jorge Orgaz, both of whom had been expelled from their positions in the local university. When the government took over the University of the Littoral, the *Federación Universitaria del Litoral* (FUL) protested against the imposed anti-Reform regulations and accused the Uriburu regime of reinstituting a spirit of reaction already rejected by the Argentine people. In La Plata the youth objected to the anti-Reform changes made in the ULP after 1930 and attacked the administration through their journal

Renovación. Gaceta universitaria, organ of the medical students center of the University of Buenos Aires, also published many articles criticizing the actions of university and government officials.

In the early 1930's the students continued to employ the political methods developed during the struggles for the University Reform. They sent petitions of protest to the Minister of Education, distributed leaflets in the streets, requested interviews with the national executive, held public meetings with political parties and labor organizations, and often resorted to the direct action of the university strike. Nonetheless, the political climate and the nature of the national administration in the early 1930's were considerably different from what they had been between 1918 and 1922: During the Uriburu administration the youth found that their actions had little effect in changing government policy. The Conservatives having regained power, their concern was to stifle opposition and to counter measures instituted by the Radicals. Consequently, student petitions were ignored, requests for presidential interviews were denied, and university groups suffered from direct government repression.

Although they failed to influence national policy in the 1930's, the Argentine university youth did play a significant part in the general opposition to the Conservative administration. The weakness of the democratic political parties during this period, combined with the clarity of student opinion and the courage of university forces in the face of repression, gave the youth a notable position and prestige among those groups which opposed the Uriburu, and later the Justo, government. This prestige was evident in a meeting of some 60,000 persons held in March, 1932, in Buenos Aires. The speakers at this anti-government rally included Reformista professors Alfredo L. Palacios and José Peco and student leader Eduardo Howard. Howard, at that time president of the FUA, called for the release of imprisoned students and the restoration of Reform principles within Argentina's universities. The inclusion of a student leader as one of the main speakers in a political meeting of this size was one indication of the stature of the university youth among the opposition.[10]

The administration of President Agustín P. Justo began in 1932. With Justo more political opposition was allowed than during the Uriburu regime, but the Conservatives, through bribery, nepotism, and fraud, kept a close control of the nation's political life. Most posts in the government bureaucracy continued to be occupied by Conservatives, and many young professional men graduating from Argentina's universities were unable to gain access to coveted public positions. During the 1930's, men trained in law or engineering were forced to find jobs in occupations far removed in nature from their academic training. Many youths responded to this situation with resigned acceptance; others, however, sought a solution through political action. In these years the Argentine student movement began to expand the scope of its program and to take on a more radical appearance. Reformista professors, who heretofore had maintained an apolitical position, began to participate actively in political parties. Reformista students also began to work more closely with political groups. Some youths who entered politics in the 1930's "joined either the extreme left, the Communists, or the extreme right, the nationalists and fascists." [11]

At the Second National Student Congress assembled in Buenos Aires in August, 1932, the Argentine student movement indicated that it was beginning to adapt and expand the original concepts of the Reform in response to the return of the Conservatives to national political power. At this meeting, modeled on the Córdoba Congress of 1918, the youth dealt with both educational and political issues. In education the students called for a reform not only in institutions of higher learning, but also throughout the entire educational system of the nation. As a part of this broader outlook, they urged secondary school students to form their own organizations and to campaign for the establishment of Reform statutes in their institutions and promised their younger colleagues the full support of the university federations in these efforts. The Second Congress also gave new and broadened definitions to the Reform articles on university extension classes, student participation in university government, and respect for university autonomy.

The Second National Student Congress, reflecting the increased national role of the Argentine university youth since 1918, concerned itself much more with political, economic, and social issues than had the First National Student Congress. Evident throughout the discussions was a tone of disillusionment with past political philosophies, which appeared to the youth to have caused the world depression and the rise of authoritarian governments in Europe and Latin America in the early 1930's. At the Second Congress the students rejected the concept of a nation based upon the principles of "private economy and individual rights," principles which had dominated Argentine thought throughout the late nineteenth and early twentieth centuries. Instead, the students urged a struggle for a completely new social, economic, and political structure for the nation. In their declarations they called for a society which would be based upon "a collective economy and social rights." On specific issues, the students urged solidarity with the working class, voiced their opposition to dictatorship, and demanded that the church not interfere in political affairs.[12]

The sentiments expressed by the youth during the Second Congress represented a significant departure from the philosophy which had dominated the Córdoba Congress fourteen years earlier. In 1918, the students had aimed at reforming the university first so as to use the renovated institutions of higher learning as a tool in transforming the nation. The argument which began to emerge from the Second Congress was almost the reverse of the original Reformista concept: Confronted with a government which did not respect university autonomy or democratic procedures and which made the implementation of Reform principles almost impossible, the youth of 1932 began to conceive a program and to formulate a plan of action which would aim at changing the nature of Argentine society first. Only after reforms had been made at the national level, it was argued, could significant modifications be made in the Republic's institutions of higher learning.

Not only in philosophy but also in other, more tangible, respects was the Second National Student Congress representative of the changes which had occurred in the Argentine student movement between 1918 and 1932. The number and variety of groups which attended the Second Congress were indicative of the expansion of the student movement and its activities since the Córdoba Reform. The Buenos Aires Congress, as had been the Córdoba conference, was composed of delegations representing all the university federations as well as the National Student Federation, FUA. Also in attendance were observers from seven labor organizations, including representatives of the influential *Confederación General del Trabajo* (CGT, General Labor Confederation) and the *Federación Obrera Regional Argentina* (FORA, Argentine Regional Labor Federation). Perhaps the clearest indication of the university movement's growth was the fact that representatives from some forty student centers and *agrupaciones* were present at the meeting.

Although the Second National Student Congress welcomed the advice and support of such older Reformistas as Saúl Alejandro Taborda, Deodoro Roca, Enrique F. Barros, and Gabriel del Mazo, it was evident that the active leadership of the student movement had passed to a younger generation. Among the principal directors of the Congress were student leaders such as Alberto May Zubiría of the UBA Faculty of Law and president of the FUA; Isidro Odena, also of the UBA Faculty of Law; Ernesto Giúdice, of the UBA Faculty of Medicine; Héctor P. Agosti, of the UBA Faculty of Philosophy and Letters; Pablo Lejarraga, of the UBA Faculty of Economic Sciences; and Augusto J. Durelli, of the UBA Faculty of Engineering. In later years, as will be seen in subsequent chapters, these men became influential intellectuals and politicians and continued to maintain close contact with university and student problems. Like the "men of '18," the "generation of '32" was largely from the middle class and relatively young in years: In May, 1932, May Zubiría was twenty-four, Odena twenty-six, Giúdice twenty-five, Agosti twenty-one, and Lejarraga twenty-nine.[13]

In the early 1930's, before and after the Second National Student Congress, many Reformistas urged the university youth of Argentina to enter actively into national politics as a means of bringing about the social, economic, and political changes necessary if the principles of the University Reform were ever to be made effective. A pamphlet drafted by Reformista professors Gabriel del Mazo, Julio V. González, Florentino V. Sanguinetti, and others in August, 1931, during the Uriburu dictatorship, advised the Republic's university students to form a "united front" with labor groups and political parties. The Reformistas argued that the nation was in a state of political crisis because of the authoritarian nature of the post-revolutionary administration. To solve this crisis, they declared that the youth should join with the "popular forces" and the democratic political parties in a coordinated effort to restore the rule of democracy, social justice, and the internal peace to the nation. The document concluded by encouraging the students to concentrate "all your force on civic action and the solution of the country's political problems."[14]

After the revolution of 1930, a number of the older Reformistas themselves entered the political parties which opposed the Uriburu and Justo administrations. Reform figures Alejandro Korn, Deodoro Roca, and Carlos Sánchez Viamonte joined the Socialist party. Other Reformistas, including José Peco, Mario Sáenz, and a former president of FUA, Eduardo Araujo, became active members of the Radical party. Joining the Socialist party in the early 1930's, Julio V. González attacked the apolitical tradition of the Reform, which in his opinion was now leading the Reformistas "straight to ruin." [15]

Another factor in the increasing "politicization" of the university groups in these years was the growing influence of Marxism among some sectors of the youth. In the 1930's, several prominent student leaders began to criticize the Reformista philosophy as being too moderate and started to analyze the condition of the Argentine society and the Argentine university in Marxist and revolutionary terms. In 1932 Ernesto Giúdice, Socialist student leader in the UBA Faculty of Medicine and later an important member of the Argentine Communist party, published *Ha muerto el dictador pero no la dictadura* from exile in Montevideo. In this work, Giúdice traced student disappointment with the failure of Irigoyen and the Radicals to implement effective social and economic reforms. Describing contemporary Argentina against the background of a Marxist interpretation of twentieth-century world history, Giúdice advised the nation's university youth to consider revolution as a response to the Conservative Justo administration.[16]

Héctor P. Agosti, student leader in the UBA Faculty of Philosophy and Letters and also editor of two Communist weeklies, emphasized social and economic factors in his analysis of the University Reform movement. In a series of articles written in the early 1930's, Agosti argued that although the Reformista program did contain revolutionary elements, such as anti-imperialism and solidarity with the proletariat, the Reform could not supply what he believed was most needed in post-1930 Argentina—"a coherent revolutionary thought." Claiming that the liberal ideas of the 1920's could not meet the problems evolving from a worldwide class struggle, Agosti reasoned that Marxism was the only course for Argentina's middle and lower classes suffering—he said—from capitalist-imperialist exploitation.[17]

In 1933, Agosti and other members of the Argentine Communist party formed a new student organization called *Insurrexit.* Critical of Reformista thought, the leaders of *Insurrexit* attacked the interpretation of the Reform put forth by Julio V. González: namely, that the student movement resulted from a conflict between new and old generations. Instead, the Communists viewed university developments in terms of class struggle. The Reform, according to *Insurrexit,* was not a fight between fathers and sons, but rather a clash between the middle sectors of the society and the privileged. Still debated, this criticism of Reformista thought was one of the most important and stimulating contributions of the Communists to the Argentine student movement.[18] Disbanded in 1935, *Insurrexit* nonetheless represented the definite introduction of Marxist influences into student political activity, influences which have persisted down to the 1960's.

While some university students began to turn toward Communism in the 1930's, others were attracted to the extreme right. After the fall of Irigoyen in 1930, various organizations of a reactionary and right-wing nature began to assume positions of prominence on the national scene. The Argentine ultra-nationalists, reacting against liberalism and stimulated by the rise of European Fascism, were composed of several elements at this time. In their ranks were the frustrated sons of *estancieros;* some intellectuals; army officers who admired the Fascist emphasis on militarism and force; and elements in the Argentine clergy who were Spanish, strongly pro-Franco, and also strongly anti-Communist. Although there were differences in emphasis and degree, the ultra-nationalists were generally anti-liberal, anti-Communist, anti-Semitic, and virulently opposed to Great Britain and the United States. Most of them glorified the Spanish colonial tradition, sought to rehabilitate the memory of the dictator Juan Manuel de Rosas, and favored the establishment of Argentine hegemony over all of South America.[19]

During the administration of Uriburu, who had once proposed the institution of Mussolini's corporate state in Argentina, organizations of an ultra-nationalist character were used by the government as shock troops (*grupos de choque*) against opposition elements. The most significant of these was the *Legión Cívica Argentina* (Argentine Civic Legion), which in the early 1930's attempted to break student strikes and to prevent student political activity. In September, 1931, for example, a raid by members of the "Civic Legion" caused considerable damage to the engineering students' center in the UBA. Neither the university officials nor the police did anything to stop the destruction and later closed the center.[20]

One of the principal tactics employed by the ultra-nationalists against liberal university groups was to accuse them of being under Communist influence. In August, 1932, at the same time as the Second National Student Congress, the *Unión Universitaria Nacionalista* (Nationalist University Union) held a conference in the UBA Faculty of Law. Carlos Ibarguren, former professor in the Buenos Aires law school and the leading theoretician of the ultra-nationalists in the 1930's, was the principal speaker. In his address, Ibarguren suggested that the model of Mussolini's corporate state would best protect Argentina from the "Red wave or anarchy" by forming a society where the "hierarchy is made by the selection of values and discipline is the base of order." [21] One week later, a spokesman for the *Acción Nacionalista Argentina* (Argentine Nationalist Action), an ultra-nationalist group headed by a former anti-Reformista dean of the UBA Faculty of Law, Juan P. Ramos, claimed that the Second National Student Congress was the focal point for a growing Communist influence in the Republic. He urged that the "patriotic youth" resist the threat to the Argentine university of a "moral contamination" presented by the alleged growth of Communism.[22]

At that time these ultra-nationalist organizations enjoyed some success in recruiting students to their ranks, particularly youths who were anti-Reformista. Their greatest stronghold among the university sectors in these years was in the UBA Faculty of Law, which by the end of the decade "had gradually come to be the intellectual seat of Argentine nationalism." [23] Anti-Reformista student groups such as the *Círculo Argentino de Estudiantes de Derecho* often reflected the thinking of the ultra-nationalists. One student newspaper of the period gave an almost mystical quality to nationalism by proclaiming in boldface lettering **"TO BE ARGENTINE** means: to feel, to think, to work Argentinely (*Argentinamente*)." Nowhere in the journal was there any mention of the concepts of democracy, social justice, or student participation in university government which characterized Reformista publications.[24]

The Reformistas, who had struggled against the *Liga Patriótica* in the 1920's, were also leaders in the opposition to the ultra-nationalist groups of the 1930's. The Reformistas certainly were nationalistic and, like the ultra-nationalists, were opposed to the economic influence of Great Britain and the United States in Latin America. But here the similarities between the two groups ended; the differences were much more striking. The Reformistas favored racial equality and respect for individual liberties. They opposed European Fascism, militarism, and the glorification of the Spanish colonial tradition. The liberal youth opposed also any idea of a Fascist-inspired stratified or hierarchical society. Instead, the *Federación Universitaria Argentina* and the *Federación Universitaria de Buenos Aires* claimed: "We aspire to work modestly and quietly in the construction of a just, equal and happy society; free from the exploitation of man by man, free from the hunger of some and the full belly of others." [25]

Throughout the 1930's, the Reformistas' political activities included criticisms of the ultra-nationalists and warnings that the policies of these rightist groups were closely connected with the threat of an increased Fascist influence in the Republic. Deodoro

Roca, a principal figure in the 1918 Reform, argued in his writings that only through a united effort by intellectuals, students, and workers to oppose Fascism would Argentina escape the fate of Germany and Italy.[26] The declarations of Argentina's student federations echoed Roca's argument. A FUA statement urged the "responsible elements" in the nation to form a "united front" to prevent an increase of Fascist influence. The Reformistas called on all Argentines to struggle against "the armed bands of the 'legión cívica' the 'acción nacionalista argentina' and other vanguards of Argentine Fascism." [27]

Another form of nationalism, economic nationalism, came to influence a large sector of the Argentine public in the years following the world depression and the 1930 revolution. The nationalism of this period was triggered in part by the concessions which President Justo made to foreign capital in an effort to ensure Argentina's rapid recovery from the effects of the depression. Under Justo, many Argentines became aware and resentful of the Republic's economic dependence upon Great Britain, which was admittedly the nation's best customer but at the same time controlled "about three-fourths of the [nation's] railroad mileage, most of the street railway systems, and much of the meat-packing industry." [28] In 1933 the Justo government underscored this dependence when it signed the so-called Roca-Runciman trade agreement with Great Britain for the continuance of commercial interchange between the two nations. The terms of the agreement were generally favorable to the British and aroused the vociferous ire of Argentine nationalists.

The Reformistas, who had attacked imperialism as early as 1920, continued to oppose European and North American interference in the political and economic affairs of Latin America in the 1930's. Deodoro Roca argued in a series of essays that the Vatican, European and North American capitalists, and Latin American landowners and militarists were working in concert to bleed the continent of its wealth. Leaving in their wake a situation of economic and social chaos, the imperialists, Roca wrote, created the conditions conducive to the rise of authoritarian regimes. Writing in the tradition of the *Unión Latino Americana,* Roca also accused imperialist powers fighting for petroleum deposits as the real instigators of the Chaco War, which took place between Bolivia and Paraguay in the late 1920's and the early 1930's.[29] Reformista student declarations echoed Roca's arguments, claiming that the Chaco War was being waged for the sole benefit of "a few industrialists who direct the destruction of humanity from the comfortable armchairs of their offices." [30] During this period, the FUA persisted in protesting North American "colonialism" and influence in the Caribbean. In 1936 the national student federation, FUA, directed a note to United States Secretary of State Cordell Hull, in which it criticized U.S. policies in Puerto Rico.

In the 1920's, the Argentine university youth had concentrated their critical fire on violations of national sovereignty in Latin America by the United States. In the 1930's, however, the Reformistas began to turn their attention to the economic influence of Great Britain in their own country. For example, a FUBA statement of 1936 claimed that "Our farm workers have to labor from sunrise to sunset because they must give one of each three harvests to the English railroads." [31] This shift in attention to Great Britain reflected the national reaction to the Republic's economic dependence upon England. Several prominent politicians and intellectuals also examined and criticized Argentina's economic relations with Britain during the 1930's. For example, Socialist Alfredo L. Palacios investigated the history of British companies in Argentina and argued that the Republic had been unfairly exploited by these concerns, which for their part realized great profits at the expense of the Argentine citizen's comfort and safety. The writings of Raúl Scalabrini Ortíz, a frequent speaker at student meetings, in exposing the historic influence of England on the economic life of the

Republic, concentrated in particular on British construction and control of the nation's railroads.

Solidarity with the working class was another theme in the Reformista program which received attention in the 1930's. The Second National Student Congress called for the renewal and expansion of university extension classes and stressed the need for social and economic reforms which would improve the condition of the workingman. When the government in 1932 threatened to deport a group of workers, the FUA protested and called for a public demonstration of support for the proletariat. Whenever the university youth urged the formation of a "popular front" to oppose Fascism, the labor groups were almost always included in the proposals.

Labor organizations, often connected with the Socialist and Communist parties, provided much of the manpower for opposition to the Uriburu and Justo administrations. As a result, the members of these organizations were frequently the victims— along with the university youth—of repression and violence from the government and ultra-nationalist organizations. In this period workers and students went to jail or into exile together. Speaking from his own considerable experience in prison, student leader Héctor P. Agosti claimed that the primary result of this "drawing together of worker and student was, for many students, a greater clarity in the understanding of social phenomena." [32] Indeed, not only was the understanding between the university youth and the workingman greater in those years, but there was also a significant increase in common concrete activity between the two groups. Students and workers participated in joint parades and meetings, used the same printing presses, signed one another's documents, and stood shoulder to shoulder against the *Legión Cívica*. The period immediately after the revolution of 1930 represented the highest point of real worker-student solidarity since the Reform of 1918.

This interaction with the proletariat, however, ordinarily remained high only during times of crisis and severe agitation. As Argentina's political situation became more stable during the latter part of the decade, and as governmental repression was gradually being lifted, the ties between worker and student once again loosened. On the verbal level the relations between the two groups remained good, but in terms of forming an effective political coalition or power bloc with the workers the students' efforts seemed doomed to failure. The basic difficulties for the Reformistas in this regard were twofold, and they were shared in large measure by Argentina's middle-sector political parties. First, the student attitude toward the workers remained basically romantic and idealistic, with programs of action directed more at visionary and long-term goals rather than the achievement of practical short-term considerations. Second, the students were simply not in a sufficiently powerful position to offer the labor groups anything beyond rhetoric and verbal sympathy. As one critic pointed out in 1938, what the students could give the working class was "Good faith, yes, but nothing more." [33] As will be seen in later chapters, when an Argentine leader appeared who could produce real and tangible results for the labor sectors, the tie between worker and student—so long pursued by the Reformistas—was easily broken, and "solidarity" between the two groups was revealed as an unrealistic concept.

The feeling of continental solidarity among Latin America's Reformista youth, encouraged by the spread of the University Reform, was deepened and expanded between 1930 and 1943. Where the unifying factor tying together the youth of various republics had been the common effort of renovating the university in the 1920's, it was in the 1930's more often the sharing of similar experiences in the struggle against dictatorship. Argentine Reformistas maintained contacts with other student federations in Latin America and directed messages of support to student groups suffering under authoritarian regimes in Peru, Brazil, and Venezuela. In turn, student federations in other countries sent notes of adherence and encouragement to the *Federación Universitaria Argentina* in its struggle against the Uriburu and Justo governments. When Argentina and Uruguay broke diplomatic relations in 1932, the university youth of both republics exchanged visits in which they repudiated the rupture and emphasized the solidarity and friendship which bound together the two student movements. A joint declaration concerning the break in relations criticized the action as the attitude of "governments unfaithful to the popular sentiment of Argentina and Uruguay." [34]

With the fundamental base of similar experiences and problems, an increasing number of continent-wide student congresses was held during the years 1930–1943. All of these meetings were quite similar as regards organization, composition, and resolutions to the First International Student Congress which had been held in Mexico in 1921. Argentina sent a two-man delegation to the first of these meetings, the *Primer Congreso Ibero-Americano de Estudiantes* (First Ibero-American Congress of Students), which convened in Mexico in 1931. The primary focus of the meeting was on the problem of dictatorship. Resolutions passed at the Ibero-American Congress supported the principle of popular rule based on universal and unlimited suffrage as opposed to any form of authoritarian government—a principle which at that time was being ignored by a number of Latin American regimes. Encouragement of social legislation, equal distribution of wealth, protection of minority rights, and separation of church and state were additional planks in the student platform. In response to imperialism, the university youth urged continental organization, economic boycotts, and national control of natural resources as measures to resist what they believed were the aggressive and exploitative tendencies of foreign powers. Argentina also sent representatives to the *Congreso Latinoamericano de Estudiantes,* which assembled in Chile in 1937 and produced resolutions similar to those of the First Ibero-American Congress of 1931.[35]

These international meetings served to increase the sense of solidarity among Latin America's youth considerably. At these congresses ideas were exchanged, experiences were shared, and students practiced the techniques of political maneuvering and in-fighting at a sophisticated international level. For the Argentine delegations, backed by their tradition as initiators of the Reform, these gatherings provided an opportunity to make significant con-tributions to student thinking. Moreover, the Argentines were able to learn firsthand of the events which had occurred and the forces which were on the move in all of Latin America.

In the late 1930's and early 1940's, Argentina was beginning to give serious consideration to the implications of World War II. President Roberto Ortiz, who had been elected in 1938 and who attempted to restore political honesty and respect for individual liberties in Argentina, was openly sympathetic to Great Britain and its allies in the conflict with the Axis. Ortiz was supported in this position by the liberal elements, including most members of the Radical and Socialist parties.

Favoring the Axis in these years were many Argentine ultra-nationalists and sectors of the military attracted to Fascism. These groups returned to national political power and influence in mid-1940, when poor health forced President Ortiz to surrender control of the government to his Conservative vice-president, Ramón S. Castillo. Castillo, who earlier had clashed with the Reformistas while dean of the University of Buenos Aires Faculty of Law in the 1920's, was clearly sympathetic to the Axis. When the Japanese attack on Pearl Harbor in December, 1941, moved the majority of Latin American nations to sever contacts with Berlin, Rome, and Tokyo, the Castillo government refused to break relations with the Axis powers. Using the "crisis" atmos-phere of the war as an excuse, the administration declared a "state of siege" on December 16, 1941. During the "state of siege," which lasted until June 4, 1943, the Castillo government restricted individual liberties, used political corruption to control the nation's elections, protected instruments of Axis propaganda in the Republic, and began to grant economic concessions to German and Italian companies investing in Argentina.

The nation's Reformista university students were prominent among the groups which opposed Castillo's policies. After the "state of siege" had come into force, several UBA students were arrested for laying a wreath at the monument of Roque Sáenz Peña "to pay homage to the man who had given Argentina the vote . . . [and] to protest against the party that had taken it away." [36] In 1942, a lead editorial in the *Revista jurídica* of the UBA Faculty of Law commented upon the national situation and concluded that the university youth demanded restored what they believed was then lacking in the Republic, "honor and dignity in the government, decency in the management of public affairs, [and] the economic emancipation of the country." [37]

The attitudes of Argentina's Reformista youth with regard to World War II underwent a significant change between 1938 and 1942. When the conflict first began to develop on a large scale, certain elements of Reformista thought caused the youth to urge neutralism as the Argentine international stand. Pacifism, long a frequent theme in student declarations, placed the youth in a posture of opposition to any policy which involved the use of force to settle international disputes. The national interests of Argentina could best be served, according to student opinion at that time, by remaining aloof from the world war, which the Reformistas viewed as essentially a conflict between imperialist powers.

When the United States entered the war in late 1941, student thinking began to shift. The Reformistas and the democratic parties, which had been at the forefront of the anti-imperialist campaigns in the 1930's, agreed to shelve the nationalist issue until the war was won. It was gradually becoming clear that the Allies were acting very much in line with prevailing Reformista principles. Identification with the forces of democracy and social justice, sympathy for the goals of the Atlantic Charter, and fear of Nazi-Fascist penetration into Argentina through the Castillo government led a majority of the university youth to give their moral support to the Allies by early 1942.

The opinions of the students in the early 1940's reflected the thinking of older Reformistas, several of whom held influential positions in the political and intellectual life of the Republic. One of these was Julio V. González, Socialist congressman in the national legislature from 1940 to 1943 and a frequent speaker at university meetings. In a lecture sponsored by the medical students' center in the University of the Littoral in 1941, González discussed the youth's relationship to the issue of Nazism-Fascism. Alluding to the Reform, he claimed that the movement's emphasis on individual liberty made it completely incompatible with any form of totalitarianism. He admitted that English and North American imperialism were threats to Argentine sovereignty. Nevertheless, he argued, Nazi-Fascist imperialism presented the more immediate danger and therefore should be the students' principal concern. Later, in a speech sponsored by the University of Buenos Aires Student Federation, FUBA, to commemorate the twenty-fifth anniversary of the Reform in 1943, González urged the youth to consider their roles as national leaders after World War II. He remarked that the nation would experience international difficulties because of the government's sympathies for the Axis powers. However, González concluded, the opportunity in the post-World War II years would be comparable to that which followed the end of World War I. A "new generation" of Argentine youth once more could offer to the world a hope for political freedom and socio-economic betterment after the evident failure of European institutions.[38]

A clear exposition of Reformista student attitudes on national and international issues was given in the resolutions of the Third National Student Congress convened in Córdoba in October,

1942. Dealing with the national problems posed by the Castillo administration, the youth pledged themselves to the defense of political democracy and proposed direct action to protect constitutional guarantees. One resolution called for the elimination of the "state of siege." Another demanded a curtailment in the activities of ultra-nationalist groups, which under Castillo had increased in size and influence. On economic issues, statements were made opposing all forms of imperialism, encouraging national control of natural resources and industry, and supporting agrarian reform. In educational matters, the need to make the principles of the 1918 Reform effective was reiterated.

The most interesting of the topics discussed at this meeting were under the heading "problemas internacionales." Evidence of the growing sympathy for the Allied cause among the university youth were resolutions which claimed that Reformista principles were completely opposed to all aspects of Nazi-Fascist philosophy. Other articles called for Argentina to break diplomatic relations with the Axis powers and to establish contacts with the Soviet Union. The youth urged a continent-wide front which would oppose *niponazifascismo* and support the Allies. Reflecting upon the disillusionment of the Reformistas with regard to World War I and the ineffectiveness of postwar settlements to insure peace, the Argentine students urged that the present struggle be "the triumph of peoples and not of governments." [39]

The years 1930–1943 were important in the history of the Argentine student movement. Where the university youth had resorted to direct action to renovate the nation's institutions of higher education in 1918, they had gone to the streets to change the national political scene in 1930. When the repressions of the Uriburu and Justo governments made it clear that reforms in the universities could not be accomplished without reforms in the social, political, and economic aspects of national life, the Reformistas abandoned their former apolitical stance and, in the words of Gabriel del Mazo, took their places "as citizens in militant political life." [40] University centers and federations became important organizations of opposition to the national government, and students suffered repression, imprisonment, and exile. The characteristics of student opinion and action, such as opposition to ultra-nationalism and imperialism, were modified and expanded to meet new conditions. Finally, the youth began to deal more fully with international issues, attending continent-wide student conferences and passing judgment on Argentina's foreign policy in national meetings.

NOTES

1. J. Beresford Crawkes, *533 días de historia argentina* (Buenos Aires, 1932), pp. 29–30.
2. *Ibid.*, pp. 59–71; and *La Prensa*, September 5, 1930, p. 16.
3. *La Prensa*, September 5, 1930, p. 18.
4. The popular reception of the military move is underscored by Alfred Hasbrouck in his article "The Argentine Revolution of 1930," *Hispanic American Historical Review*, XVIII (August 1938), 285–321.
5. Crawkes, *op. cit.*, pp. 107–108.
6. *La Prensa*, September 11, 1930, p. 15.
7. See, for example, *Gaceta universitaria* (periodical of the student center of the University of Buenos Aires [UBA] Faculty of Medicine), February 11, 1932, p. 1; and *Renovación* (periodical of the Federación Universitaria de La Plata) (FULP), September 21, 1931, p. 1.
8. See Federación de Ateneos Radicales, *La Universidad de Buenos Aires y la dictadura de septiembre* (Buenos Aires, 1940); and José Peco, *Defensa o acusación?* (Buenos Aires, 1935).
9. See Federación Universitaria Argentina (FUA) statements in del Mazo, ed., *La reforma universitaria* (1941–Vol. I), pp. 271–330.
10. Eduardo Howard, "Proceso público a la dictadura," in Federación Universitaria de Buenos Aires (FUBA), *La reforma universitaria, 1918–1958* (Buenos Aires, 1959), pp. 126–128.
11. Ysabel Fisk Rennie, *The Argentine Republic* (New York, 1945), p. 259.
12. For a review of the resolutions and actions of the Second National Student Congress see *La Prensa*, August 13–19, 1932; and "Segundo Congreso Nacional de Estudiantes Universitarios (Buenos Aires, agosto

13–18 de 1932)," del Mazo, ed., *La reforma universitaria* (1941–Vol. I), pp. 370–390.

13. "Quién es quién en la reforma argentina," in Federación Universitaria de Buenos Aires (FUBA), *La reforma universitaria, 1918–1958*, pp. 367–375.

14. *Los universitarios argentinos y el problema político nacional* (Buenos Aires, 1931).

15. Julio V. González, *Reflexiones de un argentino de la nueva generación* (Buenos Aires, 1931), p. 48.

16. Ernesto Giúdice, *Ha muerto el dictador pero no la dictadura* (Buenos Aires, 1932).

17. See Héctor P. Agosti, "Crítica de la reforma universitaria," in Federación Universitaria de Buenos Aires (FUBA), *La reforma universitaria, 1918–1958*, pp. 129–145; and "La ideología de la reforma," *El ateneo* (Rosario, March 1934), pp. 23–28.

18. Alberto Ciria y Horacio J. Sanguinetti, *Universidad y estudiantes: testimonio juvenil* (Buenos Aires, 1962), p. 14.

19. For fuller discussions of these ultra-nationalist groups and their programs see Rennie, *op. cit.*, pp. 266–275; and Marysa Navarro Gerassi, "Argentine Nationalism of the Right," in *Studies in Comparative International Development*, I (St. Louis, Mo., 1965).

20. "Síntesis cronológica del centro estudiantes de ingeniería y de su revista," *Ciencia y técnica* (October 1950), pp. 289–290.

21. *La Prensa*, August 13, 1932, p. 13.

22. *Ibid.*, August 21, 1932, p. 10.

23. Rennie, *op. cit.*, p. 359.

24. *Correo universitario* (Buenos Aires, August 1936).

25. "Contra el chauvinismo universitario," *Revista jurídica y de ciencias sociales* (September 1932), pp. 92–93.

26. See the series of essays on Fascism in Deodoro Roca, *El difícil tiempo nuevo* (Buenos Aires, 1956), pp. 207–228. In the 1930's Roca helped to organize a group of intellectuals into a "popular front" against Fascism. He was aided by others who had participated in the 1918 Reform, particularly his fellow "Cordobeses," Enrique F. Barros and Gregorio Bermann. The "men of '18," under the leadership of Roca, were among the principal figures of the liberal opposition to conservatism in the city of Córdoba throughout the 1930's.

27. "Frente el fascismo (manifiesto de F.U.A., septiembre 1933)," in Federación Universitaria Argentina (FUA), *Mensaje a los estudiantes argentinos* (Rosario, 1950), p. 14.

28. Hubert Herring, *A History of Latin America: From the Beginnings to the Present* (2nd ed., New York, 1962), p. 672.

29. Roca, *op. cit.*, pp. 171–205 and 229–263.

30. "La guerra," *Gaceta universitaria* (February 11, 1932), p. 5.
31. "Manifiesto antiimperialista de la Federación Universitaria de Buenos Aires (25 de mayo, 1936)," del Mazo, ed., *La reforma universitaria* (1941–Vol. I), pp. 412–413.
32. Hector P. Agosti, "Crítica de la reforma universitaria," p. 138.
33. Noel H. Sbarra, "La reforma: evocación y presencia," *Revista de la facultad de ciencias médicas y del centro de estudiantes de medicina* (La Plata, May–June 1938), p. 100.
34. "Las federaciones universitarias del Uruguay y de la Argentina hicieron una declaración," *Gaceta universitaria* (August 3, 1932), p. 3.
35. For more complete descriptions of these meetings and the resolutions which they produced, see del Mazo, ed., *La reforma universitaria* (1941–Vol. II), pp. 506–527 and 534–543.
36. Rennie, *op. cit.,* p. 288.
37. Alberto Antonio Spota, "Agitación juvenil," *Revista jurídica y de ciencias sociales* (August–September 1942), p. 200.
38. Julio V. González, "Vigencia de la reforma universitaria y la lucha contra el totalitarismo," in *La universidad: teoría y acción de la reforma* (Buenos Aires, 1945), pp. 145–167; and Julio V. González, *Proposiciones para una empresa nacional de la juventud argentina* (Buenos Aires, 1943).
39. *Tercer Congreso Nacional de Estudiantes Universitarios (Córdoba, 2 al 5 de octubre de 1942): Resoluciones adoptadas en los siete puntos del temario* (seven-page document from the personal archive of Gabriel del Mazo).
40. Gabriel del Mazo, *Le reforma universitaria y la universidad latinoamericana,* p. 27.

Students and Perón, 1943–1955

6

From 1943 until 1955, Argentina's political life was controlled by authoritarian governments. The Argentine university youth consistently opposed the repressive measures of these regimes and during these years carried on one of the most courageous struggles against dictatorship in the annals of Latin American student political activity. In many respects the student struggle in this thirteen-year period was a continuation of the university resistance to José F. Uriburu, Agustín P. Justo, and Ramón S. Castillo. Strikes, interventions, arrests, and exiles punctuated university politics between 1943 and 1955.

Government repression was more intense in this period than it had been under the *Concordancia*. Totalitarian techniques, copied from the German and Italian examples, were introduced to silence anti-government activities. Moreover, the national administrations attempted to use the Republic's universities to indoctrinate the youth with official propaganda. Nevertheless, although often forced to operate clandestinely, student federations maintained a constant stance of opposition and, on several occasions, managed to make their influence felt throughout the Republic.

On June 4, 1943, a group of army officers, led by Generals Arturo Rawson and Pedro P. Ramírez, replaced the government of Ramón S. Castillo in a swift and bloodless coup d'état. Rawson and Ramírez headed a clique within the Argentine army, the *Grupo de Oficiales Unidos* or GOU (Group of United Officers), which included Colonel Juan D. Perón, the man destined to rule Argentina between 1946 and 1955. The army group moved against the Castillo government when it appeared that the civilian administration was losing all popular support and was no longer able—in the eyes of the military—to lead the nation. At first, public opinion generally supported the June revolution, most Argentines believing that any change from the political repression and unsound policies of the Castillo regime was a change for the better.

However, it soon became apparent that instead of establishing a responsible regime, the new military government was planning to continue and to intensify those aspects of the preceding administration which the liberal sectors in Argentina opposed. Under Ramírez, the new chief executive, Congress was dissolved and the President ruled by decree. National elections scheduled for September, 1943, were canceled, critics of the administration were jailed, and the opposition press was censored. Internationally, the GOU regime proved itself more pro-Axis than Castillo. Many of the army officers influential in the new administration had received training in Germany and Italy and had come to admire the ideas and methods of Hitler and Mussolini. After the GOU revolt, anti-Semitism increased, pro-Allied organizations were hindered in their activities, and the government appointed openly pro-Axis sympathizers to important national positions. German propaganda was spread throughout the Republic, and Ramírez allowed Axis spies and conspirators to operate freely.

Argentina's student federations were among the first to oppose the June 4 revolt. A declaration by the *Federación Universitaria de Buenos Aires* (FUBA), issued shortly after the military take-over, emphasized the university youth's opposition to the Castillo regime which—according to the students—lacked a popular base of support and was anti-democratic and sympathetic toward the Axis. Nevertheless, the document continued, the youth also supported the Republic's tradition of civilian government, and, perhaps having learned from the lesson of September, 1930, opposed any military junta regardless of its stated intentions. The FUBA urged the new leadership to surrender control of the government to civilian authorities and to allow the Republic to return to rule by constitutional procedures.[1]

Professors joined with the youth in opposing the policies of the GOU government. In October, 1943, several prominent faculty members co-operated with some 150 professional and business leaders to issue a "Democratic Manifesto," calling for the restoration of "effective democracy," respect for individual political rights, and solidarity with the American republics supporting the Allies in World War II. Acting through their new minister of education, ultra-nationalist Gustavo Martínez Zuviría, the military leaders dismissed from the university those who had signed the statement.[2] The respected and world-renowned physiologist Bernardo Houssay of the University of Buenos Aires (UBA) Faculty of Medicine, and pro-Reform faculty members Nicolás Romano, José Peco, and Nicolás Besio Moreno of the University of La Plata were among those fired from their teaching posts. In protest of these dismissals, Reformistas Alfredo L. Palacios and Gabriel del Mazo resigned their positions as president and vice-president of the University of La Plata (ULP).

Student reaction to the removal of the pro-democratic professors was to initiate protests throughout the nation's university system. The government moved quickly against this student agitation in a two-pronged attack. First, pressure was brought to bear upon the *Federación Universitaria Argentina* (FUA). A statement issued from the office of Martínez Zuviría on October 23, 1943, accused the FUA of "subversive" activities and a close connection with Communism. The youth were warned not to disturb the normal functions of the University and were advised that the police had been given "precise orders" to prevent any disturbances. On November 6, 1943, another bulletin from the Minister of Education declared the national student organization and all the centers affiliated with it illegal and dissolved. The FUA and its branches were prohibited from functioning in any capacity. Despite the government order, most student organizations continued to operate in secret. Large federations were split into smaller and more mobile groups, and leaflets and other publications were circulated quietly as student opposition was maintained.[3]

The second arm of government policy was simply to intervene in and take control of Argentina's universities. A few months after the June 4 revolution the GOU administration had taken over all of the Republic's institutions of higher learning, save the University of La Plata, and had replaced university officials with Conservative and anti-Reformista intervenors. Once in office, the intervenors, acting on government orders, adopted strict measures to eliminate student agitation. In all the institutions intervened in by the government, student participation in university administration was terminated. An order from the office of the Minister of Education authorized the suspension of any professor or student who "within or outside of the classroom made ideological propaganda contrary to the social order." [4]

On the national level, the continuance of repressive and authoritarian actions paralleled the GOU regime's activities in Argentina's universities. In the last days of December, 1943, the country's political parties were dissolved by government order and rules restricting the freedom of the press even further were applied to the Republic's newspapers. Another important development at this time was the renewed influence of reactionary Catholic and ultra-nationalist elements in the country's public life. Closely involved with the new leadership, particularly through Minister of Education Martínez Zuviría, these forces sought to tie together an ultra-nationalist revolution and a Catholic spiritual renovation in Argentina. Their program was characterized by anti-Semitism, distrust of democracy, the establishment of aristocratic and elite rule, close ties between church and state, and the use of violence to usher in a new order.[5] A reflection of their influence within the new regime was a government decree issued in late 1943, which for the first time since the nineteenth century made the teaching of the Catholic religion a required part of the curriculum in Argentina's primary and secondary schools. The government argued, in a rather tortured fashion, that a school without religious training was "anti-democratic and unconstitutional" because it did not prepare young men to aspire to the Republic's presidency, one of the requisites for that office being profession of the Catholic faith.[6]

Throughout 1944 the university youth opposed the interventions in the universities, the attempts to influence Argentine education with ultra-nationalist and Catholic dogma, and the domestic and foreign policies of the national administration. Despite the arrest and imprisonment of hundreds of their number, the students managed to apply sufficient pressure to force the resignation of some reactionary professors and administrators. During this period, the national student federation, FUA, published a declaration which forecast "the triumph of the solidarity of the students purified in struggle, and the moral triumph of raising themselves against oppression and force." [7]

As the year 1944 came to a close, it became obvious to the military leaders of Argentina that the Axis powers were doomed to defeat in World War II. With an Allied triumph impending, the Argentine government shifted from its previous international policy. In the last months of the world conflict, Argentina joined the pro-Allied Latin American republics which had declared war on the Axis. This move was intended to improve Argentina's position with regard to the approaching peace settlements and changing alliances in the postwar period.

The change of stance on the international scene at this time was paralleled by a "liberalization" on the national level. Political restrictions were relaxed, political parties were allowed to reorganize, elections were promised, and some press censorship was lifted. In February, 1945, the professors who had been dismissed a year and a half earlier for signing the "Democratic Manifesto" were allowed to return to their teaching posts. University autonomy was restored, and university elections were held to choose new officials. In all six of the nation's institutions of higher learning these elections returned to office men who opposed the national government. On August 7, 1945, the decree which had made the FUA illegal was revoked. A FUBA declaration claimed that this government measure recognized once more "the complete inability of violence to subject the forces of the spirit." [8]

The return of Reformistas to university positions and the restored legality of student organizations gave the university sectors opposed to the authoritarian, ultra-nationalist, anti-democratic, and pro-Axis military regime a national forum from which they could express their ideas. Their words reflected the prevailing mood among the liberal elements of the Argentine university at that time and helped to stimulate the thinking and activities of the student groups in mid-1945. The basic issue most commonly discussed was the role of the university groups after the end of World War II, and how these elements might best take advantage of the Allied and democratic victory over the Axis and dictatorship. A typical example of this concern was an address by Reformista professor Carlos Sánchez Viamonte to a group of Buenos Aires students in May, 1945. Reiterating a 1918 theme, Sánchez Viamonte stated that World War II, as had World War I, underscored the failure of European ideas and institutions and claimed that the hope for the future of Western civilization now lay in the success of a

democratic America. He believed that the end of the ongoing conflict would bring with it the triumph of liberty and justice throughout the world. Sánchez Viamonte foresaw great changes occurring
both on the international and the national level and advised the
youth to remain alert to the new responsibilities and opportunities
which the end of the world war would bring.[9]

Stimulated by the return of liberal professors and administrators
to academic positions and by the soon to be expected victory of the
Allied forces in World War II, the university groups in mid-1945
intensified their efforts to change the undemocratic nature of the
Argentine government. A conference of rectors of the nation's universities, which met in Buenos Aires the last week in July, 1945,
issued a declaration urging a return to institutional normality in
the Republic and supporting the concept of American solidarity
against the Axis. Student organizations backed the pro-Allied and
pro-democratic stand of the rectors. In August, 1945, when the
Japanese surrender was announced, groups of university youth led
popular demonstrations celebrating the Allied victory. Secondary
students in the *Colegio Nacional de Buenos Aires* (National College of Buenos Aires) organized a demonstration supporting
democracy and liberty. Students in La Plata held a parade of celebration for the democratic triumph and in opposition to the national government. University groups in Buenos Aires led several
well-attended public demonstrations.

The military regime attempted to prohibit the celebrations of the
Allied victory and used ultra-nationalist groups such as the
Alianza de la Juventud Nacionalista (Alliance of Nationalist
Youth)—an outgrowth of the *Legión Cívica Argentina*—to break
up public meetings. Pro-Axis organizations, shouting anti-Semitic
and anti-democratic slogans, attacked demonstrators with clubs,
stones, and revolvers. Violent clashes continued for several days,
resulting in numerous injuries and some deaths. In answer to the
violence employed against them, the nation's university organiza-

tions resorted to their familiar tactics of protest. Strikes were called, public rallies were held, and notes objecting to the treatment of the persons celebrating the Japanese surrender were sent to government officials. A FUBA declaration stated that while "the free peoples of the world celebrate the coming of democratic order, our country faces the arduous task of recovering its liberty." [10]

At the end of August, the FUA called a week-long university strike to protest government support of the violence against pro-Allied demonstrators and to urge the return of the nation to normal constitutional rule. As was usual, foreign student groups in Uruguay, Paraguay, and Peru sent messages of encouragement and solidarity to their Argentine colleagues. Chilean students held a torchlight parade protesting the anti-Allied and anti-democratic actions of Argentina's President Edelmiro Farrell, who had replaced Ramírez as chief executive in February, 1944. At home, however, the *Sindicato Universitario Argentino* (Argentine University Syndicate), the student branch of the ultra-nationalist *Alianza de la Juventud Nacionalista,* repudiated the university strike, because—in the opinion of the *Sindicato*—the strike utilized the students "in maneuvers which it [the Syndicate] does not consider of university origin." [11]

During the disturbances of August, 1945, the acting head of the Argentine government was Vice-President Juan D. Perón, who served in the president's office while Farrell was traveling in other areas of Latin America. A prominent member of the *Grupo de Oficiales Unidos,* Perón had emerged as the strongest man in the administration by mid-1944, and much of the student discontent was directed against him and his policies. On August 28, the Vice-President spoke to the nation's youth by radio with regard to the recent student activities. Perón claimed that he, too, favored the ideals of democracy and justice championed by the university groups, and he denied any government connection with the violence committed during the pro-Allied demonstrations. He argued that the nation could not return to normal constitutional rule until the goals of the June 4, 1943, revolution were achieved. In conclusion, Perón advised the youth to return to their studies and to forget political activity.

The FUA published an immediate reply, in which it rejected Perón's words as those of a dictator, criticized GOU repression in the university, accused the government of replacing democratic professors with men of totalitarian sympathies, and warned the "ambitious colonel" that the university youth intended to continue to struggle for individual liberty and constitutional government.[12]

An interesting feature of the student activity in opposition to the Farrell-Perón regime at this time was the increased participation of women's university groups in political affairs. Argentina's female students were beginning to organize and to act in student politics for the first time. In September, 1945, the *Agrupación Femenina Universitaria* (Women's University Group) of La Plata was formed. The La Plata *Agrupación* supported the rectors' pronouncement for return to constitutional normality and urged the women of Argentina to help restore individual liberties to the nation. A group with similar principles, the *Agrupación Femenina de Estudiantes de Medicina* (Women Medical Students Group) was established at the University of Buenos Aires at the same time as the La Plata organization. *Las Alumnas Democráticas de la Facultad de Derecho* (Democratic Women Students of the Faculty of Law) in Buenos Aires urged the return to constitutional government and supported the movements of national feminine groups for women's suffrage, a provision which had not been included in the Sáenz Peña electoral law of 1912.

Throughout September, 1945, the Republic's student organizations, both male and female, continued agitational activities against the government. On September 19, many university groups joined with representatives of Argentina's political parties in the

Marcha de la Constitución y la Libertad (March for the Constitution and Liberty). The purpose of the "Marcha," a parade through the streets of Buenos Aires, was to gain popular support by means of a mass demonstration against the national administration, and in turn to force a restoration of constitutional guarantees. The university youth were well represented in the demonstration, and Germán O. López, president of the FUA, marched with major political leaders in the front file of the parade. Generally, the "Marcha" was successful in attracting the support of thousands of representatives of Argentina's middle classes. However, the parade did not receive support from the country's growing and potentially powerful urban working class and hence was not successful in arousing the broad base of popular backing it had sought.[13]

Nonetheless, increasing discontent and dissatisfaction with the Argentine government, highlighted by the "Marcha," did lead the military regime to declare a "state of siege" throughout the country on September 26, 1945. Officials in the Republic's universities were told to quiet anti-government activities or face new interventions. Against the threat of an attack on university autonomy, students and professors resorted to direct action. On October 1, youths and faculty members took control of the University of La Plata. The next day the Faculty of Exact Sciences of the UBA was occupied by students, professors, and administrators. Other faculties and universities soon followed suit, and by the end of the first week in October anti-government elements controlled all the Republic's institutions of higher learning.

Student actions in the Faculty of Exact Sciences in the UBA were typical of the Argentine university youth's defense of their institutions in early October, 1945. Fearing a new government intervention, students in that Faculty joined with their professors and deans to protect the autonomy of their school. Forgetting internal political differences, all factions united to barricade the doors and windows of the Faculty on October 2, and proceeded to organize a makeshift administration to direct the resistance. Government police and ultra-nationalist groups surrounded the Faculty building and fired indiscriminate shots into the structure, pelted the windows with stones, and cut off water and electricity. The approximately 500 students in the Faculty, including some 60 women, arranged cable and pulley systems which allowed them to receive water and food supplies from across neighboring roofs without risking harm from the streets. Chemistry students prepared tear gas bombs and bottles of acid to resist any violent attack. Government newspaper censorship prevented the story of the university occupation from getting a wide hearing, but students in the Faculty of Exact Sciences set up a short-wave transmitter and notified other countries of their situation. After three days of siege, during which one youth was killed by a shot fired into the university building, government police entered the Faculty and arrested all those within. According to Professor Augusto J. Durelli, who participated in the occupation, faculty members and students were then taken to nearby jails and submitted to physical abuse before being imprisoned.[14]

Government intervention and arrests were repeated in all universities. In the University of the Littoral, five days of occupation were ended when 300 police entered the various faculties and arrested some 1,300 students and professors. The University of La Plata was surrounded by police armed with rifles, machine guns, and tear gas. When finally given the order to enter the ULP, the armed police inflicted wounds on some 80 defenseless faculty members and university youth. Official figures released by the government indicated that totals of 1,445 male and 149 female students, six professors, and thirty-nine "agitators" had been detained in connection with the student occupation of the University of Buenos Aires.[15]

After detentions ranging from a week to ten days, the students, professors, and administrative officials arrested in early October were released and the universities were restored to the control of their elected officials. A statement signed by several rectors and by the FUA president, Germán O. López, after their release from imprisonment, protested the measures taken by the government and claimed that the students and professors who took over the academic buildings had resorted to such action only for the noble purpose of defending university autonomy. A FUA declaration promised that the university youth would continue their fight for justice and liberty despite the arbitrary actions of the government officials. The national federation stated its responsibility to carry out the "mandate of history and of those who fell for an ideal." [16]

The October, 1945, interventions in Argentina's universities occurred at the same time as a significant crisis in the national political structure. Vice-President Juan D. Perón, already a student nemesis because of his authoritarian measures as a member of the GOU regime, had emerged as the dominant figure on the Argentine political scene. After the revolution of June 4, 1943, Perón had chosen an assignment as head of the national Labor Department, an office which previously enjoyed little influence or prestige. From that position he began to cultivate the political support of the working class. War-time prosperity, a shift in economic emphasis from agricultural to industrial concerns, and the rapid growth of Buenos Aires and other cities, largely from internal migration, led to a significant increase in the size of Argentina's urban proletariat during the World War II years. Coming to the cities, the workers felt a sense of isolation in a new environment. Moreover, they failed to find their desires for social justice and improved social status fulfilled by either the established labor unions or the ineffective political parties.

It was to these discontented masses that Perón made his appeal. As head of the Labor Department, a post he raised to cabinet rank, Perón introduced new social legislation, enforced previously neglected labor measures, and promised the workingman a sense of dignity in the impersonal urban social structure of Argentina. Perón combined his activities among the labor groups with skillful political maneuvering within the military administration. By mid-1944 he had taken the post of acting minister of war and was named vice-president of the Republic in addition to his position in the Labor Department.

On October 9, 1945, a rebellious group of military officers, fearful of Perón's growing strength, forced the "ambitious colonel" to resign from his three government offices and placed him under arrest. Faced with this crisis, Perón's able consort, María Eva Duarte, soon to become Eva (Evita) Perón, went with other supporters and aides to the working-class districts of Buenos Aires to capitalize upon the carefully nurtured political backing of the proletariat. Aroused by the eloquent words of Eva Duarte, a huge crowd of workers jammed the streets and squares of Buenos Aires on October 17 in support of their imprisoned leader. The demonstration of widespread popular backing forced the release of Perón, who shortly thereafter resigned from the army and announced himself a candidate for the Republic's presidency in elections to be held in February, 1946.[17]

The nation's political parties and university groups fully appreciated the political strength revealed by the October 17 demonstrations. During the latter part of 1945 and the early months of 1946, these elements attempted to form a united front against the threat represented by the dictatorial Perón. With this purpose in mind, the established parties, including Socialists, Communists, Democratic Progressives, Radicals, and some Conservatives, joined together in a *Unión Democrática* (Democratic Union). The *Unión* nominated Radicals José Tamborini and Enrique Mosca for president and vice-president of the Republic. Recognition of individual liberties, political rights for women, and adherence to the principles of the University Reform were among the planks of the *Unión's* platform.[18]

Argentina's student federations gave their backing to the political coalition and campaigned actively for the Tamborini-Mosca ticket. During these months, university strikes were called and anti-government manifestoes from the youth flooded the nation. Student newspapers and magazines compared Perón with Mussolini and Hitler and lamented the fact that democratic victories in the rest of the world were being overshadowed by the threat of a new dictatorship at home. In addition, the university youth criticized the frequent use of force and violence against anti-Perón elements, highlighted by student arrests, and the attacks of ultra-nationalist groups.

A declaration by the University of Buenos Aires Student Federation (FUBA) accused the Buenos Aires police of being "the most effective shock troops of the official candidate" and of acting as part of "a plan of pre-electoral public intimidation." [19]

One of the gravest problems confronting the university youth in late 1945 and early 1946 was the need to adjust to Perón's control of the working classes and his ability to turn the workers against the students. Peronist mobs, largely composed of workers, attacked university groups with the cries "alpargatas sí, libros no" (sandals yes, books no) and "haga patria, mate un estudiante" (be a patriot, kill a student). Proud of their historical interest in the proletariat, the student groups attempted to meet this challenge by emphasizing the tradition of student-worker solidarity and by arguing that real social justice could not be achieved under the leadership of a man like Perón. A FUA declaration of the period underscored the national federation's long-standing interest in the betterment of working-class conditions and the organization's desire to see real social, economic, and political justice achieved in the nation on democratic bases. Articles in *Renovación,* official organ of the *Federación Universitaria de La Plata* (FULP), accused Perón of being a demagogue not capable of implementing real social reforms. The La Plata students printed historical statements relative to student-worker solidarity and called for "an intelligent and sincere closeness between student and worker organizations." [20]

In reviewing the documents of the university sectors during the pre-election months, it seems clear that, essentially, student opposition to Perón at that time was not based on differences of opinion with regard to social and economic policies, but rather on political grounds. Both Perón and the university groups spoke in favor of better conditions for the proletariat and significant changes in the nation's distribution of income. However, most of the youth saw Perón as basically anti-intellectual, and they distrusted his pro-Axis sympathies. The students had already felt the effects of his authoritarian measures as a member of the GOU government, and they foresaw a dictatorship if he were to take national control. Furthermore, the university groups believed that Perón was a demagogue and a political opportunist, incapable of implementing a really profound social and economic reform in Argentina.

Despite the sound political objections to Perón presented by Argentine liberal elements, the working class was not swayed from its devotion to its new leader. Whether he was sincere in his desires for social improvements or not, Perón had provided concrete benefits to the workers while head of the Labor Department and promised more betterments if elected. The university youth, along with Argentina's political parties, had failed until too late to appreciate the profound social and economic changes which had occurred in the Republic during the World War II years. Moreover, the students were not in a position, as was Perón, to offer real improvements to the proletariat. Once again, all that the university federations could give the workers were good intentions, sympathy, and words. In practical terms these could not compete with the enforcement of the eight-hour day, the higher wages, and the insurance and retirement benefits which Perón had introduced.

By using his support among the labor groups and also by attracting the Argentine ultra-nationalists, large sectors of the military, and some segments of the Catholic church, Juan D. Perón captured more than half the popular vote and was elected president of the Republic on February 24, 1946, in what was generally considered one of Argentina's most honest elections.

Argentine student political activity in 1945 and 1946 may be compared in many respects with the actions of the youth during the University Reform. The post-World War II period, as had the years immediately after World War I, seemed to the youth to present hope for a liberal and democratic America subsequent to the defeat of the reactionary forces in Europe. In 1918, this hope had helped to stimulate the movement to reform the nation's institutions of higher learning. In 1945, it moved the youth to attempt reform of the national government. Student activity in 1945 and 1946 was characterized by the same methods of organization, patterns of action, and political maneuvers used in the Córdoba movement. Newspapers, sharing government repression with the liberal sectors in 1945 and 1946, lent editorial support to the student actions and provided as much space as possible for university problems. Political parties, particularly the Radicals and the Socialists, worked closely with the students in opposition to the military government and Perón. In fact, the support of the university federations for the *Marcha de la Constitución y la Libertad* and the *Unión Democrática* marked one of the highest points of student co-operation with national political groups since 1918.

There were also interesting differences between the two periods. In 1945, most professors and administrative officials were on the side of rather than opposed to the actions of the university youth. As World War II came to a close, the entire university, including the principles of autonomy and academic freedom, were threatened by the Argentine government, and faculty members and students joined forces to resist this threat. Many professors and administrators—for example, Alfredo L. Palacios, Gabriel del Mazo, and Carlos Sánchez Viamonte—had either participated in or been influenced by the Reform. It was natural, therefore, that they were more sympathetic to student opinions than had been the professorial bodies of 1918.

One of the most significant aspects of this period, 1945–1946, was the emerging role of women in university politics which was mentioned earlier in this chapter. From 1918 to 1943, the names of female students or female organizations rarely appeared in the chronicle of student political activities. However, by 1945, young ladies were forming university groups, issuing manifestoes, agitating for particular political reforms, supporting movements to restore constitutional normality, and entering the prisons of the Republic because of their beliefs and actions. In part, the increased feminine political activity in the university at this time reflected the growing political and economic influence of women in many areas of Latin America. In Argentina, President Perón in 1947 recognized the importance of this new political force by extending to women the same political rights heretofore enjoyed only by men.

Soon after the presidential election of Juan D. Perón, the fears of the liberal opposition with regard to political repression were realized. Perón and his advisers moved swiftly to impose a dictatorship upon the Argentine Republic. Through coercion, manipulation of the law, and outright violence Perón managed to extend his personal control over all of the Republic's institutions. The national bureaucracy was filled with loyal followers of his. Congress and the Supreme Court became rubber stamps, manned by pro-Perón stooges. By 1951, the Radicals were the only opposition party represented in the national legislature. The nation's constitution was revised to give the president increased power over the Republic's affairs.

Controlling the army and police, Perón moved to eliminate all individual liberties and possibilities of opposition. Secret police,

government espionage agents, and an efficient intelligence apparatus were organized to locate and control persons or groups who
voiced their objections to the government. Those who dared
express anti-Perón sentiments were often subjected to arrest, imprisonment, or exile. Censorship was widespread and thorough.
Anti-government periodicals and newspapers were forced either to
cease operations or to publish official propaganda. *La Prensa,* the
great independent daily of Buenos Aires, with a worldwide reputation of journalistic excellence, was expropriated by the government
in 1951. *La Nación,* the other internationally respected paper of
the capital city, was severely restricted and regulated under Perón.
Other means of mass communication, radio, movies, and tele-
vision, became propaganda instruments of the national administration.[21]

Argentina's institutions of higher education had been among the
leaders of the anti-Perón forces and were therefore given special
attention when the dictatorial regime came to power. Late in
April, 1946, two months before Perón was officially inaugurated,
members of the Labor party, which had been organized to promote
Perón's presidential candidacy, requested lame-duck President
Farrell to take over the nation's universities. Ostensibly, the purpose of the request was to facilitate the reorganization of the
schools on the basis of new legislation to be considered in the
National Congress. In reality, the government interventions were
intended to eliminate the university groups as centers of anti-
government activity. Despite the objections of administrators, professors, and student federations, the chief executive took control of
the Republic's six universities on May 2, 1946.

In the wake of the interventions, the Peronists purged the universities of more than 70 per cent of their faculty members. Many
professors resigned in protest of the new government violation of
university autonomy. Others were forced to surrender their chairs
because of new, government-imposed regulations. For example,

retirement was made obligatory under certain conditions broadly interpreted by administrative officials. At the end of 1946, more than 1,000 professors had lost their jobs.

A list of those separated from their university teaching posts in 1946 was like the "Who's Who" of Argentine higher education. Most of the professors were supporters of Reform principles, many of them had opposed the government actions of 1943–1946, and nearly all of them were among the finest scholars and most prestigious academicians in the Republic. Gone from the University of Buenos Aires were Carlos Sánchez Viamonte, Bernardo Houssay, Osvaldo Loudet, José María Monner Sans, Alfredo L. Palacios, and Florentino V. Sanguinetti; ousted from the University of Córdoba were Arturo Orgaz and Gumersindo Sayago; lost to the University of La Plata were Julio V. González and José Peco. Meeting in Rosario in December, 1946, hundreds of the ousted professors signed a declaration criticizing the interventions and attacking the government's failure to respect university autonomy and academic freedom. The Rosario conference especially praised the students for their resistance to the measures taken against the universities.[22]

Some of the dismissed professors took teaching positions in universities outside Argentina. From their foreign posts they criticized the Perón government and informed other countries of the Republic's loss of academic freedom. Others returned to professional life in Argentina, often working closely with student groups in anti-government activity. Their university places were taken by men who supported the Perón government, many of them coming from the ultra-nationalist and Catholic circles, and most of them clearly inferior to their predecessors in terms of intellectual ability and scholarly achievement.[23]

Having rid Argentina's institutions of higher learning of opposition professors, Perón moved to consolidate his control over the universities even further. On October 9, 1947, the National Congress ratified a new university law which allowed the President of the Republic to choose the rectors of the universities. The legislation also provided that deans be selected by Directive Councils from a list submitted by the rector, thereby in fact giving the chief executive control over the selection of all university officials. Student participation in university government was limited by a provision which permitted only one student representative on the Directive Councils, that student with voice but without vote in administrative proceedings.[24]

After assuming control of the universities and filling them with his own followers, Perón attempted to use the Argentine educational system, along with the mass media, for indoctrination in official philosophy. As most dictators do, he hoped to develop a loyal following among the youth which could be used to perpetuate his regime. As part of this campaign, statues of the President and his first lady were placed in the faculties. Professors were "encouraged" to emphasize the benefits of Peronism in their lectures, and texts were rewritten glorifying the role of Juan and Evita in national life, comparing their contributions to those of the Argentine liberator and military hero, General José de San Martín. Classes in Peronist political philosophy were made obligatory in all universities.

During his administration Perón took elaborate precautions to prevent anti-government activity on the part of the university federations. As leaders among the opposition, students often bore the brunt of arrest, physical violence, and imprisonment. University centers were raided and closed by government agents, and many student leaders spent years in hiding or in exile during Perón's rule. Before they were permitted to enter the university or take examinations, youths were required to obtain from the police a "good-conduct pass," which was a card certifying that they had not engaged in any form of anti-government political activity. Penalties for non-compliance with the new regulations included suspension for year-long periods, prohibition from entering another Argentine university, and loss of credit for examinations previously passed.[25]

While he made liberal use of the "stick," Perón also offered a "carrot" to the university youth in the form of officially created and sponsored student organizations, once again reflecting the dictator's desire to attract support from the young people of Argentina. In 1950 Perón created the *Confederación General Universitaria* (CGU, General University Confederation), intended as an alternative to the *Federación Universitaria Argentina* (FUA). Branches of the CGU were established throughout the Republic's universities. Although disavowing connection with any political party, the new *Confederación* was clearly a front organization for the national government, for it proudly stated its support for "the man who made it possible for the nation to recover its dignity and justice. The CGU will never deny the admiration and the support which the figure of Perón deserves." [26]

Although the CGU was well financed by the Perón government and offered attractive athletic facilities and social advantages, few students were drawn to its ranks. The official nature of the organization was well known among the university youth, the great majority of whom continued to oppose Perón until his overthrow in 1955. In the UBA Faculty of Engineering, a survey taken in 1954 revealed that, whereas the Reformista student center had about 4,000 members, the CGU organization had only 200. The same survey showed that some 1,600 students belonged to the established center in the UBA Faculty of Architecture, in contrast to the 400 associates of the CGU group in the same Faculty.[27]

The police terrorism, restrictive regulations, and government-sponsored organizations under Perón proved no more successful in fully halting university student activity than had similar measures taken by Argentine authoritarian regimes from 1930 to 1946. Throughout the years of the Perón administration the university youth continued to carry out anti-government activities.

Immediately after Perón's election victory and the university interventions of May, 1946, student federations and centers passed through a period of fragmentation and reorganization. However, the danger to the entire university community posed by the Argentine dictatorship eventually led students of various political affiliations to unite in the common cause of opposition to Perón. By 1950, student groups—often operating clandestinely—were preparing to act openly against the national administration. An article published by students of the UBA Faculty of Law in 1950 attacked the government's repressions within the universities and criticized the officially sponsored university organizations and the youths who supported the Perón regime. In June, 1950, a declaration by the *Federación Universitaria Argentina,* commemorating the thirty-second anniversary of the Córdoba Reform, demanded the restoration of university autonomy, the renewal of student participation in university government, the removal of repressive devices such as the "good-conduct certificate," and the re-establishment of constitutional guarantees in the nation.[28]

Clear evidence that Argentina's student movement was still very much alive, despite all Perón's efforts to hinder its operation, was the student strike to free from imprisonment Ernesto Mario Bravo. Bravo, a politically active chemistry student in the Faculty of Exact Sciences in Buenos Aires, was arrested and detained by Peronist police in the middle of May, 1951. When youths from several faculties were unable to get information concerning the condition of the imprisoned student, who—it was rumored—was being tortured, they petitioned university and government authorities to release Bravo immediately.

On June 9, the students in the UBA Faculty of Exact Sciences agreed to strike until the government freed Bravo. The strike soon spread throughout the University of Buenos Aires. The Peronist rector of the University blamed the boycott on small groups of "Communist" agitators and warned the student leaders that they would be severely punished for their actions. During the disturbances, which lasted for several days, government police arrested some 50 students, including the leading officers of the UBA centers. Police action, however, did not halt university agitation. The *Federación Universitaria de Buenos Aires,* in a public statement, demanded the release of Bravo and others who had been arrested, the removal of police forces from all faculties, and government guarantees that the strikers be permitted to return to their studies once the boycott had been ended.[29] On June 21 the demands of the university youth were met when Ernesto Mario Bravo was released from police custody. His release represented a significant victory for the Argentine student movement, which under extreme repressive conditions had been able to achieve a stated goal through political action.

Subsequent to the Bravo strike, an interesting development occurred within the Argentine student movement when Communist university students began to sympathize with and to support the Peronist CGU. The Communists had participated actively in the 1951 activities to free Bravo and their shift was a rather sudden one, but not out of character for many Communist organizations that followed the pragmatic policies of the national Communist party and the international movement.

The Argentine Communist party, which had strongly opposed pro-Axis Perón before the end of World War II, began to modify its attitude toward the dictator after his election in 1946. Although still classified as a member of the anti-government opposition, the party attempted to establish some kind of practical working relationship with the new President. Perón, always ready to use "Communism" as a smear label for opponents, was more judicious when dealing with the Communist party on a practical political basis. Attempting to improve relations with the Soviet Union to further his foreign policy of "third position" neutrality, Perón seemed willing to follow a policy of "peaceful co-existence" with regard to Argentina's Communists. As a result, the Communist "press and public activities were not submitted to the same kind of persecution as those of other opposition groups." [30]

The move of the Communist student sectors to a more pro-Perón position in 1952 was apparently a reflection of the national Communist party line at this time. In 1952 the Argentine party, under the temporary leadership of an interim secretary general, moved from a stance of "constructive opposition" to one of full backing for many of the dictator's policies. This attitude did not endure for long, and by 1953 the party had returned to a more neutral position with relation to the national government. However, for the Communist students, the effects of the change were more lasting. Having attacked the *Federación Universitaria Argentina* as a tool of "Yankee Imperialism," the Communists were read out of the Argentine university movement by the FUA late in 1952.

While the FUA was losing the support of the Communists in 1952, it was gaining strength from the youth of the Republic's secondary schools. Students in the nation's *colegios* had given sporadic support to the university groups since 1918. In 1946 they had organized a group to join with the university youth in the *Unión Democrática,* and in 1951 they participated in the strike to free Ernesto Mario Bravo. To co-ordinate these activities, the *Federación de Estudiantes Secundarios* (FES, Federation of Secondary Students) was formed in December, 1952. Members of the university federations helped the young students to organize their activities, and the program of the FES was similar in spirit and detail to that of the FUA. The new *Federación* favored defense of political liberties, a more equal distribution of national income, and student participation in secondary school administration.[31] With the leadership of the FES, these youths continued to aid the university federations in the struggle against the Perón dictatorship between 1952 and 1955.

The Perón regime, based on the support of labor, the military, and the church, was beginning to show signs of strain by 1953.

With the death of his wife Evita in July, 1952, Perón lost his most valuable aide and adviser. Beloved by the masses, Evita had been an important figure in her own right and had helped her husband maintain his political and moral equilibrium. After Evita's death, the Argentine dictator began to alienate the Catholic church with measures legalizing divorce and removing restrictions on prostitution. In April, 1953, Perón whipped a large crowd of followers into a frenzy of violence lasting several days, during which the Jockey Club—symbol of the Argentine oligarchy—was sacked and the headquarters of opposition political parties were burned. Discontent spread among many sectors of the population when it became gradually apparent that Perón's unsound economic policies were not bringing the promised prosperity. Many who had favored the harsh political measures of the regime in its early stages were humiliated by the excesses of the Peronists in controlling the political life of the nation.

Against this larger picture of gradual political decay, Argentina's university circles continued to act in opposition to the national administration. In late 1954, a nationwide university strike revealed the widespread and profound dissatisfaction with the Perón government among the Republic's students. The university agitation began on October 5, 1954, when an assembly was held in the UBA Faculty of Engineering to present achievement awards to graduating members of the student center. Halfway through the ceremony the meeting was interrupted by armed police, who attempted to arrest the presiding officer. The youths resisted the authorities and a general riot ensued. After the breakup of their meeting, the engineering students formed a column and marched through the streets of Buenos Aires to protest the police action. The officers of the center then decided to call a general university strike, which in a few days spread throughout the UBA. The government's reaction was to close all student centers and to arrest university leaders.

As had become common in student political activity, agitation in one part of the Republic quickly spread to all of Argentina's universities. Within a week after the disturbances in Buenos Aires, the student federations in Rosario, Santa Fe, Córdoba, Tucumán, and La Plata supported the youth of the capital with protest meetings, strikes, and messages of solidarity. Methods of student activity were adapted to evade the repressive nature of the Perón dictatorship. University youths painted slogans on walls at night, held "lightning meetings" which could be dispersed at the first sound of a police whistle, and distributed fliers in crowded public places where escape was easy. The student leaflets included a chronological summary of the October events, listed the number of youths arrested, and criticized the authoritarian nature of the government. A typical FUBA leaflet ended with the observation that "liberty is an essential condition for living, without liberty one does not live, one vegetates." [32]

An important aspect of the student resistance at this time was the activity of exile groups, especially those in Uruguay, to stimulate international interest in the Argentine situation. Youths who had fled the Perón dictatorship kept other Latin American nations informed of the university repression in Argentina and sent detailed reports of their resistance to the Co-ordinating Secretariat of National Unions of Students (COSEC), an international student organization located in Leiden in the Netherlands. [33] When the FUA called a nationwide university strike late in October, 1954, to protest the arrests of student leaders and the closing of centers, the *Grupo Universitario Argentino en el Exilio* (Argentine University Group in Exile) in Montevideo directed a message to COSEC requesting the support of youth groups from all parts of the globe. The exiles suggested that students in other nations publicize the Argentine situation, send protest cables to the Argentine government and the United Nations, and picket Argentine embassies. [34]

Abel Alexis Lattendorf, a former student officer in the University of Buenos Aires who was forced to flee to Montevideo because of his opposition to the Perón government, was one of the principal leaders of the resistance outside Argentina. Letters sent in early 1955 by Lattendorf to FUA secretary Gerardo A. Andújar indicated exile methods of arousing foreign interest in the Argentine situation. Contact was maintained through clandestine correspondence between Lattendorf and student leaders in Argentina. Those operating in the homeland sent written reports, pamphlets, and other information on the university struggle to Montevideo. Lattendorf, in turn, passed these facts on to foreign federations and international organizations in the hope they would be spread throughout the world by means of student propaganda. A letter from Lattendorf to Andújar, dated January 28, 1955, explained:

> Avrea Ingram [COSEC official] in a personal letter asks me for more information about the latest arrests, especially that of Amanda Toubes [woman student leader in the UBA Faculty of Philosophy and Letters, arrested during the October strike] which they hope to spread widely. They are preparing a "general release" to send to all the National Unions and world student press. The details of police persecution, prison treatment, the Haramboure [president of the FUA] case, etc., they need so that the large European periodicals might publish this news.[35]

The work of the exile groups in publicizing these events eventually resulted in the sending of a Chilean-Uruguayan student commission to Argentina in late January, 1955, to investigate the condition of the Republic's university youth subsequent to the October strike. The visiting youth discovered that 253 students had been imprisoned as a consequence of the October disturbances, and that most of these victims were suffering under miserable conditions. It was revealed that imprisoned youths were not allowed to receive extra food or clothing from family or friends, that medical services were inadequate, and that female students in jail were refused sanitary materials. The Chilean-Uruguayan commission, in a report to the Argentine Minister of

Justice, requested the release of the imprisoned students, the reopening of university centers, and the removal of disciplinary sanctions. Their findings were then submitted to COSEC for publication and distribution to student organizations throughout the world.[36]

Another result of exile activities, plus the influence of the Reform tradition of continental student solidarity, were the manifestations of support for the Argentine youth expressed by university federations in other Latin American countries. For example, in April, 1955, the Uruguayan federation, in close contact with exile groups in Montevideo, picketed the Argentine embassy to publicize and to protest the authoritarian measures of the Perón regime. These international activities, combined with continued internal agitation, finally brought concrete results in the spring of 1955, when the Argentine government released the students arrested in October and allowed them to resume their academic careers.[37]

The October, 1954, university strike in Argentina was a significant event in the student struggle against Perón. The widespread national support given to the student actions begun in Buenos Aires revealed the failure of the Peronists to entice, coerce, or indoctrinate the youth to their way of thinking. Despite official organizations, obligatory classes in "political formation," and nine years of intervention in university affairs, most of the Argentine youth still opposed the Perón government. Moreover, at this time new elements, the influence of international opinion, foreign student pressure, and the use of a worldwide youth organization were introduced as basic techniques of Argentine student political activity. These developments took place at the same time as an increased student activism was becoming apparent throughout the world.

With the end of World War II and the formation of the United Nations, youth federations and associations in many nations made efforts to form an international student organization. By the early 1950's two principal groups, developing under the tensions created by the Cold War, had been formed. One was the International Union of Students (IUS), headquartered in Prague, Czechoslovakia. Communist-backed and inspired, the IUS served as a front organization for the Soviet Union and the international Communist movement. The second group was the International Student Conference (ISC), better known by its directing body, the Co-ordinating Secretariat of National Unions of Students or COSEC. While disclaiming political or governmental affiliations, COSEC was clearly representative of Western thought on social, economic, and political issues. Both the IUS and the ISC attempted to attract affiliates from Latin America.

From 1946 until 1950, the Argentine National Student Federation (FUA) was too disorganized and too involved in pressing domestic matters to participate actively in student affairs on the international level. In 1952 the FUA, which had been a member of the IUS, broke relations with that organization. The FUA then attacked the Prague-based Union as an instrument of Soviet foreign policy and criticized its official recognition of the Peronist *Confederación General Universitaria.*[38] By 1953, the Argentine youth began to consider COSEC a possible ally in their struggle against Perón. Although concerned that the ISC might be merely a Western-bloc answer to the IUS, the Argentine federation decided to send a delegate to the Third International Conference of Students, sponsored by COSEC and held in Copenhagen, Denmark, January 12-17, 1953.

The Copenhagen meeting was the first opportunity for the FUA to express its plight to a worldwide student audience. The Argentine representative presented a detailed report of university intervention and student repression under Perón. He also contacted as many foreign student groups as possible and received assurances that the Argentine situation would be featured prominently in university youth publications. Upon his return from Denmark, the FUA delegate reported that international interest had been stimulated in the youth's struggle against Perón. In addition, he indicated that the principles of the ICS would not allow that organization to admit the CGU for membership, a basic concern at this time for the anti-Peronist youth of Argentina.[39]

After the Third International Conference, contacts between COSEC and the FUA increased and led to a steady stream of correspondence between the two groups. Aware of the difficulties under which the Argentine students were forced to operate, COSEC adjusted accordingly, publishing as much information about the situation under Perón as possible. Using complicated methods of intrigue and deception to leave the country, the FUA managed in 1954 to send a delegation to the Fourth International Student Conference which met in Istanbul. At this meeting the Argentines continued to inform the world's youth of the state of their universities and their resistance to the government.

Because of its courageous struggle against the Perón dictatorship, its position as one of the world's first national student federations, and its traditional connection with the University Reform, the FUA was a prestigious group in international meetings. The Argentine youth were able to contribute substantially to the opinions and activities of COSEC. In return, the FUA received the full support of the international organization between 1953 and 1955. Furthermore, the Argentine federation benefited intellectually from increased contact with foreign youth groups. Ernesto Weinschelbaum, FUA international secretary in 1953, pointed out that attendance at the Copenhagen and Istanbul meetings gave the Argentines an intimate knowledge of the problems of countries in Southeast Asia and Africa "that struggle boldly for their independence." [40]

As the downfall of the Perón government neared in late 1955, Argentina's university youth found themselves confronted with several significant and profound problems. One obvious challenge was the need to rebuild the Argentine university system. Under

Perón, Argentine education had registered some advances. Many new academic buildings, one of them the impressive Faculty of Engineering in Buenos Aires, were constructed and work on "university cities" was begun. Also, a marked increase in the number of university students occurred during Perón's rule. From 68,460 students enrolled in Argentine institutions of higher education in 1945, the figure was more than doubled to 142,435 by 1955.[41]

However, new buildings and new students were small gains when set against the terrible retrogressions in the areas of academic freedom and intellectual quality suffered during the years 1945-1955. Perón's purge of professors left the Argentine universities without most of their finest scholars. Autonomy was abolished, and public education became an instrument for indoctrination. Success for professors and students depended not so much upon scholarly achievement as upon loyalty to the Perón government. Youths who joined the CGU were graduated after only three years of study. One doctoral thesis written during the Perón period, which I saw in the UBA Faculty of Medicine, was a ten-page study of university athletics. Corruption, terrorism, and intellectual sterility were the characteristics of a university system that once had been the finest in Latin America.

In terms of Reformista political philosophy, the students were faced with the harsh reality that by 1955 Perón had used and made effective many aspects of their own program. Despite growing disaffection within the church and the military, it was clear, even in 1955, that Perón had captured and maintained the support of the Argentine labor movement. He had improved the social and political status of the urban workers, and although his economic benefits were more illusory than real, Perón had established a relationship with the working class which neither the university groups nor the middle-sector political parties had ever been able to match. As a nationalist, Perón's policies of anti-imperialism and economic independence, underscored by his nationalization of the British-owned railroads in 1948, echoed sentiments which had characterized the university federations since 1918. Although accepting support from the elitist ultra-nationalist groups, Perón ranked as one of Argentina's great exponents of inclusive nationalism. Under his administration, two large and significant groups—the urban proletariat and Argentine women—became full participants in the national political process. Perón's policies and accomplishments, therefore, presented a serious dilemma for the university youth. Somehow they had to make clear that they opposed the dictator's repressive political measures even though they sympathized with the aims of the social revolution which so many Argentines associated with Peronism.

Another serious challenge to the Reformistas came from within the student movement itself. In 1950 the *Liga de Estudiantes Humanistas* (League of Humanist Students) was organized. At the time of its founding, the *Liga* was composed largely of liberal Catholic elements, who opposed the co-operation of Argentina's clergy with the Perón government. The Humanistas drew heavily upon the growing body of Christian Democratic thought, which was then gaining influence in many parts of Latin America. The Catholic students urged a re-evaluation of individual conduct and attitudes in relation to social duties and responsibilities and emphasized a renovation of society in concordance with basic human values. In addition, the Humanistas made some serious and well-founded criticisms of Reformista thought. They pointed out that the Reform had succeeded neither in producing a leadership group for the Republic, nor in appreciating fully the true nature of the nation's social, economic, and political development. These failures, the Humanistas argued, had contributed to Perón's rise to power.

Despite disagreeing with the Reformistas philosophically, the Humanistas joined with the university federations in opposing the Perón government. The Humanistas repudiated the *Confederación*

General Universitaria, participated in the strike to free Ernesto Mario Bravo, and were among those arrested in the 1954 university agitation. When Perón began to turn against the Catholic church in the final years of his rule, the *Agrupación Humanista Renovadora* (Renovating Humanist Group) of the UBA Faculty of Engineering objected openly to "the persecution that today affects Argentine Catholicism, and demands the liberty of all those imprisoned for ideological reasons." [42]

Student resistance to the dictatorial rule of Juan D. Perón was an important factor in keeping alive the spirit of freedom and individual rights in those years of political repression. With the end of the Perón period, the university youth could share the credit with other groups as bulwarks of opposition to the dictatorship. But as the fall of the regime neared it became apparent that new problems were appearing for the student movement. The formation of the *Liga Humanista* raised profound questions about the effectiveness of the Reform principles which had served as the basis of Argentine student activity for thirty-seven years. The economic and social revolution which came with Perón indicated that the students would have to formulate new theories and adjust old philosophies to meet the challenges of Peronism. Finally, the youth faced the problem that once the common enemy of Peronist repression was defeated, the student movement might lose its effectiveness, as it had in the past, by splitting into smaller factions as soon as the moment of crisis had passed. In the years after the fall of Perón, all of these issues were to become fundamental concerns of the Argentine university youth.

NOTES

1. "Decía F.U.B.A. el 4 de junio," *Tribuna universitaria* (Buenos Aires, January 8, 1946), p. 7.
2. Gustavo Martínez Zuviría, better known by his pen name of "Hugo

Wast," was an ultra-nationalist author who had written many works in an anti-democratic and anti-Semitic vein. His appointment as minister of education was a clear indication of the anti-Reform and anti-liberal attitude of the June 4 government.

3. William L. Munger, "Academic Freedom Under Perón," *Antioch Review*, VII (June 1947), 278–279.

4. *La Prensa*, December 2, 1943, p. 8.

5. George Doherty, "The Cross and the Sword, A Catholic View of Argentine Nationalism," *Harpers*, CXC (January 1945), 106–115.

6. *La Prensa*, January 1, 1944, p. 5.

7. "La federación universitaria y la huelga," in Federación Universitaria Argentina (FUA), *Mensaje a los estudiantes argentinos* (Rosario, 1950), pp. 15–16.

8. *La Prensa*, August 10, 1945, p. 13.

9. "Discursos pronunciados por el alumno Julio Cesar Solla y los doctores Alberto G. Spota y Carlos Sánchez Viamonte en el acto organizado por el centro estudiantes de ingeniería, en conmemoración del 135º aniversario de la revolución de mayo," *Ciencia y técnica* (June 1945), pp. iii–xv.

10. *La Prensa*, August 16, 1945, p. 9.

11. *Ibid.*, August 27, 1945, p. 9.

12. *Ibid.*, August 30, 1945, p. 9.

13. Alfredo Galletti, *La política y los partidos* (Buenos Aires, 1961), pp. 171–172. For a discussion of the attitudes and position of Argentine urban labor at this time, see *ibid.*, pp. 197–198.

14. Augusto J. Durelli, "Forma y sentido de la resistencia universitaria de octubre de 1945," *Ciencia y técnica* (December 1945), pp. 469–490.

15. See *La Vanguardia*, October 9, 1945, pp. 2, 7; and *La Prensa*, October 6, 1945, p. 8. The names, ages, and faculties of the women students arrested were published later. This tactic, combined with placing the young ladies in cells used for prostitutes, probably was intended to shame them out of their political activities. The information released revealed that, although ages for the women students ranged from 18 to 31, the great majority were between 19 and 23, and that they represented fairly evenly all the faculties of the University of Buenos Aires (UBA). See *La Prensa*, October 7, 1945, p. 10.

16. *Ibid.*, October 15, 1945, p. 8.

17. For additional information on the rise of Perón to power see George I. Blanksten, *Perón's Argentina* (Chicago, 1953), pp. 47–62; John J. Johnson, *Political Change in Latin America: The Emergence of the Middle Sectors* (Stanford, Calif., 1958), pp. 94–127; and Arthur P. Whitaker, *The United States and Argentina* (Cambridge, Mass., 1954), pp. 115–138.

18. Galletti, *op. cit.*, pp. 181–185.
19. "F.U.B.A. desconoce a la policia federal como fuerza guardiana del orden," *Tribuna universitaria* (January 8, 1946), pp. 6–7.
20. "Pan, justicia y libertad para el pueblo es nuestra consigna social," *Renovación* (November 13, 1945), pp. 4–5.
21. For a description of the repressive activities of the Perón regime see Blanksten, *op. cit.*, pp. 111–219.
22. Federación de agrupaciones para la defensa y progreso de la universidad democrática y autónoma, *Avasallamiento de la universidad argentina* (Buenos Aires, 1947).
23. Roberto Mac-Lean y Estenós, *La crisis universitaria en Hispano-América* (Mexico, D.F., 1946), p. 124.
24. Mariano R. Tissembaum, "La universidad, su misión y sus fines," *Cuaderno número 6, del Instituto de Derecho del Trabajo, "Dr. Juan B. Alberdi"* (Universidad Nacional de Tucumán, 1962), p. 223.
25. "La universidad argentina bajo la dictadura de Perón," *Revista de América,* XI (Bogotá, September 1947), 316–317.
26. Horacio E. Bordo, *Los movimientos universitarios argentinos: de la reforma a la C.G.U.* (Buenos Aires, 1954), p. 14.
27. Federación de Estudiantes Secundarios, *Guía del estudiante* (Buenos Aires, 1954).
28. Federación Universitaria Argentina (FUA), *Mensaje a los estudiantes argentinos,* pp. 7–8.
29. These Federación Universitaria de Buenos Aires (FUBA) demands were included in a leaflet entitled "La Federación Universitaria de Buenos Aires informa al pueblo la realidad en torno a los acontecimientos universitarios." From the files of the United States National Student Association, Philadelphia, Pa., January, 1964.
30. Robert J. Alexander, *Communism in Latin America* (New Brunswick, N.J., 1957), p. 174.
31. Federación de Estudiantes Secundarios, *Guía del estudiante.*
32. Federación Universitaria de Buenos Aires (FUBA) leaflet entitled "El estudiantado al pueblo." From the personal files of former Federación Universitaria Argentina (FUA) secretary Gerardo Andújar, Buenos Aires, November, 1964.
33. See pages 146–148 of this chapter for a brief discussion of the background of the Co-ordinating Secretariat of National Unions of Students (COSEC).
34. Co-ordinating Secretariat of National Unions of Students (COSEC), *Memorandum: The University Situation in Argentina* (Leiden, Netherlands, October 22, 1954).
35. Letter from Lattendorf to Andújar (January 28, 1955). From the Andújar files, Buenos Aires, November, 1964.

36. Co-ordinating Secretariat of National Unions of Students (COSEC), "Report of the Delegation of the Federación de Estudiantes Universitarios del Uruguay y de la Confederación de Estudiantes Universitarios de Chile who visited Buenos Aires, January 25–31, 1955" (Leiden, Netherlands, March 16, 1955).

37. "Informe de la F.U.B.A.," *Boletín del centro estudiantes de ingeniería la línea recta* (Buenos Aires, June 1955), p. 5.

38. Peter T. Jones, *The History of U.S. National Student Association Relations with the International Union of Students, 1945–1956* (Philadelphia, Pa., 1956), pp. 119–120.

39. "Informe del delegado argentino a la Tercera Conferencia Internacional de Estudiantes." From the Andújar files, Buenos Aires, November, 1964.

40. Ernesto Weinschelbaum, "Valoración del movimiento universitario," *Sagitario* (Buenos Aires, March–April 1956), p. 66.

41. Statistics from República Argentina, Secretaría de Educación de la Nación, *Anuario estadístico, año 1945* (Buenos Aires, 1948); and República Argentina, Ministerio de Educación y Justicia, "Hojas de apéndice correspondiente al año 1955" (Buenos Aires, 1955).

42. "Tierra de nadie," *Boletín del centro estudiantes ingeniería la línea recta* (June 1955), p. 7.

Students and Reconstruction, 1955-1964

7

In September, 1955, groups within the Argentine military, joined by sectors of the Catholic church and segments of the civilian opposition, overthrew President Juan D. Perón and forced him into exile. Perón was gone but the changes he had wrought remained. As the provisional government established after the September revolution began to reconstruct the nation, it became clear that Perón had left Argentina in a state of economic bankruptcy, institutional chaos, and political turmoil. The military and civilian administrations between 1955 and 1964 occupied themselves with these problems and attempted to promote their own solutions to the deficiencies of the nation laid bare by the rise of Perón and the Perón dictatorship.

During this period Argentina faced new problems and challenges, in addition to difficulties characteristic of the Republic's twentieth-century history. The increasing political role of the military, which governed the nation from 1955 to 1958 and overthrew civilian President Arturo Frondizi in 1962, was the dominant theme in Argentina's politics. It became clear that the military was

greatly concerned in preventing the recurrence of Peronist dominance. Any government which hoped to remain in office had to
have the support of the armed forces, and to earn this support had
to prove itself strong enough to combat a threatened Peronist
resurgence.

The status of the urban workers, who remained fervently loyal
to the exiled Perón, became a major concern. Providing a large
base of potential political support, the working class demanded
improvements in its conditions after the 1955 revolution. During
these years the Peronists, when they were allowed to participate in
the political process, showed considerable strength, registering in
some elections between 25 and 35 per cent of the total vote. These
victories were gained despite the continued absence from Argentina of Perón, who directed affairs from Madrid and on several
occasions threatened to return to the Republic. How to cope with
Peronism and Perón's continued influence among the working-
class groups was an issue which was primary in the thoughts and
actions of all Argentine administrations between 1955 and 1964.

Argentina's middle-sector political parties attempted to attract
support from the labor organizations, but generally were unsuc-
cessful in these efforts. Once again, these parties, particularly the
Radicals and the Socialists, were weakened through fragmentation.
In 1958 Radical Arturo Frondizi was elected president of the
Republic, and in 1963 still another Radical, Arturo Illia, was
chosen chief executive. However, both men were leaders of competing branches of the same party, Frondizi representing the
Unión Cívica Radical Intransigente (Intransigent Radicals) and
Illia the *Unión Cívica Radical del Pueblo* (Radical Party of the
People). Both men, because of the large number of parties entered
in elections, were able to triumph not by majority votes, but by
gaining a larger minority percentage of the total ballots than their
opponents. During their administrations they were forced to move
slowly and cautiously and to make many compromises to further

their programs. In addition to fragmentation, another factor weakening the position of these parties was the general absence of young and energetic leadership. This was underscored graphically by the Socialist party ticket of seventy-eight-year-old Alfredo L. Palacios for president and sixty-six-year-old Carlos Sánchez Viamonte for vice-president in the 1958 elections.

On the international level, Argentina experienced the repercussions of the Cold War, which was moving its battleground from Europe to the developing areas of Asia, Africa, and Latin America. Argentina, like all of Latin America, was forced to consider the implications of the Cuban revolution of 1959 and of the increasing Communist influence and strength in the hemisphere. Moreover, many Argentine leaders felt keenly the need to restore the Republic to a position of hemispheric prestige and leadership following the Perón era. All of these problems were made more complex by Argentina's failure to achieve sustained economic growth, a continuous inflation of the currency, and a growing tendency toward political apathy on the part of many of the Republic's citizens.

The activities of Argentina's university youth in the post-Perón period reflected all of these issues. Perhaps the most significant development in the history of the university groups between 1955 and 1964 was the fragmentation of the student movement into competing factions. From 1918 up to 1955, the university groups could be generally categorized as pro-Reform and anti-Reform, two basic divisions. By the early 1960's, however, as will be seen, although these labels still maintained some validity, the shadings of difference had become more subtle and more complicated.

Having been a prominent element among the forces opposed to Perón, the university youth of Argentina moved swiftly to take over the nation's universities during the September revolution. On September 21, 1955, soon after the ouster of Perón, the leadership of the *Federación Universitaria de Buenos Aires* (FUBA) resolved to occupy the University of Buenos Aires (UBA) until the provisional government made final decisions concerning the reorganization of Argentine higher education. Three days later, on September 24, groups from each student center occupied and began to administer the faculties of the UBA. The federations in all the other universities of the Republic soon followed a similar course of action.

Having occupied the universities, the youth began to make clear to the provisional administration, then under the command of General Eduardo Lonardi, just what they expected of the new government in the way of educational reform. When Lonardi addressed a public celebration of the revolution on September 23, 1955, members of the FUBA demonstrated in the Plaza de Mayo to publicize their demands with regard to the needs of the university and its members. Shouts and signs echoed sentiments of "We Want the Reform," "Professors Yes—Stooges No," and "Participation of the Students in the Election of University Authorities." [1] In more explicit terms, the *Federación Universitaria Argentina* (FUA) expressed its belief that an oppressive and corrupt regime had been overthrown by a movement for democracy and liberty. The national federation called for the full restoration of individual rights and constitutional guarantees, the repeal of repressive legislation, the destruction of Perón's espionage and enforcement apparatus, and the reopening of student centers. For the FUA, a new era had begun "in the struggle of the Argentine university youth for University autonomy, truly free and secular education, and academic freedom." [2]

Within the University of Buenos Aires, the youths held lengthy and well-attended meetings to discuss the educational needs of the Republic. A FUBA delegation suggested to the provisional government that either José Luis Romero, Vicente Fatone, or José Babini, all favorite professors with the youth, be chosen as intervenor in the UBA to direct the reorganization of the University.

Student resolutions urged the elimination of Perón-inspired university organizations, "good-conduct certificates," and classes in "political formation." The youth also recommended that students and professors expelled from the University because of their opposition to Perón be readmitted and that classes in the UBA, suspended during the revolution, be resumed as soon as possible.[3]

The prevailing spirit of the students throughout these first days after the fall of Perón was one of guarded optimism. After twenty-five years of tight political control, the Argentine youth apparently believed that the university and the nation finally could advance in a progressive and democratic manner. The first measures of the provisional government with regard to the university seemed to justify this optimism. On September 29, the Lonardi administration named student choice José Luis Romero intervenor in the UBA. In his initial speech, Romero promised to restore university autonomy as soon as possible.[4]

On December 23, 1955, the provisional government issued decree-law number 6403 on the "organization and autonomy" of Argentina's universities. Removed were the stipulations of the Perón era, and restored were the articles of the "Ley Avellaneda." Despite the generous provisions of the new statutes, which seemed to assure the full restoration of university autonomy, student groups expressed their dissatisfaction with the fact that the government had not consulted them before drafting the document. The FUBA and other student federations, while generally approving the new decree, found fault with its Article 28, which read: "Private initiative can create free universities which will be qualified to issue diplomas and titles which will always be subject to conditions expressed by a regulation that will be dictated opportunely." [5] Reformistas feared that this stipulation would allow the establishment of private Catholic universities, not regulated by the state, and capable of granting professional licenses.[6] These objections forecast a long and bitter dispute among the university sectors over the issue of private universities, an issue which, as will be seen, split Argentina's student movement severely.

Disagreement over the new university legislation indicated the Reformistas' growing discontent with the post-Perón administration. Student documents in the post-revolutionary period began to urge caution in dealing with the new regime. A statement from the student center of the UBA Faculty of Engineering in late 1955 advised the Argentine university sectors to maintain a political neutrality with regard to the provisional government.

> It is absolutely necessary to affirm the following: the students, as citizens, can look with greater or lesser sympathy upon the present government of the Revolution and personally support it or become involved with it. The student movement, on the other hand, following a perfectly independent course, cannot have any kind of commitment with it nor with any of the civilian or military sectors which support it. It follows thus a clear syndical criterion in its political action, which is totally autonomous and does not criticize nor support men, parties or tendencies but only the measures which these forces adopt.[7]

Reformista dissatisfaction with the national administration, now led by General Pedro E. Aramburu, who had replaced Lonardi as provisional president in late 1955, came to a head in the early months of 1956. Discontent continued to center on law 6403, particularly Article 28, and on the man many youths held responsible for the inclusion of that article in the new legislation, Minister of Education Atilio Dell'Oro Maini. The student federations severely criticized Dell'Oro Maini, former president of the *Liga de la Juventud Católica Argentina* (League of Argentine Catholic Youth), for his close connection with Catholic and ultra-nationalist organizations. With his clear Catholic sympathies, the university youth feared Dell'Oro Maini inevitably would encourage the founding of private religious universities in the Republic.

In April and May, 1956, the Reformistas began to take direct action to force the suspension of the new university decree and the resignation of the Minister of Education. During these months student groups sporadically took over the nation's universities, held public demonstrations in front of government buildings, including the Casa Rosada, and boycotted classes. These actions were instigated and supported by the student federations. Catholic university organizations opposed the demonstrations and sympathized with Minister Dell'Oro Maini and the provisions of law 6403. The Humanistas, who had sided with the FUA up to and through the 1955 revolution, were not in accord with the older university groups on the Dell'Oro Maini issue. When the FUBA made an early move to force the Minister of Education to resign in December, 1955, the Humanistas responded that they "energetically oppose said request for resignation." [8]

Finally, on May 16, 1956, the pressure of the student campaign had become sufficiently strong to compel Atilio Dell'Oro Maini to resign his cabinet position. However, for the Reformistas the victory was only partial. The individual university intervenors, most of whom, like José Luis Romero in the UBA, were pro-Reformista and student favorites, also resigned as a result of the youths' agitation. Furthermore, the government decree on the "organization and autonomy" of the university, including controversial Article 28, still remained. Finally, the failure of the Humanistas to back the federations on this issue was the first concrete sign of the student movement's impending fragmentation.

After the resignation of Dell'Oro Maini in mid-1956, the issue of private universities and Article 28 remained relatively dormant until the inauguration of President Arturo Frondizi in May of 1958. After three years (1955-1958) of provisional military control, Argentina had elected Frondizi as its first civilian president since 1938. Frondizi, representing a branch of the already splintered Radical party, the "Intransigents," had participated in Reformista politics in the 1930's as a student in the UBA Faculty of

Law and enjoyed general Reformista support at the time of his election. Besides university backing, Frondizi's program of economic development and national unity attracted support from the middle classes and from some of the Peronista groups. Frondizi's political base was a shaky and tenuous coalition, weakened by the splintering of his own party. Therefore, apparently as a maneuver to strengthen this base with the addition of Catholic support, Frondizi unexpectedly announced in late August, 1958, that he favored freedom of education and would encourage the implementation of Article 28 of law 6403 when this legislation came up for consideration in the National Congress. With this presidential announcement, the volatile issue of private Catholic universities became the subject of a passionate national debate and produced one of the gravest crises of the Frondizi administration (1958–1962). The debate concerning the establishment of private universities involved the Argentine university youth in their most significant political activity of the post-Perón period. The passions aroused by the struggle over Article 28 also served to split completely the already fragmenting student movement.

Among the university groups, the Reformistas, who consistently had opposed Article 28 from the time of its first appearance in law 6403, led the opposition to the Frondizi proposal of 1958. A sampling of Reformista opinion on this rather complex problem indicates that their arguments against private Catholic universities were founded in traditional aspects of student thought emanating from the Reform of 1918—particularly the characteristic themes of anti-clericalism, democratic education, and inclusive nationalism. Florentino V. Sanguinetti, who had been active as a Reformista in university politics in the 1920's, in 1956 argued in behalf of the state's traditional control of higher education and the national social responsibility of the university system in licensing professionals, a control and responsibility, he believed, which should not be surrendered even partially to private interests. He also pointed out that the national universities were organized on what he termed "principles of equality," whereas "the private universities will be a class privilege." [9] Professor José Luis Romero of the UBA Faculty of Philosophy and Letters told me in a 1964 interview that his objection to Article 28 was based on the belief that Argentina's educational institutions should serve as a "nationalizing" force for the heterogeneous elements of the Republic's population. Private universities, with high tuition fees and limited enrollment, according to Romero, tend to maintain class barriers and social stratification and impede the "nationalizing" process.

Argentina's Catholic groups as well as many Argentines who were dissatisfied with what they considered the poor academic quality and excess of political activity in the national institutions of higher learning, defended Article 28 and favored the establishment of private universities. Answering Reformista arguments, the *Corporación de Abogados Católicos* (Corporation of Catholic Lawyers) declared that the educational rights of the state were subordinate to the rights of the church and family with regard to the cultural formation of the youth. Articles in the Catholic periodical *Criterio* pointed out that private universities were a successful and integral part of academic life in the United States. The editors of *Criterio* also claimed that the dangers of a state monopoly of education were intensified under a dictator such as Perón, who was able to use the university system as his own propaganda and indoctrination vehicle. Private universities, they argued, would be more resistant to official pressures.[10]

The campaign to defeat passage of Article 28 began with agitational techniques typical of the university groups. In late August, 1958, the rectors of the Republic's universities, most of whom were of a generally Reformista persuasion, sent a statement to President Frondizi requesting that Article 28 not be approved. Reformista students paraded in front of the National Congress, carrying placards reminiscent of the 1918 Córdoba Reform, which read: "State, Yes; Private, No," "Secular, Yes; Free, No," and "Priests, No; Books, Yes." On September 4, Risieri Frondizi, rector of the UBA and brother of Argentina's president, spoke to a student gathering of the grave danger faced by the national university because of Article 28. The Rector criticized what he believed was the sectarian and dogmatic nature of private institutions and warned the chief executive to stop playing politics with educational issues. After his speech, Rector Frondizi led a noisy student parade through the streets of Buenos Aires to the Congress, where he requested that the private university law be defeated. Six days later the Buenos Aires University Assembly voted 53 to 15 to approve the Rector's actions.[11]

In response to these activities, President Arturo Frondizi on September 6, through a radio speech, defined his stand on Article 28. The chief executive reaffirmed his August declaration in favor of freedom of education. He mentioned that he was opposed to the state monopoly of higher education, but added that his position did not mean that he planned to institute any extreme measure such as obligatory religious instruction in the nation's school system, as some critics had suggested he might. In his talk, President Frondizi observed that the secondary and university youth, in recent weeks, had participated in acts of violence in collaboration with "sectors which want to create a climate of public unrest." He reminded the youth that student actions on September 6, 1930, exactly twenty-eight years earlier, had been used "as the advance of an action of force which cost the University and the entire country long years of suffering."[12]

The FUA and local university federations replied to Frondizi's speech by intensifying their efforts to defeat Article 28. General university strikes were called throughout the Republic. In front of the Congress police and students exchanged rocks and tear-gas canisters. Many faculties were the scene of bloody riots, as Reformistas and Catholics clashed in attempts to occupy academic buildings. On September 19 the FUA organized a public rally in the Plaza Congreso, attended by a crowd estimated between 250,000 and 300,000 persons. The principal speakers, representing the secondary students, university youth, alumni, political parties, and labor groups, all urged the rejection of Article 28. After reading statements of support from Risieri Frondizi and several congressmen, the meeting broke up into orderly parades through the main avenues of the capital.[13]

One week later, on September 26, the Reformistas won an apparent victory when the National Chamber of Deputies rejected Article 28 by a vote of 109 to 52—a decision which brought cheers from the university youth who packed the Chamber's galleries. However, several days later Radical Intransigent Deputy Horacio O. Domingorena, a former president of the *Federación Universitaria de Córdoba,* offered a modified version of the disputed legislation for Senate consideration. The new bill permitted the founding of private universities with the power to grant academic degrees. But the power to approve professional practice remained in the hands of the state through public examinations administered by a government-designated body. Furthermore, private institutions were not to receive national funds, and their statutes and plans of study were to be regulated by government authorities.[14] The Senate approved this version and returned the measure to the Chamber of Deputies, where the opposition failed to muster the two-thirds majority necessary to defeat the Domingorena amendment. This time the legislators were greeted with shouts and jeers from the balconies until police were able to clear the public galleries of discontented and angry Reformistas.

Despite Reformista objections, therefore, Article 28, as rewritten by Deputy Domingorena, became the law of the land. Although the main issue—the right to establish private Catholic universities—was determined against the Reformistas, the retention of state control over the qualifying of professionals gave the university federations a partial victory. As for President Frondizi, the passage of the disputed legislation provided him with a claim for Catholic support, but it also meant that he had lost most of the Reformista backing he had enjoyed before his election. The university groups were disappointed with a man who, first as a student and later as a congressman, had voiced his firm objections to private universities and religious education, but who—the university people believed—later sacrificed his principles and campaign promises for political gain.

Within the student movement itself, the struggle over Article 28 brought to a head the divisions which had been developing among the Argentine youth since the 1955 revolution. As the private university issue was debated in September and October of 1958, the Humanistas, growing in size and strength, gradually established their position in opposition to the actions and attitudes of the Reformistas.[15] After the street demonstration led by Risieri Frondizi in early September, a *Liga Humanista* meeting resolved that order should be maintained in the university and criticized the UBA officials and the University Assembly for choosing "the way of violence and street agitation to carry forward their ends." [16] When the Domingorena law was approved, the Humanistas recognized and supported the legality of the legislative process and attacked the Reformistas' reaction to the congressional decision. Protesting the attitudes of the university federations and university officials during the debate over private universities, Humanista student representatives on the UBA Directive Councils resigned from their positions in late September. On October 1, 1958, Humanista *agrupaciones* in five University of Buenos Aires faculties announced their withdrawal from the FUBA because of disagreement over the political actions surrounding Article 28.[17]

Humanista objections to a state monopoly of education had been stated during the *Convención Nacional de Estudiantes* (National Convention of Students), held in Buenos Aires on September 1, 1956. At this meeting, the bases and principles of the *Movimiento Universitario Humanista* (Humanista University Movement) were discussed and approved. Influenced by the works and ideas of Aristotle, St. Thomas Aquinas, Jacques Maritain, and Erich Fromm, whose *Escape from Freedom* was widely read and admired among the Argentine youth, the Humanistas founded their philosophy on the proposition that "the problems of the university are problems of man and of his relations with other men." They stated that improvements in the nation's institutions of higher learning depended upon betterments in society, but rejected extra-university partisan political activity as a group to achieve these improvements. The Humanistas at this time echoed many planks of the Reformista program when they planned to develop a true worker-student solidarity, urged a reorganization of work to overcome human alienation in an industrial society, supported agrarian reform and agricultural co-operatives, favored pacifism, rejected all forms of human exploitation, advocated a pluralistic society, and stated that the university should be open to all academically qualified, regardless of social and economic status.[18]

Throughout the late 1950's and 1960's, the basic difference between the Humanistas and the Reformistas remained more a disagreement over means than ends. Both groups wanted students to concern themselves with national problems and to bring about changes which would create a democratic and progressive Argentina, free from class divisions, political unrest, and economic instability. The Humanistas believed that these goals could best be reached by restricting student political activities to the university level. They believed that the increased Reformista participation in national political affairs since 1930, underscored by their actions in the 1958 campaign against Article 28, weakened the over-all student movement and distracted from the primary task of educational reform and improvement. The Humanistas also opposed the increasing Communist influence within the FUA and the local federations during this period, a subject which will be discussed more fully in this chapter. The Humanistas feared that the growing Marxist-Leninist influence among Argentina's youth would for the first time in the history of the student movement place the university federations under the direct control of a national political party. In a sense, then, the Humanista movement represented a return to some of the original concepts of the Reform—namely, that the student movement itself should remain aloof from partisan politics and that the role of the student was to work in and reform the university so as to form an institution capable of reforming the entire nation.

Humanismo, bearing the prestige of an anti-Perón stand, offering an alternative to the Reformistas which did not ignore social and economic problems, and benefiting from the increased popularity of Christian Democratic ideas in Latin America, attracted a sizable number of youths to its ranks between 1955 and 1964. During these years a nationwide group, the *Organización de Estudiantes Humanistas Argentinos* (ODEHA, Organization of Argentine Humanista Students) was established. Humanista strength was greatest in the University of Buenos Aires, where a Humanista candidate was elected rector in 1962, but branches of the national movement were also making inroads in all of the Republic's universities. As can be seen in the statistics for 1964 in the election of student delegates to the Directive Councils of the UBA, the Humanistas were representative of one out of three students who voted and had achieved a position of strength within the university groups second only to that of the Reformistas.

UNIVERSITY OF BUENOS AIRES, ELECTIONS IN 1964 FOR STUDENT REPRESENTATIVES ON THE DIRECTIVE COUNCILS

1. *Faculty of Engineering:*
   a. Agrupación Humanista Renovadora   1,565
   b. Agrupación Movimiento Universitario de
          Centro   309

c. Agrupación Movimiento Universitario
   Reformista   2,428
d. Blank ballots   50
e. Annulled ballots   8
f. Voted (total)   4,360
g. Enrolled (total)   6,129

2. *Faculty of Agronomy:*
   a. Movimiento Reformista de Agronomía   84
   b. Movimiento Unidad Estudiantil de Agronomía
      y Movimiento Unidad Estudiantil de
      Veterinaria   342
   c. Agrupación Humanista de la Facultad de
      Agronomía y Veterinaria de Buenos Aires   445
   d. Movimiento Estudiantil de Reforma
      Universitaria de Veterinaria   74
   e. Movimiento Universitario de Agronomía   133
   f. Blank ballots   12
   g. Annulled ballots   1
   h. Voted (total)   1,091
   i. Enrolled (total)   1,270

3. *Faculty of Architecture:*
   a. Lista Universitaria   1,052
   b. Agrupación Reformista   970
   c. Movimiento de Acción Popular   838
   d. Blank ballots   45
   e. Annulled ballots   1
   f. Voted (total)   2,906
   g. Enrolled (total)   3,135

4. *Faculty of Medicine:*
   a. Lista Unica Reformista   3,964
   b. Agrupación Humanista de Medicina   2,988
   c. Blank ballots   168
   d. Annulled ballots   17
   e. Voted (total)   7,146
   f. Enrolled (total)   7,800

5. *Faculty of Pharmacy and Biochemistry:*
   a. Unidad Programática Estudiantil — 819
   b. Humanismo Auténtico — 430
   c. Blank ballots — 37
   d. Annulled ballots — 7
   e. Voted (total) — 1,293
   f. Enrolled (total) — 1,395
6. *Faculty of Exact and Natural Sciences:*
   a. Lista Humanista — 930
   b. Lista Reformista — 880
   c. Frente Estudiantil de Liberación Nacional — 203
   d. Blank ballots — 39
   e. Annulled ballots — 10
   f. Voted (total) — 2,062
   g. Enrolled (total) — 2,210
7. *Faculty of Law:*
   a. Movimiento Universitario de Centro — 1,875
   b. Humanismo, Movimiento Humanista de Derecho — 1,046
   c. Sindicato Universitario de Derecho — 276
   d. Movimiento Universitario Reformista, Lista de la Reforma Universitaria — 2,124
   e. Movimiento Social Cristiano — 1,063
   f. Agrupación Reformista de Derecho — 351
   g. Blank ballots — 103
   h. Annulled ballots — 69
   i. Contested ballots — 7
   j. Voted (total) — 6,914
   k. Enrolled (total) — 8,229
8. *Faculty of Economic Sciences:*
   a. Frente Independiente — 366
   b. Agrupación Humanista de Ciencias Económicas — 5,006
   c. Renovación Reformista — 4,478
   d. Blank ballots — 178

e. Annulled ballots   48
f. Voted (total)   10,076
g. Enrolled (total)   11,743

9. *Faculty of Philosophy and Letters:*
Completed figures not available

TOTALS:

Voted	35,848	
Humanista	12,410	(34%)
Reformista	17,002	(49%)
Others	6,436	(17%)

Source: *La Nación,* November 11, 1964, and November 21, 1964.

The split of the Humanistas from the university federations in 1958 was only part of a confusing and complex picture of student political affiliations in the post-Perón years. Between 1955 and 1964 a multiplicity of groups, representing every political tendency from Trotskyism to Fascism to Peronism, began to appear in the faculties of the Argentine universities. As can be seen in the above statistics, in the Buenos Aires Faculty of Law no less than six different organizations participated in the 1964 elections. One of these, the *Movimiento Universitario de Centro* (MUC, University Movement of the Center), which in 1964 gathered 1,875—or about one-fourth—of the total 6,914 votes cast in the law school, followed in the tradition of other Conservative groups which historically had found strength in the UBA Faculty of Law. The MUC principles at this time emphasized respect for individual rights based on natural law, supported economic activity free from state intervention or direction, and opposed collectivist and Marxist-influenced philosophies. The *Movimiento* did support university autonomy and student participation in university administration, but opposed a state monopoly of education.[19]

Although faced with a fragmentation of the student movement and divisions within their ranks, the 1964 UBA election results revealed that those groups which followed closely the principles of the Córdoba Reform still were the strongest and the largest among the Argentine youth in the post-Perón years. In general, the Reformistas continued to emphasize the themes and to display the characteristics which had marked their activity from 1918. Reformista documents continued to express faith in the efficacy of democracy, social justice, and self-determination of peoples. Reform concepts intended to improve the nature of higher education were reiterated between 1955 and 1964. The Reformistas led the student campaign against Article 28. During this period, the Reformistas repeatedly underscored the belief that the Argentine university should concern itself with the problems of Argentine society. Although not openly adhering to actual partisan political activity, the Reformistas made clear their belief that the student should act in national affairs as well as on the university level. Educational reform could be achieved only through national reform. According to student leader Arnoldo Siperman, "The mission of the Reformista students is to join the popular classes in an ascent which will form an authentic New Argentina." [20]

Confronted with a political challenge to their right from the Humanistas, the Reformistas were threatened also from the left by the increased influence of Communism in the national student movement. Between 1955 and 1964, as international Communism began to gain prestige in Latin America after the launching of the first Soviet space satellite in 1957, as the appeal of Fidel Castro's revolution began to spread throughout the area, and as fragmentation weakened student organizations, some segments of the Argentine youth began to adopt Marxist-Leninist theory and Communist students began to take control of university federations. In local and national elections for student federation officials, hard-working Communist youths, aided by the national Communist party, campaigned diligently and thoroughly, were the first to arrive at and the last to leave meetings, and through pressure and determination took control of key offices. A National Student Association (NSA) memorandum reported that in October, 1959, a well-disciplined group of Communists had taken control of the FUA at the Fourth National Student Congress held in Córdoba. During the Fourth Congress, twenty-four Reformista delegations, representing several universities, withdrew in protest of the obvious Communist influence in the meeting. These delegates later reported that in the student conference they had found themselves facing "an evident and dirty maneuver of a partisan political type, designed to convert our national federation into a parallel organism of certain political parties." [21]

Sampling the writings of Marxist thinkers in the post-Perón period, it is clear that the Communists were attempting to adopt and to identify closely with elements of Reformista thought. Communist thinkers argued that Argentine higher learning should be made more accessible to the lower class, not only by making university education free but also by actually paying less affluent students to attend. The Communists encouraged university extension courses, urged university groups to combat all forms of ideological discrimination, supported student participation in university government, and stood completely opposed to private universities. [22]

Although statistics on the percentage of Communists within the Argentine student movement were not available, it seems clear that by 1964 their control was of the university federations but not of the entire movement itself. They dominated a leadership controlling the *Federación Universitaria Argentina* and most affiliated local federations, but it was a leadership which was rapidly losing its following. The Humanistas, representing about one-third of the UBA students in 1964, had withdrawn from the federations in 1958. Other centers and *agrupaciones,* including many Reformista groups, also disaffiliated from the FUA and local federations as Communist influence became clear. In 1964 there was much talk among Reformista elements of forming a new, non-Communist national student organization. Moreover, in the early 1960's the Communists themselves, reflecting the growing splits in the international movement, began to divide into various factions representing Trotskyites, Maoists, Stalinists, Castroites, and followers of the "Khrushchev line," in this manner weakening their political position among the Argentine youth. Nevertheless, there seemed no doubt, despite these weaknesses, that in the post-Perón years the Communists enjoyed their greatest influence in the history of the Argentine student movement.

The fragmentation of the university groups into roughly four general categories—Reformista, Humanista, Conservative, and Communist—stemmed not only from philosophical differences as to the solution of educational and national problems but also from several other factors. First, most of those youths who had led the resistance to Perón moved out of the university political picture soon after the 1955 revolution. Having already spent valuable years either in jail or in exile, they were anxious to return to their studies after Perón's fall. This resumption of careers, in turn, left a vacuum of leadership and a lack of continuity in the student movement, as new leaders of differing views, not molded by the common experience of struggle against a dictator, took control of the student federations. Second, splintering among the organizations of the university youth reflected a similar process among the Argentine political parties. Between 1955 and 1964 the Radical and Socialist parties divided into various groups, usually following the leadership of one man or a small nucleus of men. Third, the very size of the Argentine university system, numbering more than 150,000 students by 1960, made it difficult for any one group to represent all shades of student opinion.

Argentine participation in international student conferences after Perón's overthrow reflected the developing split among the university groups, the increasing influence of Communism, and a growing interest on the part of the youth in world affairs and foreign relations. In late 1955 the Communist International Union of Students, with two permanent officials in Latin America, attempted to gain the affiliation of the *Federación Universitaria Argentina*. Once again the Argentine student federation refused to join an organization which was used as an instrument of Soviet foreign policy and which had failed to support the student struggle against Perón.[23] The reluctance of Argentina's youth to affiliate with the Communist organization was typical of the reaction of most Latin American students in the years 1955–1956. Despite energetic efforts in the area by the Prague-based group, the only Latin American member of the International Union of Students (IUS) in these years was the national student union of Ecuador.[24]

In 1956 the FUA sent a delegation to the Sixth International Conference of Students sponsored by the Co-ordinating Secretariat of National Unions of Students (COSEC) and held in Ceylon. There the Argentines supported the seating of an Algerian student representation, arguing that one of the essential aims of the meeting was to encourage "the effort of the students of the colonial countries to obtain their political and cultural independence." The FUA representatives displayed an interest in establishing and maintaining contacts with student groups in Asia and Africa, particularly those they believed were struggling against oppressive regimes. As regards specific issues, the Argentines opposed any recognition of the Franco-backed *Sindicato Español Universitario* (Spanish University Syndicate) and the entrance into the International Student Conference (ISC) of student organizations from Eastern Europe, because of their "total identification with the dictatorial policies of their respective governments." In their final report, the FUA delegates argued that attendance at international meetings was invaluable in learning of world problems through joint discussion, analysis, and criticism with foreign contemporaries. Thereupon, the representatives to the Ceylon meeting suggested a possible reconsideration of establishing contacts with the IUS. This move would not indicate ideological approval, the delegates contended, but might improve international understanding and put Argentina in a more neutral position vis-à-vis the East-West conflict than its heretofore "almost dogmatic: COSEC yes, IUS no." [25]

Increased Communist activity in Latin America, particularly at the student level, began to strengthen the position of the IUS in the developing areas by 1957. At this time observers began to notice that student opinion in Latin America was becoming more critical of the United States and more receptive to Communist propaganda and Marxist-Leninist theories. A FUA report presented at the *Segundo Congreso Latinoamericano de Estudiantes* (Second Latin American Congress of Students), held in La Plata in April, 1957, indicated that Argentina was beginning to feel the influences of the "third-area radicalism" developing in the student world. The points of the report, however, were also reflective of four decades of Reformista thinking on national and international issues.

The Argentine paper to the Second Congress, prepared and presented by FUA representative Gregorio Selser, blamed the nefarious influence of the United States for most of Latin America's social, economic, and political problems.[26] According to this report, which traced alleged United States economic and political infiltration in the area from the time of the Spanish-American War, it was not the people of North America but a ruling elite represented by the members of President Dwight Eisenhower's cabinet, who wished to dominate and exploit Latin America. In particular, the FUA criticized the United States emphasis on "anti-Communism," which had led to the extremes of Senator Joseph McCarthy, North American support for military dictators in Latin America in the 1950's, and the failure of the United States to appreciate the social and economic needs of the continent after World War II. Selser's presentation urged the youth of Latin America to lead the battle against imperialism, and to struggle for the full economic and political independence of their nations. He also suggested that universities be made propaganda centers to inform the public of the effects of foreign control in Latin America, and he argued in favor of trade with the countries of the Soviet bloc as a means of achieving economic independence.[27]

When the Communists began to take control of the FUA in the late 1950's and early 1960's, the position of that Argentine federation in international student relations was correspondingly affected. At subsequent continent-wide conferences the FUA became more and more virulent in its attacks on the United States and simultaneously more and more open in its praise for the policies of the Soviet Union and its support for Fidel Castro's revolution. During this period the national organization also began to loosen its bonds with COSEC and to initiate ties with the IUS. In 1959, at a national student meeting, the FUA voted to send "observers" to the conferences of the Communist organization. Two years later, in 1961, the *Federación Universitaria Argentina* officially joined the International Union of Students, arguing that this decision arose in part from an attempt "to strengthen the ties of solidarity with the great transforming movement which Fidel Castro is directing." [28]

On the domestic scene at this time, Argentina's student federations began to criticize particularly the economic policies of the Aramburu and Frondizi administrations. Attempting to restore the economic balance of the nation, left in a state of bankruptcy by Perón's measures, the Aramburu government made Argentina a member of both the World Bank and the International Monetary Fund and established trade agreements with several European nations. President Frondizi instituted austerity measures to stabilize the economy and, abandoning his pre-electoral nationalist stance, sought to encourage private foreign investment. His most controversial move came soon after his inauguration, when he signed contracts with foreign-owned oil companies, mostly firms from the United States, to develop Argentina's petroleum resources.

The student federations, drawing upon their long tradition of economic nationalism and coming more and more under the influence of radical elements, opposed what they considered the "imperialistic penetration" of their nation. In 1958, when President Frondizi negotiated the contracts with foreign oil companies, the university federations were among the first to protest. Five years later, in 1963, when the contracts were still in effect, the Reformista and non-Communist *Unión Universitaria* of La Plata published a pamphlet dealing with the petroleum contracts and their influence on the Republic. In their preface the *Unión* summed up the leftist student opinion of the Frondizi government, whose term in office (1958–1962)—they said—represented "one of the saddest periods in the history of the Republic." Under Frondizi, they argued, had occurred "the surrender of the economy, of the culture (with the creation of private universities), and the dignity of the nation." [29] When Radical President Arturo Illia finally annulled the petroleum contracts in November, 1963, the leftist university youth were among the most prominent in supporting the action.

In the post-Perón years much of the critical fire of the nationalist youth was directed against the United States, which was gradually replacing Great Britain as the principal foreign investor in Argentina. Not only were the foreign policies of the United States criticized, but also certain aspects of the internal affairs of the North American republic began to be considered. Between 1955 and 1964, the problem of racial discrimination became a prime concern for many of the nation's youths. Articles on the struggle of the American Negro to achieve full equality in the United States appeared in student publications, and incidents of racial violence were discussed by university groups. Having combated discrimination and anti-Semitism in their own country, the

Argentine youth offered their solidarity with the Negro students of the United States and voiced confidence that the United States National Student Association "will continue struggling to reach a real and definitive racial integration in that country." [30]

Student-worker solidarity, the concept so profoundly shaken by the rise of Perón, continued to be a principal issue for the Argentine university organizations in these years. All student groups attempted to establish contacts with the broad masses of Argentine society. Many federations began to play down their role in the resistance to the ex-dictator, as Perón's continued hold on an important sector of the labor organizations was obvious throughout this period. Many manifestoes declaring the need for student-worker ties were issued, and the Reformistas made the opening of the university to the working class one of their prime objectives. Labor union strikes were supported by student groups, which sometimes joined the workers in their boycotts. Moreover, Reform-inspired university extension experienced a resurgence in the post-Perón years. A university extension department was established in the University of Buenos Aires in 1956. Describing its mission as "the integration of the University with its social environs," the department, with the aid of students, professors, and graduates, began a successful program of social welfare. Between 1956 and 1962 university extension in Buenos Aires aided community development, established adult education classes, opened libraries and cultural centers, offered technical training opportunities, and initiated public health services.[31]

University extension and manifestoes of solidarity improved worker-student relations on the personal level, and programs of assistance represented an encouraging attitude on the part of the university groups to deal with national social and economic problems in practical terms. Nevertheless, the political relationship between university groups and the powerful labor unions still remained weak. The FUA and the local federations experienced no better success than the middle-sector parties in prying the Argentine proletariat away from its attachment to Perón and Peronism. The good intentions of the youth once again seemed no match for the concrete gains the working class had achieved from Perón and expected to win again through support for Peronism.

The attitudes and opinions of the university youth with regard to student-worker solidarity and numerous other issues were debated and discussed at the Fourth National Student Congress, held in Córdoba, October, 1959. The resolutions which finally emerged from this meeting represented FUA thinking on a series of social, economic, political, and educational problems.[32] Resolutions on economic problems opposed foreign intervention in Argentine affairs and favored agrarian reform, nationalization of resources and industry, and trade with all the countries of the world on the basis of mutual benefits. Politically, the FUA backed the right of all political parties to operate freely; freedom of the press, speech, and association; and the release of all persons imprisoned for political reasons. On social issues, the national federation advocated the passage of legislation beneficial to the working class and urged closer student-worker ties.

Much of the Fourth Congress dealt with the situation of the university and the position of the student within Argentina's institutions of higher learning. According to the *Federación Universitaria Argentina* interpretation, the economic structure of the nation, which was held back from developing to its full potential because of foreign control and the continued concentration of land ownership in a few hands, prevented the university from progressing and deprived many potential students of a university degree because of lack of funds. Accordingly, the national federation advocated reforms in these areas, reforms which would in turn improve the economic aspects of higher education. A possible way of improving the quality of the universities—the acceptance of financial grants from North American foundations such as Ford and

Rockefeller—was rejected by the FUA, because it saw these agencies as instruments of imperialistic penetration. On a more specific level, the FUA supported development of "university cities"; establishment of cafeterias offering food at reduced prices for students and professors; provision of student housing, student health services, and more scholarships; improvement of libraries; and the creation in each university of a department of physical education.[33]

Intellectual stimulation for the attitudes of Argentina's leftist students, as expressed in the Fourth National Student Congress and on other occasions, came from a variety of sources in this period. Of the Argentine thinkers, living Reformistas such as Alfredo L. Palacios and Carlos Sánchez Viamonte no longer seemed to exert much influence on student opinions or actions. In contrast, the writings of other Reformistas—Aníbal Ponce, Marxist author and university professor in the 1920's and 1930's, Deodoro Roca, and José Ingenieros among others—enjoyed a new popularity among the youth. Their works and thoughts were re-examined by student leaders and applied to the conditions of contemporary Argentina.[34] For the radical leftists, Argentine Communist writers Héctor P. Agosti and Ernesto Giúdice were influential. Many youths read Marx and Lenin, and the Socialist *Monthly Review* in Spanish translation was a popular periodical among the Republic's university students at that time.

In many respects the attitudes of Argentina's youth with regard to the United States reflected the works dealing with North America which were current in the Republic. In literature, the themes of poverty, decadence, and discrimination evident in the works of John Steinbeck, William Faulkner, and Tennessee Williams—authors very popular with students—often were taken seriously as valid descriptions of typical conditions in the United States. One of the most influential writers for the Argentine youth was sociologist C. Wright Mills, whose theory of the "power elite" fitted in well with many of the students' preconceived notions of North American society. Even earlier critics of the United States —Ida Tarbell and Thorstein Veblen, to name but two—were found in Spanish translation in many bookstores. The universities offered few courses on United States history or government. Moreover, up-to-date and objective studies of the United States being commonly available only in English and only at high prices, they were not widely read.

By the mid-1960's, the Argentine student movement clearly had entered into a state of crisis. Many of the challenges confronting the students at the end of the Perón period still remained. Fragmentation had allowed Communist elements to take control of the national federation and had weakened the over-all effectiveness of the university groups. Although the federations had helped in the reconstruction of the Republic's universities, they had failed to make any successful or meaningful inroads into Peronist control of the urban working classes. Between 1955 and 1964, the student movement also failed to make any significant contributions to national policy. Other than their role in helping to rebuild the nation's institutions of higher learning and opposing Article 28, which was a costly campaign of doubtful worth, the part played by the youth in national affairs was slight when compared with what it had been in the past. Indeed, many students began to question the value of student political activity during a time of relative institutional normality. Having been in a position of opposition to national governments for almost twenty-five years (1930–1955), the student federations seemed to have great difficulty in moving away from this stance and in adopting positive rather than negative solutions to national issues.

NOTES

1. "En esta hora histórica el 23 de septiembre," *Revista del mar dulce* (Buenos Aires, October 1955), p. 2.

2. "Declaración de la Federación Universitaria Argentina," in *Federación Universitaria de Buenos Aires* (FUBA), *La reforma universitaria, 1918–1958* (Buenos Aires, 1959), pp. 199–200.

3. "Informe de la mesa directiva de la Federación Universitaria de Buenos Aires (FUBA)," *Tribuna universitaria* (October 1955), p. 2.

4. "Discurso del interventor, Doctor José Luis Romero," *La revolución libertadora y la universidad, 1955–1957* (Buenos Aires, 1957), pp. 17–19.

5. "Organización y autonomía, decreto-ley No. 6403, Buenos Aires, 23 de diciembre de 1955," in *La revolución libertadora y la universidad, 1955–1957*, pp. 61–70.

6. In Argentina there are no state boards to administer legal or medical qualifying examinations after university graduation, as is done in the United States. Graduation from a national university is all that is required for licensed practice in these professions.

7. "Programa de acción estudiantil," *Boletín del centro estudiantes ingeniería la línea recta* (Buenos Aires, December 1955), p. 3.

8. "Tierra de nadie: ante un pedido de renuncia," *Boletín del centro estudiantes ingeniería la línea recta*, p. 18.

9. Florentino V. Sanguinetti, "Las universidades privadas," in *Federación Universitaria de Buenos Aires* (FUBA), *La reforma universitaria, 1918–1958*, pp. 203–231.

10. "Educación y libertad," *Criterio* (Buenos Aires, September 25, 1958), pp. 683–687.

11. "La Universidad de Buenos Aires y la libertad de enseñanza," *Revista de la Universidad de Buenos Aires* (Buenos Aires, July–September 1958), p. 521. A survey conducted in the University of Buenos Aires (UBA) Faculty of Philosophy and Letters in school term 1955–1956 revealed that 59 per cent of those interviewed favored "enseñanza laica," while 33 per cent supported "enseñanza privada." Percentages for the UBA Faculties of Economic Sciences and Architecture were in similar proportion. These statistics, plus the vote of confidence for Rector Frondizi, provide a rough approximation of the division of feeling among the university groups over Article 28. For the results of the survey in the UBA see A. M. Eichelbaum de Babini, *Algunas características de los estudiantes de la Universidad de Buenos Aires* (Buenos Aires, 1958), p. 32.

12. *La Prensa*, September 7, 1958, p. 1.

13. *Ibid.*, September 20, 1958, p. 1.

14. Horacio O. Domingorena, *Artículo 28: universidades privadas en la Argentina, sus antecedentes* (Buenos Aires, 1959), pp. 76–77.

15. As early as 1947, Augusto J. Durelli, whose writings had considerable influence in Humanista circles, had advocated an end to the state monopoly of education and the foundation of private universities. See

Augusto J. Durelli, "Plan para facilitar la creación de universidades libres en la Argentina," *Ciencia y técnica* (December 1947), pp. 402–405.

16. *La Prensa*, September 13, 1958, p. 5.
17. *Ibid.*, October 2, 1958, p. 1.
18. Movimiento Humanista de Derecho, Secretaría de Cultura, *Que es el humanismo* (Buenos Aires, 1960).
19. From a leaflet entitled "Movimiento Universitario de Centro–Declaración de principios." From the files of the United States National Student Association.
20. Arnoldo Siperman, "Reflexiones de un reformista," *Revista de derecho y ciencias sociales* (Winter 1958), p. 116.
21. Centro de Estudiantes de Derecho de la Universidad del Litoral, *Informe sobre el IV Congreso Nacional de Estudiantes de la F.U.A.* (Rosario, November, 1959), p. 8.
22. Héctor P. Agosti, Paulino González Alberdi, y Leonardo Paso, *Los comunistas y el problema universitario* (Buenos Aires, 1956).
23. Letter from Federación Universitaria Argentina (FUA) international secretary Gerardo A. Andújar to International Union of Students (IUS) president Jiri Pelikan, December 23, 1955. From the Andújar files.
24. Peter T. Jones, *The History of U.S. National Student Association Relations with the International Union of Students, 1945–1956* (Philadelphia, Pa., 1956), pp. 117–118.
25. "Informe de la delegación argentina a la Sexta Conferencia Internacional de Estudiantes, Ceylón, septiembre, 1956." From the Andújar files.
26. It should be noted that this report was drafted only after discussion and debate among Argentina's student organizations, and that the *Liga de Estudiantes Humanistas* and the *Movimiento Universitario Reformista de Ingeniería* (Reformista University Movement of Engineering) of the UBA objected to several points in the FUA document. See Gregorio Selser, *Situación político-social de América Latina* (Buenos Aires, 1957), pp. 11–12.
27. For a full report on the resolutions of the Second Congress see Selser, *op. cit.*, pp. 55–97.
28. *La Razón* (Buenos Aires), February 6, 1961.
29. Unión Universitaria, *Los contratos petroleros* (La Plata, 1963), p. 5.
30. Leaflet entitled "Declaración de la Federación Universitaria Argentina." From the personal files of Horacio J. Sanguinetti.
31. Universidad de Buenos Aires, Departamento de Extensión Universitaria, *Memoria 1961* (Buenos Aires, 1962).
32. FUA thinking at this time was strongly influenced by the growing Communist strength in the student movement. The Congress was not repre-

sentative of the Humanistas nor of the previously mentioned twenty-four dissident Reformista groups which withdrew from the meeting (see p. 173 this chapter). Nevertheless, many of the resolutions still retained a heavy Reformista flavor. See Alberto Ciria y Horacio J. Sanguinetti, *Universidad y estudiantes: testimonio juvenil* (Buenos Aires, 1962), pp. 26–27.

33. Federación Universitaria Argentina (FUA), *Resoluciones del IV Congreso Nacional de Estudiantes* (Córdoba, 1959).

34. See, for example, Alberto Ciria, "Veinte años después, Aníbal Ponce vive," *Revista de derecho y ciencias sociales* (Winter 1958), pp. 91–98; and Carlos A. Solis, "Ingenieros y la juventud actual," *Revista del mar dulce* (December 1955), p. 6.

Conclusions

8

Argentina's university youth often played a significant role in the history of their nation between 1918 and 1964. Perhaps the single most important result of student activity in these decades was the University Reform of 1918. The effects of this movement changed the orientation and nature of higher education not only in Argentina but throughout Latin America. With the Reform, the Argentine universities were changed from oligarchically controlled institutions of limited enrollment to schools more representative of all the Republic's citizens, especially of the middle sectors. As previously mentioned, between the year of the Reform, 1918, and the year 1964, the enrollment in Argentina's universities grew from 14,745 to 155,004 students, a rate far outstripping the over-all population growth in these years. Also, as the University of Buenos Aires (UBA) census of 1958 revealed, more than 90 per cent of the 58,684 students in the University in that year were from the middle classes. Furthermore, the Reform made Argentina's universities more concerned with the solution of national social, economic, and political problems than they had been in the past.

The Córdoba movement also has been credited by most observers with improving the quality of higher education in Argentina to a considerable degree, at least for the period between 1918 and the rise of Perón in the 1940's. Historian Arthur P. Whitaker, speaking of the Reform, has noted that "In the next two decades [1920–1940] the Argentine university system was without a peer in the rest of Latin America." [1]

The efforts to reform the Republic's universities between 1918 and 1922 introduced Argentina's university youth to political activity on the national scene. In those years the students successfully achieved stated goals, established methods of political action which have been followed for more than four decades, and formulated attitudes on social, economic, and political issues which have continued to the 1960's. Much of the student activity between 1918 and 1964 has centered on defense of Reform principles, and the Reform has acquired an almost mystical quality as an ideal worth defending. The anniversaries of the Córdoba revolt have been celebrated with meetings, speeches, and special publications, and the ideas and principles emanating from the movement have continued to influence a large sector of the Argentine youth.

Student activities have contributed to Argentine political life in several other areas. In the revolutions of 1930 and 1955, the university youth were influential in arousing public opinion to the side of the revolutionary forces. The September, 1930, street demonstrations of the students were instrumental in the overthrow of President Irigoyen. The October, 1954, university strike, arousing national and international sympathy for the plight of the Argentine youth, was a significant antecedent to the end of the Perón regime in September, 1955. It is interesting to note that after both these revolutions the students soon became disillusioned with and opposed to the post-revolutionary regimes, which indicates their propensity to favor rapid action and change and their corollary failure to anticipate or consider long-term effects and consequences.

One of the most characteristic positions of the university youth, not only in Argentina but throughout Latin America, has been its opposition to dictatorship. For most of the period between 1930 and 1955, the Argentine university youth were influential in the resistance to regimes which restricted political rights and individual liberties in their nation. Suffering imprisonment and exile, the students, through their local and national organizations, kept alive a spirit of freedom and a faith in democracy despite the authoritarian leaders who ruled their land.

Another contribution of the student movement to Argentine national life has been to serve as a training ground for political leaders. The university federations and the Reform movement produced many men who later took important positions in the Republic's political parties. Julio V. González and Carlos Sánchez Viamonte, both active in university affairs in the UBA Faculty of Law in the 1920's, became important figures in the Socialist party in ensuing decades. Gabriel del Mazo, participant in the 1918 Reform and president of the *Federación Universitaria Argentina* (FUA), and Arturo Frondizi, Reformista student in the UBA Faculty of Law in the 1930's, both served as Radical party deputies in the National Congress in the 1940's. Elected president of the Republic in 1958, Frondizi appointed del Mazo minister of defense in his cabinet. In addition to Frondizi, other student leaders active in the 1930's moved into political positions. Héctor P. Agosti and Ernesto Giúdice became important figures in the Argentine Communist party. Pablo Lejarraga, student leader in the early 1930's, was a Socialist party deputy in 1964. Isidro Odena, active in Reformista politics in the late 1920's and early 1930's, became an important member of the Radical party in later years.

Because of the nature of Argentina's political structure, which between 1930 and 1958 was controlled largely by military and

Conservative groups, most of those men who have made the transition from student leadership to national politics have joined the ranks of the opposition. Nearly all have entered the Radical and Socialist parties—the two political organizations which have given the greatest support to the principles of the University Reform and to the positions of the university youth throughout the years 1918–1964. As a result, except for the presidential election of Arturo Frondizi in 1958, the contribution of the student movement has not been to the leadership of the nation per se but rather to the leadership of the political opposition.

Another important aspect of student activity in Argentina has been the part played by the university youth in introducing new ideas to the political, social, and economic thought of the Republic. For example, the Reformistas emphasized the need for social justice and improved conditions for the workingman twenty-five years before these issues became current in the Republic. This position of being "ahead" of the thinking of the bulk of the population has been expected from a group which usually has been the first to hear, study, and be stimulated by new theories, both national and international, which have been introduced into the Republic. Moreover, being at an age of self-discovery and experimentation, the university youth probably have been more inclined than their elders to adopt and try out ideas which might have seemed revolutionary and advanced. Attendance at international student meetings also has placed the youth in a position of being among the first groups in the Republic to become familiar with foreign developments and thinking.

In reviewing more than forty-five years of student activity in Argentina, several principal points appear to have consistently characterized the thinking of the university youth. A majority of the students and the university federations have been opposed to imperialism, dictatorship, militarism, conservatism, ultra-nationalism, and the influence of the Catholic church in public affairs.

They have favored protection of individual rights, democratic processes, social justice, pacifism, educational improvement, solidarity with other Latin American youths, and close relations with the working class. Between 1918 and 1964, most student groups were idealistic and nationalistic and assumed a generally leftist position on the Argentine political spectrum.

Besides characteristic attitudes and opinions, student political activity in Argentina also has been marked by common tendencies and actions. The methods of political agitation, including the issuance of manifestoes, leaflets, and posters; the use of street demonstrations and university strikes; the sending of petitions to government officials; the acquiring of messages of support from foreign student groups, political parties, and international organizations—all these tactics generally have followed the pattern established by the 1918 Reform. The university youth themselves have never been in a position of national decision making. Accordingly, they have tailored their political methods to applying pressure upon those national groups which do have the power to set policy.

Some of the traditional characteristics of student activity in Argentina have tended to weaken the political influence and position of the university youth. First, the student movement often has fragmented into small and competing groups after a moment of crisis has passed or a common effort, such as the resistance to the Perón dictatorship, has been made. In part, this tendency has resulted from the continuous change of membership and leadership in the university movement, as students have graduated after five or six years of activity and new youths have taken their places. Moreover, the numerous groups which have appeared in the university have indicated the diversity of ideas and opinions which exist among any large body of intellectuals. The splintering of the student movement also reflects the pattern of Argentina's political parties, which historically have weakened their positions both by fragmenting and by failing to make compromises or to form coalitions.

Second, the Argentine university youth many times have resorted to direct action—and even violence—to achieve their ends, belying their own faith in democratic procedures. This tendency was evident in the Reformista capture of the University of Córdoba in September, 1918, the student participation in the 1930 revolution, the occupation of the Republic's universities in October, 1945, and the Reformista campaign to defeat Article 28 in 1958. The use of direct action on the part of the youth may be beneficial or harmful, depending on the circumstances of the situation and its eventual results. However, this tendency to strike action and violence can become a dangerous reflex action which places the youth in the position of performing in the same manner as the groups they have historically opposed. Furthermore, the student stand in favor of democratic procedures and respect for individual liberties can be greatly weakened when direct student action in public life infringes on the liberties of others and ignores the very principles which the youth themselves profess. The tradition of violence within the student movement, which could be seen emerging as early as the personal attack on the president of the *Federación Universitaria de Córdoba* (FUC), Enrique F. Barros, during the 1918 Córdoba Reform, has been a characteristic which has endured and which must be overcome if the Argentine university youth hope to play an influential and respected role in the national life of the Republic.[2]

Third, because the university students were under the control of authoritarian governments for most of the twenty-five-year period 1930–1955, their position, which was constructive and positive in the years immediately after the Reform, has become one of an almost impulsive negativism in the post-Perón era. Between 1955 and 1964, the Reformista students generally opposed the economic and political policies of the national government, campaigned against Article 28, and disagreed with most measures of the Argentine administration which dealt with education. During this period the youth themselves seldom offered any sound and practical alternatives for the solution of national problems.

In surveying student activity in Argentina between 1918 and 1964, some answers have emerged with regard to the questions posed in the introduction of this work. I have based these conclusions on a study of the historical material and the available evidence. In some instances, the available evidence is sufficient for only a partial answer to these complex problems.

1. *What have been the ages and socio-economic backgrounds of student leaders?*

As previously mentioned (Chapters 3, 4, and 5), the leaders of the 1918 Reform—Julio V. González, Gabriel del Mazo, Enrique F. Barros, Guillermo Watson, and Gregorio Bermann among others—and the leaders of the student movement in the early 1930's—Pablo Lejarraga, Isidro Odena, Héctor P. Agosti, and Ernesto Giúdice—were generally between the ages of twenty and twenty-five when they were active in student politics.[3] Likewise, student activists of the 1945–1960 period, such as Abel Alexis Lattendorf, leader of the exile and anti-Perón students in Uruguay in the early 1950's; Gerardo Andújar, secretary of the FUA during the Perón period; Amanda Toubes, president of the *Federación Universitaria de Buenos Aires* (FUBA) from 1954 to 1955; and Alberto Ciria and Horacio J. Sanguinetti, leaders in the UBA Faculty of Law between 1955 and 1960, were all in their early or mid-twenties when active in the university groups.[4] There is no evidence that "professional students" have had much influence in the history of Argentine student politics. The leaders of the major movements and the officials of the university federations who have been most prominent in student activities have been those who generally have followed the normal time span for university careers. That most leaders have been in their early or mid-twenties, rather than in the eighteen to nineteen age bracket, is not surprising, as it usually takes several years of political activity to reach a position of leadership in the university groups.

The question of the social and economic backgrounds of student leaders is complicated by a lack of extensive data, but there is some information available for a tentative conclusion. A survey of four faculties in the UBA and a sample from the University of the South in Bahía Blanca for the school year 1955–1956 reveal the largely middle-class composition of the student body. In the University of Buenos Aires, 93 per cent of the students in the Faculty of Philosophy and Letters were from the middle class, and only 7 per cent from the working class. The UBA Faculty of Economic Sciences survey revealed that 83 per cent were from the middle class, 15 per cent from the working class, 2 per cent being unclassifiable. The class ratios for the UBA Faculties of Exact Sciences and Architecture were almost exactly the same as those for the Faculty of Philosophy and Letters. In the University of the South, 87 per cent of the students surveyed were from the middle class and only 13 per cent from the working class.[5] A more complete survey, the UBA census of 1958, revealed that of the 58,684 students polled, more than 90 per cent were from middle-class families.[6] The overwhelming middle-class representation in the university, therefore, would seem to indicate that this is the group from which student leaders are recruited. Furthermore, students from the working class, none of whom to my knowledge held leadership positions in the university movements during the years 1955–1964, would necessarily be under greater financial strain and have to devote more time to earning an income than their middle-class colleagues. This, in turn, would limit time for political activities.

Unfortunately, survey materials for the years 1918–1955 are not yet available. However, certain propositions suggest that during this period the student leadership, particularly the Reformista leadership, was also of middle-class origin. First, as mentioned in Chapter 3, historians of and participants in the Reform movement have underscored the middle-class origins and orientations of the Reformistas. Second, those university and student leaders who entered politics, entered parties which were representative of the middle class and its program. Third, the careers of the Reformista leaders after graduation were in professions which in Latin America have been associated with the middle class. Most of the "generation of '18" and of the student leaders of the early 1930's became practicing lawyers or physicians and maintained their contacts with the university groups by becoming professors in Argentina's institutions of higher learning. The above propositions, however, still are largely speculative and impressionistic. The problem of the socio-economic backgrounds of Argentina's student leaders, both past and present, offers many opportunities for further and more detailed research.

2. *What factors have made students politically influential?*

During times of institutional crisis, when political parties have been fragmented and ineffective, the university youth of Argentina have represented a fairly cohesive group which has been able to act in a united and decisive manner. This was particularly true at certain points between 1930 and 1955, when the students were a leading group in the political opposition. Moreover, courage in the resistance to dictatorship has given the university youth a special prestige in Argentine politics. However, it should also be noted that one of the periods of greatest student achievement, the era of the Reform between 1918 and 1922, was a period of institutional normality. The important factor in those years was the existence of a national administration which sympathized with the goals and permitted the activities of the university groups.

In Argentina, as elsewhere in Latin America, the university youth have represented an educated group being trained to accept the responsibilities of national leadership. Furthermore, throughout much of the literature dealing with the Reform movement, the theme that Argentina's students represent the "hope for a better future" has been emphasized. Because of this position and this prestige, the students have represented an influential and important group in Argentine society. Nevertheless, these aspects of student politics seem somewhat less important in Argentina than in some other Latin American republics. In countries such as Venezuela and Bolivia, for example, where literacy rates have been low and the number enrolled in universities has been small, the students have represented an elite of educated men who have enjoyed high social, economic, and political prestige and have been looked to as leaders of national thought and action. However, in Argentina, a country which has had one of the highest literacy rates and the greatest number of university students in Latin America, the university youth seem to have held a less influential position because of these factors than have their counterparts in less developed countries. In other words, Argentina's students have not represented an elite group to the same extent as have students in other Latin American republics.

In considering the factors in the Argentine political, social, and economic structure which have made students influential, it is also necessary to mention those conditions which have hindered the effectiveness of student action. One of these is the constantly changing composition of university group leadership. Unlike a political party, which can maintain a cohesive leadership over long periods, the student movement depends upon the direction of a constantly changing executive, as students periodically and regularly graduate from the university. Also, unlike political parties, the university federations are not represented in Congress, nor in the governmental bureaucracy. At times, the university sectors have wielded power by acting much in the manner of an interest group, applying pressure for change through petitions, personal interviews with government officials, and public demonstrations.

Nevertheless, the university youth have neither the time nor the resources to engage in these activities on the same level as more powerful interest groups such as labor and business. Finally, in the face of the increasing political role of the military, not only Argentina's students, but many other groups in the Republic, have found it more and more difficult to effectuate the changes they desire when the elements which control the nation's armed might have been arrayed against them. As one student told me in 1964, when the university youth clashes with the army in the streets, the army will inevitably emerge the victor.

With regard to the actual political influence of the students in national affairs, some qualifying remarks should be made at this point. In a work of this kind, concentrating as it does on one particular group, the historian runs the risk of overemphasizing the role and contributions of the group he is studying, much the way a biographer might inflate the importance of the personality about whom he is writing. Student activity in Argentina historically has been significant, but, as I have indicated, significant at certain times, in certain situations, and in certain areas. In the long run, the students have not been so important in bringing about changes on the national level in Argentina as have other groups, particularly the military and the established political parties. To rank the university groups as to influence and importance in Argentina would be a complex and largely subjective process and beyond the scope of this work. It is interesting to note, however, that in a recent and important study of the groups which have enjoyed power and influence in Argentina in the past several decades, the student federations were not included. The groups which were considered were the armed forces, the church, the political party leadership, representatives of the large landowning interests, representatives of the commercial and industrial interests, representatives of the labor unions, and members of the executive branch of the government.[7]

3. *Have there been connections between national political parties and student organizations?*

The Argentine student movement historically has attempted to remain free from national political affiliation. During moments of crisis and political change, particularly during the resistance to the Uriburu and Perón dictatorships, the university federations have worked closely with national parties, particularly with the Radicals and the Socialists. Moreover, Argentina's political parties have attempted to recruit members from the university population and have made efforts to support and identify with the principles of the University Reform. Individual students have affiliated with national parties while pursuing their careers, once again particularly with the Radicals and the Socialists. But the university federations themselves, despite the political inclinations of their individual members, generally have remained independent of the influence and program of national political groups. In the future, however, this conclusion might need revision if the Communist control of Argentina's student federations continues. Under the Communists, the university students become direct agents of a political group.

4. *How influential have been professors, national political leaders, and intellectuals on student thought and action?*

Certain intellectuals, who at various times were also professors and political activists—for example, José Ingenieros, Julio V. González, Deodoro Roca, and Alfredo L. Palacios—were clearly quite influential in helping to formulate the attitudes of Argentina's university youth. The ideas outlined in the speeches, essays, and books of these men often have been reflected in student documents or translated directly into action. This influence was especially great between 1910 and 1930, when Argentine thinkers produced a significant body of introspective and critical literature. Between 1930 and 1945, the men who had been active in the University Reform provided much of the intellectual stimulation and inspiration for the Argentine youth. After the fall of Perón in 1955, the influence of contemporary national thinkers and political leaders diminished, and the university students began to look abroad or to the past for their ideas.

The working relationship between professors and students, particularly between pro-Reform professors and students, generally has been a close one since the 1918 Córdoba revolt. In the 1920's, Reformista professors in the University of Buenos Aires Faculty of Law led the university youth in the struggle against the counter-Reform. In the 1930's, students supported professors who had been dismissed from their teaching posts by the Uriburu government. During the resistance to Perón in the mid-1940's, students, faculty members, and administrative officials worked in close co-operation. In 1958, rectors, professors, and the university youth demonstrated together in the streets during the campaign to defeat Article 28.

5. *What percentage of the university youth have participated in political activities?*

The number of students who have engaged in political activities has varied with historical circumstances and the nature of the issue. During the Reform movement of 1918, the revolution of 1930, the resistance to Perón in 1945 and 1946, and the campaign to defeat Article 28 in 1958, a majority of the university youth were involved in one way or another in political activities. However, during those times when a relatively normal situation prevailed and no transcendent issue was being debated, the number of students who were active in organizational activities, served as student officers, and participated in university affairs usually was only about 10 per cent of the total student body. A survey conducted among students of the Faculties of Medicine, Exact Sciences, and Economic Sciences of the UBA, soon after the termination of the campaign for private universities, revealed that:

> The level of overt public activity is quite low among all the groups, although well over half of all respondents report that they argue politics with friends and acquaintances. Party activity, on the con-

trary, involved only six per cent of the freshmen, eight per cent of the seniors, and six per cent of the graduates. Of the latter only 17 per cent attended a meeting of their professional associations in the six months preceding the questionnaire, while only 15 per cent of the seniors and 20 per cent of the freshmen attended a student association meeting.[8]

6. *Has the student movement been of one defined political tendency?*

Although the Reformistas and Reform thought have dominated Argentina's student movement, the university youth seldom have been monolithic politically. Within the Reformista ranks themselves, various splinter groups have appeared, as in the early 1920's, and attempted to outline new and different approaches to university and national problems. From the establishment of the Committee for the Defense of the University in Córdoba during the 1918 movement down to the more recent *Movimiento Universitario de Centro* in Buenos Aires, there frequently were groups of a conservative nature within the university which have opposed the liberal Reformistas. Moreover, two other important groups, the Communists, first showing strength in the 1930's, and the Humanistas, organized in the 1950's, have presented serious challenges to Reformista dominance of the university sectors.

In Argentina the student has played a dual role: He has been both a citizen of the nation and a member of the university community. As a citizen he has tended to follow lines which have reflected the political composition of the nation. A survey of the student center of the Faculty of Philosophy and Letters in the UBA, conducted during the school year 1955–1956, revealed the following breakdown of national political affiliations among the youth: Christian Democrats, 19 per cent; Radicals, 17 per cent; Socialists, 15 per cent; Communists, 7 per cent; Conservatives, 3 per cent; Democratic Progressives, 3 per cent; and Peronistas, 1 per cent. In the survey, 19 per cent answered they did not know their political affiliation; the remaining 16 per cent polled did not answer this question.[9] The results of this poll indicate that, although the Faculty of Philosophy and Letters has the general reputation of being very leftist, in truth, the political preferences of its members correspond very closely to the political affiliations of Argentina's middle class in general. As Kalman H. Silvert has noted:

> The Latin American university student is the child of his parents. To assume that the student is but a hot-eyed revolutionary is to presume that somehow registering in a university is sufficient to cut family ties, break class and other group identifications, and produce a special kind of creature divorced from his society.[10]

While as a citizen the Argentine student has reflected the fragmentation of the Republic's political parties, as a member of the university he has shown more solidarity on certain issues—particularly issues related to education. Referring once again to the 1955–1956 survey at the University of Buenos Aires, 86 per cent of the first-year students questioned in the Faculty of Philosophy and Letters and 90 per cent of those interviewed in the Faculty of Architecture agreed with the principle of student participation in the administration of the nation's institutions of higher learning. Only 5 per cent in each school opposed this Reform concept, which has been supported by Humanistas as well as Reformistas.[11]

7. *What has been the relationship between the quality of education and student political activity in national affairs?*

The relationship between university issues and national issues has always been an important one with regard to student political activity in Argentina. Throughout the history of the student movement, from the 1918 Reform to the 1958 campaign over Article 28, one of the basic aims of the youth has been to improve the quality of their educational institutions and to correct what they have considered the faults of higher learning in the nation. Most of the national student congresses, a majority of the reports from university organizations, and a large number of the speeches by student leaders have been concerned more with educational than with political issues. However, in their actions to improve the Republic's universities the youth often have discovered that this goal cannot be achieved without their participation in national political affairs. For example, no improvements, at least along Reform lines, could be made within Argentina's universities between 1945 and 1955 until the Perón regime was overthrown.

8. *What have been the political attitudes and activities of student leaders after graduation from the university?*

The *leaders* of Argentina's student movement generally have tended to maintain the attitudes and positions established during their years of university activity. This has been particularly true of the group of men who participated in the 1918 Reform. Political activists such as Reformistas Gregorio Bermann, Julio V. González, Gabriel del Mazo, and Deodoro Roca were greatly affected by the political philosophy associated with the Córdoba movement, and they continued to base their actions and thoughts on their earlier university experience after they had become members of Argentina's Socialist (González and Roca), Radical (del Mazo), and Communist (Bermann) parties. The student leaders of the 1930's, among them Héctor P. Agosti (Communist), Ernesto Giúdice (Communist), Pablo Lejarraga (Socialist), and Isidro Odena (Radical), also maintained their liberal positions after graduation.

It seems likely that in the 1960's Argentina's university students will continue to play an important role in the national life of the Republic. In particular, the youth will continue in attempts to improve the quality of the nation's universities by applying pressure on the national government to pay more attention to the needs of higher education. On the national economic and political levels, student success will depend greatly upon the youth's ability to overcome fragmentation and to present a coherent and positive program for the solution of the nation's problems. Events on the national scene will largely determine the possibilities of the student federations to overcome their differences and to form a more united movement. If some sort of national consensus is achieved, or if one political party should emerge dominant, these developments will be reflected among the university youth. On the other hand, if authoritarian rule should return to the Republic and threaten the entire university system, then—judging from the pattern of past actions—students, professors, and administrative officials will at some point submerge their political differences and form a united opposition.

One of the great challenges for Argentina's student movement in the 1960's, particularly for the Reformistas, will be to meet the growing criticism of the principles of the University Reform. In many instances these criticisms are well founded and have come not only from anti-Reformista sources but also from men who generally have sympathized with student aspirations. If the Argentine university is to be a key instrument in the social, economic, and political development of the nation, these critics argue, the Reform must be adjusted to meet new conditions. The political activities of the students, particularly within the university, they point out, often became more important than attention to academic concerns. The principles of the Reform, it is said, have not improved the quality of higher education but have instead had the opposite effect of downgrading academic standards and worsening the very conditions they were intended to better.

The fact that many of the deficiencies of higher education in Argentina remain, as seen in Chapter 1 of this work, more than four decades after the 1918 Reform, lends great weight to these arguments. Part-time professors, poor and repetitious lectures, and courses unrelated to national realities continue to plague Argentina's university system. Furthermore, in many instances, Reform principles have led to results unforeseen by the "men of '18." Professors often have been forced to cater to the whims of students to avoid being fired from the university by the student representatives on the administrative councils. The principle of periodic review of professorial posts can be heavily influenced by political considerations. Similarly, an academically qualified teacher may lose his position simply because during the time of his review he gave a low grade to a politically influential student. Periodic review, which means there is no tenure system in Argentine higher education, also discourages professors from abandoning the relative security of a career outside the university in favor of the instability and insecurity of full-time university teaching.

Two more Reform principles have come under severe attack. One is unregulated attendance at classes, which—it is claimed— prevents a consistent and meaningful intellectual dialogue in the classroom. The other is the Reform ideal that the university of Argentina should be open to all citizens. On this point, critics underscore the lack of space and facilities, the large classes which make student-professor contact and intensive learning impossible, and the extremely high drop-out rate in Argentina's universities. To improve Argentine higher education, they argue, entrance requirements should be toughened and enrollment should be limited to those with the capability and the dedication to complete their studies. Historically, the Reformistas have opposed any and all measures to limit or restrict university enrollment.[12]

Another important problem for Argentina's student movement in the 1960's, affecting both Reformistas and Humanistas, will be the increased influence of Communism within the university federations. The Humanista position in this regard has been somewhat clearer than that of the Reformistas. The Humanistas have established their own organizations, independent of the national and local university federations, which by the early 1960's were largely under Communist control. They also have formulated a program considerably distinct from that of the leftist university groups.

Humanista success in the future will depend to a great extent upon the success of the Christian Democratic movement in the nation as a whole. Furthermore, the Humanistas must prove that they can offer a viable alternative to the Reform philosophy, an alternative which considers the solution of national social and economic problems. Finally, they must prove with practice their belief that university problems can best be solved by acting primarily within the institutions of higher learning rather than on the national scene.

For the Reformistas, the majority of whom are still affiliated with the Communist-controlled federations in the 1960's, the problems they must face in the future are profound and impressive. In the first place, they must determine their position with regard to Communism, making clear the line where Reform philosophy ends and Marxist theory begins. By clarifying their program in a clear-cut manner, they can establish the distinctions between their movement and the Communists. Second, the Reformistas will have to decide whether to intensify their political activities within the established organizations to defeat the Communists who have captured the student movement's leadership, or whether to break away from the federations and establish a new and completely independent organization. Much of the Reformista's future success depends upon the various liberal and leftist sectors' of the university youth overcoming their tendency to fragment. Instead, they must agree upon a basic program and an organizational plan which will permit the non-Communist youth who believe in the Reform principles to play a constructive and effective role in the university and the nation.

In the 1960's the Reformistas must re-examine the basic points of their philosophy in relation to the economic, social, and political conditions of post-Perón Argentina. They must consider whether the Reform principles which were applied to a university system of 14,500 students in a nation of eight million in 1918 are still applicable for a university system which in 1960 numbered 150,000 students in a nation of twenty million. In light of poor facilities, high drop-out rates, and lack of personal attention, will Reform principles of unregulated attendance at classes, unrestricted enrollment, and student participation in university government serve to better or worsen the academic quality of Argentina's institutions of higher learning? The Reformistas also will have to re-examine the consequences of their actions with regard to national developments between 1918 and 1964 and will have to determine where their activities have been beneficial and where they have been detrimental to the Republic's long-term interests. Finally, the Reformistas will have to confront the argument that during times of institutional normality, the proper role of the student is that of student, not of political activist.

The fate of the Reform and the Argentine student movement will hang upon the ability of the university youth to meet the serious and challenging problems which confront their universities and their nation in the 1960's. One of the aspects of student political activity which has prevailed from the days of the Córdoba Reform movement into the 1960's, has been the claim that the youth have acted to promote the best interests of the nation. This principle should be a prime consideration for the Argentine youth in the future and should guide them in the difficult and important decisions they will have to make in the years to come.

NOTES

1. Arthur P. Whitaker, *The United States and Argentina* (Cambridge, Mass., 1954), p. 74.
2. From my own personal experience I can testify to the continued existence of violence within the Argentine student movement. On June 26, 1964, I attended a meeting of the *Federación Universitaria Argentina* (FUA), held in the auditorium of the University of Buenos Aires (UBA) Faculty of Law. During the course of the ceremony, intended

to celebrate the University Reform, some twenty youths entered the hall and fired shots indiscriminately into the crowd. A general disorder ensued, and the participants fled the building. The police, not permitted into the Faculty, were not able to halt the shooting. Fortunately, this time no one was injured. However, in recent years similar episodes have led to serious damage to property and persons.

3. See "Quién es quién en la reforma argentina," in Federación Universitaria de Buenos Aires (FUBA), *La reforma universitaria, 1918–1958* (Buenos Aires, 1959), pp. 367–375.

4. Abel Alexis Lattendorf's age was obtained from a biographical note in Carlos Strasser, *Las izquierdas en el proceso político argentino* (Buenos Aires, 1959), p. 298. Ages for the others—Andújar, Toubes, Ciria, and Sanguinetti—were taken from personal interviews I had with them in Buenos Aires in 1964.

5. A. M. Eichelbaum de Babini, *Algunas características de los estudiantes de la Universidad de Buenos Aires* (Buenos Aires, 1958), p. 17.

6. Universidad de Buenos Aires, *Censo universitario* (Buenos Aires, 1959), pp. 111–114.

7. José Luis de Imaz, *Los que mandan* (Buenos Aires, 1964).

8. Frank Bonilla and Kalman H. Silvert, *Education and the Social Meaning of Development: A Preliminary Statement* (New York, 1961), p. 104.

9. Eichelbaum de Babini, *op. cit.,* p. 36.

10. Kalman H. Silvert, "The University Student," in John J. Johnson, ed., *Continuity and Change in Latin America* (Stanford, Calif., 1964), p. 225.

11. Eichelbaum de Babini, *op. cit.,* p. 31.

12. For a knowledgeable North American observer's comprehensive and searching criticism of Argentina's university system in the post-Perón period, see Kalman H. Silvert, "Other People's Classrooms," in his *The Conflict Society: Reaction and Revolution in Latin America* (New Orleans, La., 1961), pp. 162–182.

Bibliography

The research for this work on student political activity was carried out both in the United States and in Argentina. In the United States I used the facilities of the Stanford University Library, the Library of Congress in Washington, D. C., the Columbus Memorial Library of the Pan American Union, the New York Public Library, and the Latin American Division of the United States National Student Association in Philadelphia. I also spent twelve months in Buenos Aires, where I gathered materials from the *Biblioteca del Congreso de la Nación,* the *Biblioteca Nacional,* the *Biblioteca "Juan B. Justo"* of the Argentine Socialist party, and the libraries located in the Faculties of Medicine, Law, Philosophy and Letters, Engineering, and Economic Sciences of the University of Buenos Aires.

Although extensive use was made of public research facilities, many of the materials collected came from private libraries. One of the principal characteristics of student activity in Argentina has been resistance to authoritarian regimes. This position has meant that student centers and organizations, including libraries and files, often have been destroyed by police and government officials. As a result, many important documents were available only through private sources.

I was most fortunate in being allowed to use the personal library of Florentino V. Sanguinetti and his son, Horacio J. Sanguinetti. Both father and son were active student leaders in the law school of the University of Buenos Aires, and their collection of documents, periodicals, and articles on university issues is one of the most extensive in the Republic. Gerardo A. Andújar, secretary of the national student federation and a leader in the Faculty of Philosophy and Letters in Buenos Aires between 1950 and 1956, kindly permitted me the use of his materials covering the period when he was active in the student movement. Gabriel del Mazo, author of many extensive works on educational and political issues, provided me with several important documents from his large library. Carlos S. Bianchi, president of the University of La Plata, lent me a collection of his speeches and essays dealing with university matters. David Richardson, Latin American correspondent for *U.S. News and World Report*, permitted me to use his personal file on student activity in Argentina. In addition to using their personal documents, I also spoke at length with Florentino and Horacio Sanguinetti, Gerardo A. Andújar, and Gabriel del Mazo about the various issues considered in this work. I also held interviews with historian José Luis Romero, Dean of the Faculty of Philosophy and Letters in Buenos Aires, Amanda Toubes, student leader in the mid-1950's, and Carlos Sánchez Viamonte, Socialist politician and active participant in university affairs for more than forty years. Finally, I spoke with approximately 100 Argentine university students about their actions and attitudes with regard to educational and national concerns. The majority of the youths contacted were from the Universities of Buenos Aires, La Plata, and the Littoral.

PUBLIC DOCUMENTS

República Argentina, Secretaría de Educación de la Nación. *Anuario estadístico, año 1945*. Buenos Aires, 1948.

República Argentina, Ministerio de Educación y Justicia. *Estadística educativa*, "Establecimientos, alumnos y profesores" (cifras provisionales). Buenos Aires, 1960.

República Argentina, Ministerio de Educación y Justicia. "Hojas de apéndice correspondiente al año 1955." Buenos Aires, 1955.

República Argentina, Ministerio de Justicia e Instrucción Pública. *Estadística*. Buenos Aires, 1919.

República Argentina, Ministerio de Justicia e Instrucción Pública. *Estadística, año 1930*. Buenos Aires, 1933.

Universidad de Buenos Aires. *Censo universitario*. Buenos Aires, 1959.

LEAFLETS AND REPORTS FROM PRIVATE COLLECTIONS

From Gerardo A. Andújar

F.U.B.A. "El estudiantado al pueblo."

"Informe de la delegación argentina a la Sexta Conferencia Internacional de Estudiantes, Ceylón, Septiembre, 1956."

"Informe del delegado argentino a la Tercera Conferencia Internacional de Estudiantes."

"La Federación Universitaria Argentina ante la titulada pacificación nacional."

"Nota de la Federación Juvenil Comunista."

"Resolución de la J. R. de F.U.A. (Córdoba, 28 de noviembre, 1953)."

"Reunión de Junta Representativa de F.U.A. (15 de diciembre, 1952)."

From Gabriel del Mazo

Grancelli Chá, Héctor. *Retiro de las delegaciones argentina y uruguaya ante la pretensión de que el Congreso obrará segun consignas.*

Tercer Congreso Nacional de Estudiantes Universitarios (Córdoba, 2 al 5 de octubre de 1942): Resoluciones adoptadas en los siete puntos del temario.

From Horacio J. Sanguinetti

"Carta abierta al Ingeniero Gabriel del Mazo (La Plata, 28 de octubre, 1958)."

"Declaración de la Federación Universitaria Argentina."

"La Federación Universitaria, ante la reglamentación del artículo 28."

From the United States National Student Association

Co-ordinating Secretariat of National Unions of Students. *Memorandum: The University Situation in Argentina.* Leiden, Netherlands, 1954.

COSEC. "Report of the Delegation of the Federación de Estudiantes de Uruguay y de la Confederación de Estudiantes Universitarios de Chile who visited Buenos Aires, January 25–31, 1955." Leiden, Netherlands, 1955.

Einaudi, Luigi. "Perón's Secret Files on Students Opened to U.S.N.S.A. Representatives." (1956)

"La Federación Universitaria de Buenos Aires informa al pueblo la realidad en torno a los acontecimientos universitarios."

"Movimiento Universitario de Centro–Declaración de principios."

"National Federation of Argentine Students."

"No se deje engañar."

"Universidad Nacional de Buenos Aires, La Nación Argentina, November 10, 1960."

NEWSPAPERS

La Nación, 1951–1964. Buenos Aires.
La Prensa, 1918–1964. Buenos Aires.
La Vanguardia, 1918, 1945. Buenos Aires.

COLLECTIONS OF DOCUMENTS, ESSAYS, SPEECHES, AND ARTICLES

Co-ordinating Secretariat of National Unions of Students. *University Reform in Latin America.* Leiden, Netherlands, 1959.

Federación Universitaria de Buenos Aires. *La reforma universitaria, 1918–1958.* Buenos Aires, 1959.

Gollán, Josué. *La universidad al servicio de la democracia: una experiencia en política universitaria.* Santa Fe, 1945.

González, Julio V. *La reforma universitaria.* Buenos Aires, 1927. 2 vols.

Ingenieros, José. *La universidad del porvenir y otros escritos sobre filosofía, educación y cultura.* Buenos Aires, 1956.

Ingenieros, José. *Los tiempos nuevos: reflexiones optimistas sobre la guerra y la revolución.* Madrid, 1921.

Kautsky, John H., ed. *Political Change in Underdeveloped Countries: Nationalism and Communism.* New York, 1962.

Korn, Alejandro. *Influencias filosóficas en la evolución nacional.* Buenos Aires, 1936.

La reforma universitaria: en la Universidad de Córdoba: en la Universidad de Buenos Aires, año 1918. Buenos Aires, 1919.

La revolución libertadora y la universidad, 1955–1957. Buenos Aires, 1957.

Lipset, S. M., and S. S. Wolin, eds. *The Berkeley Student Revolt: Facts and Interpretations.* New York, 1965.

Mazo, Gabriel del, ed., *La reforma universitaria.* Tomo I. "Juicio de hombres de la nueva generación acerca de su significado y alcances (1918–1926)." Buenos Aires, 1926.

Mazo, Gabriel del, ed., *La reforma universitaria*. Tomo II. "Documentos relativos al movimiento estudiantil en las Universidades de Córdoba y Buenos Aires (1918)." Buenos Aires, 1927.

Mazo, Gabriel del, ed., *La reforma universitaria*. Tomo III. "El Primer Congreso Nacional de Estudiantes Universitarios (Córdoba, 1918)." Buenos Aires, 1927.

Mazo, Gabriel del, ed., *La reforma universitaria*. Tomo IV. "Documentos relativos al movimiento estudiantil en La Plata (1919–1920)." Buenos Aires, 1927.

Mazo, Gabriel del, ed., *La reforma universitaria*. Tomo V. "Documentos complementarios que se refieren a la acción directamente social del movimiento estudiantil argentino (1918–1921)." Buenos Aires, 1927.

Mazo, Gabriel del, ed., *La reforma universitaria*. Tomo VI. "Documentos relativos a la propagación del movimiento en América Latina (1918–1927)." Buenos Aires, 1927.

Mazo, Gabriel del, ed., *La reforma universitaria*. Tomo I. "El movimiento argentino." La Plata, 1941.

Mazo, Gabriel del, ed., *La reforma universitaria*. Tomo II. "Propagación americana." La Plata, 1941.

Mazo, Gabriel del, ed., *La reforma universitaria*. Tomo III. "Ensayos críticos (1918–1940)." La Plata, 1941.

Mazo, Gabriel del. *La reforma universitaria y la universidad latinoamericana*. Buenos Aires, 1957.

Mazo, Gabriel del. *Reforma universitaria y cultura nacional*. Buenos Aires, 1955.

Repetto, Nicolás. *Hombres y problemas argentinos*. Buenos Aires, 1945.

Roca, Deodoro. *Ciencias, maestros y universidades*. Buenos Aires, 1959.

Roca, Deodoro. *El difícil tiempo nuevo*. Buenos Aires, 1956.

Sánchez Viamonte, Carlos. *La cultura frente a la universidad*. Buenos Aires, 1928.

Sanguinetti, Florentino V. *Temas universitarios*. Buenos Aires, 1960.

Selser, Gregorio. *Situación político-social de América Latina*. Buenos Aires, 1957.

Strasser, Carlos. *Las izquierdas en el proceso político argentino*. Buenos Aires, 1959.

Taborda, Saúl Alejandro. *Facundo*. Buenos Aires, 1959.

Tomasek, Robert D., ed. *Latin American Politics: Studies of the Contemporary Scene.* Garden City, New York, 1966.

PERIODICALS

Boletín del centro estudiantes ingeniería la línea recta, 1955–1956. Buenos Aires.
Boletín de la federación universitaria, 1918. Buenos Aires.
Boletín de la Federación Universitaria Argentina, 1920. Buenos Aires.
Brecha, 1939. La Plata.
Ciencia y técnica, 1944–1950. Buenos Aires.
Contorno, 1953. Buenos Aires.
Correo universitario, 1936. Buenos Aires.
Criterio, 1958. Buenos Aires.
El ateneo, 1934. Rosario.
Gaceta universitaria, 1930–1939. Buenos Aires.
Lecciones y ensayos, 1959. Buenos Aires.
Nosotros, 1918–1924. Buenos Aires.
Renovación, 1931, 1945. La Plata.
Revista de ciencias económicas, 1927. Buenos Aires.
Revista de derecho y ciencias sociales, 1956–1958. Buenos Aires.
Revista de filosofía, 1918–1928. Buenos Aires.
Revista de la facultad de ciencias médicas y del centro de estudiantes de medicina, 1938–1941. La Plata.
Revista del mar dulce, 1955–1959. Buenos Aires.
Revista jurídica y de ciencias sociales, 1922–1942. Buenos Aires.
Sagitario, 1925–1927. La Plata.
Sagitario, 1956. Buenos Aires.
Tribuna universitaria, 1946, 1955–1957. Buenos Aires.
Universidad, 1945. Santa Fe.

ARTICLES

Agosti, Héctor P. "La ideología de la reforma," *El ateneo* (March 1934), pp. 23–28.
Bagú, Sergio. "La pre-reforma." *Revista de la facultad de ciencias*

médicas y del centro de estudiantes de medicina (May–June 1938), pp. 131–136.

Bakke, E. Wight. "Students on the March: The Cases of Mexico and Colombia." *Sociology of Education,* XXXVII (Spring 1964), 200–228.

Beals, Carleton and E. K. James. "Students Carry Guns," *Yale Review,* XXIV (September 1934), 14–33.

Bermann, Gregorio. "El conflicto universitario de Córdoba," *Nosotros,* XXVIII (1918), 517–524.

Besio Moreno, Nicolás. "Centro estudiantes de ingeniería de Buenos Aires," *Ciencia y técnica* (September 1944), pp. 280–290.

Bonilla, Frank. "The Student Federation of Chile: 50 Years of Political Action," *Journal of Inter-American Studies,* II (July 1960), 311–334.

Botana, Natalio and C. A Castilla. "Situación del humanismo," *Lecciones y ensayos* (1959), pp. 153–156.

Brainerd, Heloise. "Higher Education in the Argentine Republic," *Bulletin of the Pan American Union,* LXIII (January 1929), 31–41.

Brenner, Anita. "Student Rebels in Latin America," *The Nation,* CXXVII (December 12, 1928), 668–669.

Ciria, Alberto. "Veinte años después, Aníbal Ponce vive," *Revista de derecho y ciencias sociales* (Winter 1958), pp. 91–98.

Corcella, Ismael R. "Anhelos de libertad en la música del pueblo negro norteamericano," *Revista del mar dulce* (May 1956), pp. 25–26.

Doherty, George. "The Cross and the Sword, A Catholic View of Argentine Nationalism," *Harpers,* CXC (January 1945), 106–115.

Durelli, Augusto J. "Del universo de la universidad al universo del hombre," *Ciencia y técnica* (August 1946), pp. 159–171.

Durelli, Augusto J. "Forma y sentido de la resistencia universitaria de octubre de 1945." *Ciencia y técnica* (December 1945), pp. 461–490.

Durelli, Augusto J. "Plan para facilitar la creación de universidades libres en la Argentina," *Ciencia y técnica* (December 1947), pp. 402–405.

Freyre, Felipe F. "La defensa del petroleo es posición irrenunciable de los argentinos," *Revista del mar dulce* (June–July 1958), pp. 25–26.

Frondizi, Risieri. "La universidad y sus misiones," *Comentario* (Buenos Aires, October–December 1956), pp. 3–9.

Frondizi, Risieri. "Las universidades argentinas bajo el régimen de Perón," *Cuadernos americanos,* XXXVIII (México, D.F., March–April 1948), 40–60.

Gerassi, Marysa Navarro. "Argentine Nationalism of the Right," *Studies in Comparative International Development,* I (St. Louis, Mo., 1965).

Germani, Gino. "Informe preliminar del Instituto de Sociología sobre las encuestas entre estudiantes universitarios," *Centro* (Buenos Aires, October 1956), pp. 34–46.

Germani, Gino. "La movilidad social en la Argentina," *Revista de derecho y ciencias sociales* (Summer 1956–1957), pp. 40–51.

Gollán, Josué. "La Universidad del Litoral y la reforma universitaria," *Universidad* (April–June 1945), pp. 21–35.

González, Julio V. "El partido nacional reformista," *Revista de ciencias económicas* (September 1927), pp. 1093–1098.

González Alberdi, Paulino. "La reforma universitaria," *Revista de filosofía* (1928), pp. 255–265.

Grundfest, Harry. "The Situation in Argentine Universities," *Science,* CVII (February 13, 1948), 167–168.

Hasbrouck, Alfred. "The Argentine Revolution of 1930," *Hispanic American Historical Review,* XVIII (August 1938), 285–321.

Haya de la Torre, Victor R. "En el XI aniversario de la reforma," *Revista de filosofía* (September–November 1928), 121–133.

Haya de la Torre, Victor R. "The Student Movement of Latin America," *Bulletin of the Pan American Union,* LX (November 1926), 1105–1108.

Hernández Urbina, Alfredo. "Las dos ideologías del Congreso Americano de Estudiantes," *Hombre libre* (Santiago de Chile, February 1944), pp. 17–18.

Herrero, Antonio. "Acción universitaria de Alfredo L. Palacios," *Nosotros,* XLVII (1924), 372–387.

"La C.G.U. argentina frente al comunismo," *Boletín de la Organización Mundial Universitaria* (Buenos Aires, August 1953), p. 10.

"La crisis de 1930," *Revista de historia* (Buenos Aires, 1958).

" 'La Nación' y la reforma universitaria," *Revista del centro estudiantes de ingeniería* (Buenos Aires, October 1918), pp. 9–11.

"La universidad argentina bajo la dictadura de Perón," *Revista de América,* XI (Bogotá, September 1947), pp. 314–319.

"La Universidad de Buenos Aires y la libertad de enseñanza," *Revista de la Universidad de Buenos Aires* (Buenos Aires, July–September 1958), 506–522.

Lipset, Seymour Martin. "University Students and Politics in Underdeveloped Countries," *Minerva,* III (Autumn 1964), 15–56.

Loudet, Osvaldo. "Los orígenes de la Federación Universitaria Argentina," *Revista de psiquiatría y criminología* (Buenos Aires, May–June 1946), pp. 173–184.

Martz, John D. "Venezuela's 'Generation of '28': The Genesis of Political Democracy," *Journal of Inter-American Studies,* VI (January 1964), 17–32.

Mazo, Gabriel del. "Homenaje a José Ingenieros," *Revista de la facultad de ciencias médicas y del centro de estudiantes de medicina* (January–March 1941), pp. 73–78.

Mezzadri, Francisco A. "El gasto en educación en la Argentina," *La Nación* (December 6, 1964), Sec. 4, p. 6.

Munger, William L. "Academic Freedom Under Perón," *Antioch Review,* VII (June 1947), 275–290.

Pinner, Frank A. "Student Trade-Unionism in France, Belgium and Holland: Anticipatory Socialization and Role-Seeking," *Sociology of Education,* XXXVII (Spring 1964), 177–199.

Plá, Cortés. "La Universidad del Litoral y la intervención de 1943," *Universidad* (April–June 1945), pp. 13–19.

Sánchez Viamonte, Carlos. "La lucha por la reforma," *Sagitario* (January–March 1926), pp. 248–258.

Sanguinetti, Horacio J. "Datos para una historia de la revista del centro de estudiantes de derecho (1906–1958)," *Revista de derecho y ciencias sociales* (Winter 1958), pp. 117–122.

Sanguinetti, Horacio J. "El estado y las universidades privadas, notas para un estudio," *Lecciones y ensayos* (1959), pp. 185–201.

Sbarra, Noel H. "La reforma: evocación y presencia," *Revista de la facultad de ciencias médicas y del centro de estudiantes de medicina* (May–June 1938), pp. 94–130.

Scheman, L. Ronald. "The Brazilian Law Student: Background, Habits, Attitudes," *Journal of Inter-American Studies,* V (July 1963), 333–356.

Simon, S. Fanny. "Anarchism and Anarcho-Syndicalism in South

America," *Hispanic American Historical Review,* XXVI (February 1946), 38–59.

Siperman, Arnoldo. "Reflexiones de un reformista," *Revista de derecho y ciencias sociales* (Winter 1958), pp. 106–116.

"Situación estudiantil argentina," *Jornada* (Montevideo, April 1955), p. 9.

"Solidaridad del Comité Nacional de la Unión Cívica Radical," *Política* (Buenos Aires, October 1954), p. 2.

Solis, Carlos A. "Ingenieros y la juventud actual," *Revista del mar dulce* (December 1955), p. 6.

"Student Activities in South American Revolutions," *School and Society,* XXXIII (January 10, 1931), 61.

Tissembaum, Mariano R. "La universidad, su misión y sus fines," *Cuaderno número 6, del Instituto de Derecho del Trabajo, "Dr. Juan B. Alberdi,"* Universidad Nacional de Tucumán (1962), pp. 199–236.

"Universidad: un polígono de tiroteo ideológico," *Primera plana* (Buenos Aires, June 30, 1964), pp. 20–22.

Viñas, Ismael. "La traición de los hombres honestos," *Contorno* (November 1953), pp. 2–3.

Weinschelbaum, Ernesto. "Valoración del movimiento universitario," *Sagitario* (March–April 1956), pp. 62–66.

"Y España?" *El despertador* (Buenos Aires, December 1955), p. 1.

PAMPHLETS

Agosti, Héctor P., P. González Alberdi, and Leonardo Paso. *Los comunistas y el problema universitario.* Buenos Aires, 1956.

Argentino, Julio. *Meditación en la madrugada: el movimiento estudiantil de 1943,* Buenos Aires, 1943.

Bianchi, Carlos S. *En el XXVII aniversario de la reforma universitaria.* La Plata, 1945.

Bordo, Horacio E. *Los movimientos universitarios argentinos: de la reforma a la C.G.U.* Buenos Aires, 1954.

Centro de Derecho y Ciencias Sociales. *Guía al nuevo compañero.* Buenos Aires, 1960.

Centro de Estudiantes de Derecho de la Universidad del Litoral.

Informe sobre el IV Congreso Nacional de Estudiantes de la F.U.A. Rosario, November 1959.

Centro Estudiantes de Ciencias Económicas. *Conferencias.* Buenos Aires, 1929.

Centro Estudiantes de Derecho y Ciencias Sociales. *Memoria y Balances.* Buenos Aires, 1926.

Comisión argentina del Segundo Congreso Mundial de la Juventud. *Movimiento del Congreso Mundial de la Juventud: Resoluciones del II Congreso, Nueva York, agosto de 1938.* Buenos Aires, 1938.

Confederación General Universitaria. *Congreso Mundial de la Juventud Universitaria.* Buenos Aires, 1952.

Conferencia Internacional de Dirigentes Universitarios. Convocado por la Organización Mundial Universitaria. San Carlos de Bariloche, Argentina, 1955.

Cossio, Carlos. *La reforma universitaria, desarrollo histórico de su idea.* Buenos Aires, 1930.

Cossio, Carlos. *Le reforma universitaria y la reacción.* Buenos Aires, 1930.

Dana Montaño, Salvador M. *Problemas generales y particulares de las universidades argentinas.* Santa Fe, 1943.

Eichelbaum de Babini, A. M. *Algunas características de los estudiantes de la Universidad de Buenos Aires.* Buenos Aires, 1958.

Federación de agrupaciones para la defensa y progreso de la universidad democrática. *Avasallamiento de la universidad argentina.* Buenos Aires, 1947.

Federación de Ateneos Radicales. *La Universidad de Buenos Aires y la dictadura de septiembre.* Buenos Aires, 1940.

Federación de Estudiantes Secundarios. *Guía del estudiante.* Buenos Aires, 1954.

Federación Universitaria Argentina. *Estatutos.* Buenos Aires, 1958.

Federación Universitaria Argentina. *Mensaje a los estudiantes argentinos.* Rosario, 1950.

Federación Universitaria Argentina. "Situatión económica, social y política del país." *Resoluciones del IV Congreso Nacional de Estudiantes.* Córdoba, 1959.

Federación Universitaria Argentina. "Situación educacional, científica y cultural de las universidades nacionales y del país." *Resoluciones del IV Congreso Nacional de Estudiantes.* Córdoba, 1959.

Federación Universitaria Argentina. "Situatión social de los estudiantes." *Resoluciones del IV Congreso Nacional de Estudiantes.* Córdoba, 1959.

Federación Universitaria de Buenos Aires. *Crítica al decreto ley de organización de las universidades.* Buenos Aires, 1955.

Federación Universitaria de Buenos Aires. *Por la nacionalización del petroleo argentino.* Buenos Aires, 1928.

Federación Universitaria de Córdoba. *Memorial de cargos de la F.U.C. presentado a los poderes públicos el 1 de junio.* Córdoba, 1932.

Giúdice, Ernesto. *Reacción clerical-rosista, ó laicismo y universidad nacional.* Buenos Aires, 1958.

Goldrich, Daniel. *Radical Nationalism: The Political Orientations of Panamanian Law Students.* East Lansing, Mich., 1962.

González, Julio V. *Proposiciones para una empresa nacional de la juventud argentina.* Buenos Aires, 1943.

Graciarena, Jorge P. *La universidad y el desarrollo de un estrato profesional urbano en la Argentina.* Buenos Aires, 1963.

Justo, Juan B. *El conflicto universitario de Córdoba.* Buenos Aires, 1918.

Kleiner, Bernardo. *En defensa de la universidad argentina.* Buenos Aires, 1957.

Los universitarios argentinos y el problema político nacional. Buenos Aires, 1931.

Malvicino, Francisco M. *La universidad y el momento argentino.* La Plata, 1945.

Monner Sans, José María. *Historia del "Ateneo Universitario" (1914–1920).* Buenos Aires, 1930.

Movimiento Humanista de Derecho, Secretaría de Cultura. *Que es el humanismo.* Buenos Aires, 1960.

Palacios, Alfredo L. *La juventud y la moral política.* La Plata, 1943.

Palacios, Alfredo L. *La Unión Latino-Americana y el imperialismo yanqui.* Buenos Aires, 1927.

Palacios, Alfredo L. *La universidad y los problemas nacionales.* La Plata, 1942.

Palacios, Alfredo L. *Mensaje a la juventud de Ibero-América.* Montevideo, 1944.

Partido Reformista–Centro Izquierda. *Memorial.* Buenos Aires, 1930.

Partido Socialista. *La reforma universitaria y el partido socialista.* Buenos Aires, 1945.

Rodríguez Tarditi, José. *Páginas de acción estudiantil.* Buenos Aires, 1937.

Romano, Nicolás. *Hipólito Yrigoyen y la reforma universitaria.* La Plata, 1958.

Sanguinetti, Horacio J. "Exposición y actualidad de algunos problemas universitarios," separata de la *Revista de la Universidad Nacional de Córdoba* (September–December 1961).

Sanguinetti, Horacio J. *Régimen administrativo de la universidad.* Buenos Aires, 1963.

Unión Universitaria. *Los contratos petroleros.* La Plata, 1963.

Universidad de Buenos Aires, Departamento de Extensión Universitaria. *Memoria 1961.* Buenos Aires, 1962.

Universidad de Buenos Aires, Departamento de Extensión Universitaria. *Primer año de extensión universitaria.* Buenos Aires, 1957.

Williamson, Robert C. *El estudiante colombiano y sus actitudes, un análisis de psicología social en la universidad nacional.* Bogotá, 1962.

GENERAL WORKS

Agosti, Héctor P. *José Ingenieros, ciudadano de la juventud.* Buenos Aires, 1945.

Alexander, Robert J. *Communism in Latin America.* New Brunswick, N.J., 1957.

Bagú, Sergio. *Vida ejemplar de José Ingenieros, juventud y plenitud.* Buenos Aires, 1936.

Bermann, Gregorio. *José Ingenieros, el civilizador, el filósofo, el moralista, lo que debe nuestra generación.* Buenos Aires, 1926.

Bermann, Gregorio. *Juventud de América: sentido histórico de los movimientos juveniles.* México, D.F., 1946.

Blanksten, George I. *Perón's Argentina.* Chicago, 1953.

Bonilla, Frank and K. H. Silvert. *Education and the Social Meaning of Development: A Preliminary Statement.* New York, 1961.

Bunge, Carlos Octavio. *Nuestra América.* Barcelona, 1903.

Caballero Martín, Angel S. *La universidad en Santa Fe.* Santa Fe, 1931.

Ciria, Alberto. *Partidos y poder en la Argentina moderna (1930–46).* Buenos Aires, 1963.

Ciria, Alberto and H. J. Sanguinetti. *Universidad y estudiantes: testimonio juvenil.* Buenos Aires, 1962.

Cossio, Carlos. *La reforma universitaria: el problema de la neuva generación.* Buenos Aires, 1927.

Crawkes, J. Beresford. *533 días de historia argentina.* Buenos Aires, 1932.

Domingorena, Horacio O. *Artículo 28: universidades privadas en la Argentina, sus antecedentes.* Buenos Aires, 1959.

Fillol, Tomás Roberto. *Social Factors in Economic Development: The Argentine Case.* Cambridge, Mass., 1961.

Galletti, Alfredo. *La política y los partidos.* Buenos Aires, 1961.

Giúdice, Ernesto. *Ha muerto el dictador pero no la dictadura.* Buenos Aires, 1932.

Giúdice, Ernesto. *Problemas ideológicos, científicos, técnicos y filosóficos en la universidad.* Buenos Aires, 1959.

González, Julio V. *La revolución universitaria, 1918–1919.* Buenos Aires, 1922.

González, Julio V. *La universidad: teoría y acción de la reforma.* Buenos Aires, 1945.

González, Julio V. *Reflexiones de un argentino de la nueva generación.* Buenos Aires, 1931.

Halperin Donghi, Tulio. *Historia de la Universidad de Buenos Aires.* Buenos Aires, 1962.

Hernández Arregui, Juan José. *La formación de la conciencia nacional.* Buenos Aires, 1960.

Herrero, Antonio. *Alfredo L. Palacios: caracteres, valores y problemas de su personalidad y su acción.* Buenos Aires, 1925.

Herring, Hubert. *A History of Latin America: From the Beginnings to the Present.* Second edition. New York, 1962.

Imaz, José Luis de. *Los que mandan.* Buenos Aires, 1964.

Ingenieros, José. *El hombre mediocre.* Buenos Aires, 1917.

Ingenieros, José. *La evolución de las ideas argentinas.* Buenos Aires, 1918–1920.

Ingenieros, José. *Los tiempos nuevos: reflexiones optimistas sobre la guerra y la revolución.* Madrid, 1921.

Johnson, John J., ed. *Continuity and Change in Latin America.* Stanford, Calif., 1964.

Johnson, John J. *Political Change in Latin America: The Emergence of the Middle Sectors.* Stanford, Calif., 1958.

Jones, Peter T. *The History of U.S. National Student Association Relations with the International Union of Students, 1945–1956.* Philadelphia, Pa., 1956.

Kantor, Harry. *The Ideology and Program of the Peruvian Aprista Movement.* Berkeley, Calif., 1953.

Kleiner, Bernardo. *20 años de movimiento estudiantil reformista, 1943–1963.* Buenos Aires, 1964.

Korn, Guillermo. *La resistencia civil.* Montevideo, 1945.

Kornhauser, William. *The Politics of Mass Society.* Glencoe, Ill., 1959.

Lassalle, Edmundo. *The Universities in Argentina.* Washington, D.C., 1944.

Lazarte, Juan. *Líneas y trayectoria de la reforma universitaria.* Rosario, 1935.

Lipset, Seymour Martin, ed. *Student Politics.* New York, 1967.

Mac-Lean y Estenós, Roberto. *La crisis universitaria en Hispano-América.* México, D.F., 1956.

Mazo, Gabriel del. *El radicalismo: notas sobre su historia y doctrina (1922–1952).* Buenos Aires, 1955.

Mazo, Gabriel del. *Estudiantes y gobierno universitario.* Second edition. Buenos Aires, 1955.

McGann, Thomas F. *Argentina, the United States and the Inter-American System, 1880–1914.* Cambridge, Mass., 1957.

Palacios, Alfredo L. *La universidad nueva.* Buenos Aires, 1925.

Peco, José. *Defensa o acusación?* Buenos Aires, 1935.

Ramírez Novoa, Ezequiel. *La reforma universitaria.* Buenos Aires, 1956.

Rennie, Ysabel Fisk. *The Argentine Republic.* New York, 1945.

Rodríguez Bou, Ismael. *La educación superior en América Latina.* Washington, D.C., 1963.

Rojas, Ricardo. *La restauración nacionalista.* Buenos Aires, 1909.

Rojas, Ricardo. *Memoria del rector.* Buenos Aires, 1930.

Romano, Nicolás. *Dichos y hechos al servicio de la universidad.* Buenos Aires, 1942.

Romero, José Luis. *A History of Argentine Political Thought.* (Translated from the Spanish by Thomas F. McGann). Stanford, Calif., 1963.

Sánchez, Luis Alberto. *La universidad latinoamericana.* Guatemala City, Guatemala, 1949.

Scobie, James R. *Argentina: A City and a Nation.* New York, 1964.

Silvert, Kalman H. *The Conflict Society: Reaction and Revolution in Latin America.* New Orleans, La., 1961.

Ugarte, Manuel. *El destino de un continente.* Madrid, 1923.

Whitaker, Arthur P. *The United States and Argentina.* Cambridge, Mass., 1954.

Index

Acción Nacionalista Argentina, 104
Agosti, Héctor P., 95, 101–102, 108, 181, 189, 193, 202
Agrupación(es), 79, 100
Agrupación de Izquierda del Partido Unión Reformista, 79
Agrupación Femenina de Estudiantes de Medicina, 127
Agrupación Femenina Universitaria, 127
Agrupación Humanista de Ciencas Económicas, 170
Agrupación Humanista de la Facultad de Agronomía y Veterinaria de Buenos Aires, 169
Agrupación Humanista de Medicina, 169
Agrupación Humanista Renovadora, 151, 168
Agrupación Movimiento Universitario de Centro, 168
Agrupación Movimiento Universitario Reformista, 169
Agrupación Reformista, 169
Agrupación Reformista de Derecho, 170
Alberdi, Héctor Ripa, 66–67, 70–71
Alem, Leandro N., 26
Alianza de la Juventud Nacionalista, 125–126
Alianza Popular Revolucionaria Americana (APRA), 69, 81
Alvear, Marcelo T. de, 64–65, 80, 82, 88
American Negro, solidarity with, 178–179
Anarchists, in Reform of 1918, 59
Anarcho-Syndicalism, 25, 75
anarchy, Latin American type, 30–31

Andújar, Gerardo A., xvii, 145, 193
anti-clericalism, 35, 79
anti-colonialism, 107; *see also* anti-imperialism; colonialism
anti-Communism, 103; *see also* Communism and Communists
anti-dictatorship, 77–79, 109–110, 189–191
anti-government activity, in Perón regime, 139–140
anti-imperialism, 77–79, 89, 102–103; nationalism and, 71; Perón and, 149–150
anti-positivism, 65–66, 71
anti-Reform movement, 44–45, 157; *see also* counter-Reform
anti-Semitism, 103, 125
Aprista party, 69–70
Aquinas, St. Thomas, 167
Aramburu, Gen. Pedro E., 160, 177
Araujo, Eduardo, 102
Argentina: "hegemony over all South America," 104; as pro-Allies in World War II, 123
Argentine Communist Party, 26, 90, 102–103, 108, 141–142, 172–173; *see also* Communism and Communists
Aristotle, 167
Article 28 (of "Ley Avellaneda"), Reformista opposition to, 161–165, 167, 182, 192–193, 199
Ateneo Universitario group, 32, 34
Atlantic Charter, 113
attendance, unregulated, 50, 65
autonomy, university, *see* university autonomy
Avellaneda, Nicolás, 4
Axis propaganda, "protection" of, 111–112

Babini, José, 158
Bakke, E. Wight, xi
Barros, Enrique F., 44, 48, 51, 54, 58, 73, 100, 192–193
Bas, Arturo N., 54
beef production, 23–24
Bermann, Gregorio, 41–42, 58, 73, 96, 193, 202
Bernstein, Eduard, 25
Besio Moreno, Nicolás, 121
Betancourt, Rómulo, 78
Blanco, Antonio Guzmán, viii
Bolshevik Revolution, 28, 31, 76; see also Russian Revolution
Bonilla, Frank, xiii
Bordabehere, Ismael, 41, 44, 58
Bravo, Ernesto Mario, 46, 140–142, 151
Buddhist religion, 34
Buenos Aires: 1910 meetings in, 49; revolution of September 5, 1930, 91
Buenos Aires, University of (UBA), 4–18, 28–32, 42, 65, 71, 75, 79, 81, 84, 92, 94–97, 100–102, 105, 111–112, 121, 127–128, 137, 139–141, 143–145, 149, 151, 158–161, 163–164, 166, 168, 171, 173, 179, 187, 189, 193–194, 199–201; "Civic Legion" raid at, 104; "faculties" of, 7; socio-economic class and, x, 10, 194; student dismissals from, 82–83; student march on, 90–91
Bunge, Carlos Octavio, 30

campus social life, 10
Capdevila, Arturo, 34, 41, 54, 67
capitalism, failure of, 28
capitalist-imperialist exploitation, 103; see also anti-imperialism; imperialism
Caraffa, Belisario, 44, 54
Casa Rosada (executive HQ in Buenos Aires), 52, 91–92, 95, 161
Castillo, Ramón S., 82–83, 88, 111, 119–120; and World War II, 112–113

Castro, Fidel, vii, 172, 177
Catholic Church: Perón and, 134, 151, 155; renewed influence of, 122–123; resistance to change in, 56; supports Frondisi, 161
Catholic-oriented groups, in student strikes, 47
Catholic religion, in Cordoba University, 34
Catholic universities, private, 159
cattle breeding, 23–24
caudillismo, 30
census, first, 25; see also population
Centeno, Alejandro, 44
centro (student center), 13
Chaco War, 107
Chambers, William N., xvii
Chile: Latin American Congress in, 110; reform principles in, 64, 69–71
Chilean Student Federation, xiii
Chilean-Uruguayan student commission, 145–146
Christian Democratic movement, 205; youth and, 200
Church, new liberalism and, 34; see also Catholic Church
Círculo Argentino de Estudiantes de Derecho, 83, 93, 105
Ciria, Alberto, 193
civil rights movement, U.S., vii
class attendance, unregulated, 50, 65
class privilege, 163; see also socio-economic class
Cold War, 146–147, 157
colegio, 9
Colegio Nacional de Buenos Aires, 125
colonialism: break with, 48; condemnation of, 71–72, 107
Comité por Defensa de la Universidad, 45–47, 52, 54–57, 200
Comité pro-Reforma, 40–41, 43
Communism and Communists: "coexistence" with, 141–142; Concordancia and, 88; increase in strength of, 172–177; Reformistas and, 59, 172; Reform of 1918

and, 59; student membership in, 98, 141–142; super-patriots and, 76; tolerance of, xiii; youth and, 200

Communist International Union of Students, 175

Communist Party, 26, 90, 102–103, 108, 141–142, 172–173

Concordancia, 87–89, 119

Confederación General del Trabajo, 100

Confederación General Universitaria, 139, 141, 147–151

Congreso Latinoamericano de Estudiantes, Chile, 110

Conservatives and Conservative policies, 24–28, 33–35, 44, 52–53, 56, 59, 63–64, 75, 83–84; *Concordancia* and, 88–89; control of national life by, 98, 190–191; in counter-Reform, 80; in Democratic Union, 131; increased strength of, 65; resurgence of, 80–81; in revolution of 1930, 90–93; students and, 97–115; youth and, 200

Convención Nacional de Estudiantes, Buenos Aires (1956), 166

Co-ordinating Secretariat of National Unions of Students (COSEC), 144–148, 175–177

Copenhagen Conference, 1953, 147–148

Corda Fratres group, 34, 44

Córdoba, University of, 3, 23, 28, 33–35, 40–46, 48, 52, 54–56, 137, 144, 192, 200; changes made as result of Reformista action, 53–54; counter-Reform and, 80; professors ousted from, 60

Córdoba Congress (1918), 98

"Córdoba Manifesto" (1918), 48

Córdoba Reform (1918), 23, 27, 39–40, 55, 64–65, 77, 140, 172, 199, 207; counter-Reform and, 80–81; important results of, 56–58; *see also* Reform; Reformistas; Reform of 1918

Corporación de Abogados Catolicos, 163

corporate state, 104

corruption, political, 64–65

counter-Reform (1918–1930), 63–84; second, 94

Crawkes, Col. J. Beresford, 92

Criterio (pub.), 163

Cuban Revolution (1959), 157, 172

Cultura (pub.), 34

Cuyo, University of, 5

Darwin, Charles, 33

Defense Committee, *see Comité por Defensa de la Universidad*

degree (diploma): number granted, 18; prestige of, 11–12

de la Torre, Lisandro, 26

de La Torre, Victor Raúl Haya, 69, 77–78

Dell'Oro Maini, Atilio, 160–161

del Mazo, Gabriel, xvii, 27, 42, 58, 69, 73, 77, 96, 100–101, 115, 121, 135, 189, 193, 202

democracy: faith in, 56; rule of, 101; in World War II period, 125–126

"Democratic Manifesto," 121, 124

Democratic Progressives, 130, 200

Democratic Union, *see Unión Democrática*

dictatorship: following revolution of 1930, 94; imperialism and, 77; Perón regime as, 127; Reformistas opposition to, 74, 102; student opposition to, 77–79, 109–110, 189–191

direct action, results of, 192; *see also* political activism

Directive Council (*Consejo Directívo*), 7–8, 29, 43, 82–83, 138, 166, 168

Domingorena, Horacio O., 165–166

drop-outs, in Argentine universities, 18, 206

Duarte, Maria Eva, *see* Perón, Eva

Durelli, Augusto J., 101, 129

economic growth: nineteenth century, 23–24; twentieth century, 5
economic nationalism, 106
education: criticism of, 15; law and medicine emphasized in, 15; modernization and, 28–29, 50–51; national funds for, 16; political activism and, xiv; Reform of 1918 and, 49
Eisenhower, Dwight D., 176
Engels, Friedrich, 25, 33
Escape from Freedom (Fromm), 167
Escuela Superior de Guerra, 82
estancias, 24, 87, 103
exiles, during Perón regime, 144–145
expansionism, threat of, 72

"faculties," University of Buenos Aires, 6
Fagen, Richard, xvii
farm population, 25
Farrell, Edelmiro, 126–127
Fascism, 103–108, 171
Fatone, Vicente, 158
Faulkner, William, 181
FECH (National Student Federation of Chile), xiii, 69
Federación de Estudiantes Catolicos, 34–35
Federación de Estudiantes de Chile (FEC), xiii, 69
Federación de Estudiantes de Peru (FEP), 69
Federación de Estudiantes Secundarios (FES), 142
Federación Obrera Regional Argentina (FORA), 25, 100
Federación Universitaria Argentina (FUA), 14, 42–45, 49, 55, 58, 65, 67, 69, 71, 78–79, 81, 95–97, 100, 102, 105–106, 108, 110, 121–124, 126–128, 130, 132, 134–140, 142, 144–145, 147–148, 158, 161, 164–165, 167, 173–176, 179–181, 189
Federación Universitaria de Buenos Aires (FUBA), 14, 29, 41–42, 49,

65, 93, 105, 107, 113, 120, 124, 126, 132, 141, 144, 157–159, 161, 166, 193
Federación Universitaria de Cordoba (FUC), 14, 43–46, 48, 51–54, 58, 75–76, 165, 192
Federación Universitaria de La Plata (FULP), 14, 66, 132
Federación Universitaria de Littoral (FUL), 14, 96
Federación Universitaria North-Tucumán (FUN), 14
Federación Universitaria Northeast-Resistencia (FUNR), 14
Federación Universitaria Sur-Bahia Blanca (FUS), 14
federation, university, 14
FEP, FUA, etc., *see under Federación*
finances, in student life, 10
First International Student Congress (Mexico, 1921), 110
First National Congress of University Students (Córdoba, 1918), 48–51, 67–68, 75, 99
Ford Foundation, 180
Fourth International Student Conference (Istanbul, 1954), 148
Fourth National Student Congress (Cordoba, 1959), 173, 180–181
Franciscan order, 4
Franco, Francisco, 103, 175
fraternities and sororities, absence of, 10
Frente Estudiantil de Liberación Nacional, 170
Frente Independiente, 170
Fromm, Erich, 167
Frondizi, Arturo, 155–156, 161–162, 177–178, 189–190; and Article 28 struggle, 163–164
Frondizi, Risieri, 164–165

Gaceta universitaria (pub.), 97
Gálvez, Manuel, 31
Giúdice, Ernesto, 100–102, 181, 189, 193, 202
Goldrich, Daniel, xiv
Gómez, Juan Vicente, 71

Gonzáles, Joaquín V., 5, 30, 35
Gonzáles, Julio V., 28, 58, 67, 79,
   81, 84, 96, 101–103, 113, 137,
   189, 193, 198, 202
Great Britain, dependence on, 106
Grupo Concordia, 79
Grupo de Oficiales Unidos (GOU),
   120–122, 126, 130
Grupo Universitario Argentino en
   el Exilo, 144
Guzmán Blanco, Antonio, viii

Haramboure case, 145
Haya de la Torre, Victor Raúl, 69,
   77–78
higher education, criticism of, 15;
   see also university
Hitler, Adolf, 120, 132
Houssay, Bernardo, 121, 137
Howard, Eduardo, 97
Hull, Cordell, 107
Humanismo (Movimiento Humanista de Derecho), 170
Humanismo Auténtico, 170
Humanistas, 150–151, 161, 166,
   171; challenge from, 172, 204–
   205; Communism and, 173; goals
   of, 167–168; political tendency
   of, 200; versus Reformistas, 166–
   168, 172, 204–205 youth and,
   201

Ibarguren, Carlos, 104
idealism: versus materialism, 56,
   70–72; "rebirth" of, 70; Reform
   principles and, 204
ideas, students' rights to, 33
Ideas (pub.), 34, 47
Illia, Arturo, 156, 178
immigrants, increase in number of,
   25
imperialism: dictatorship and, 74;
   economic chaos and, 106–107; see
   also anti-imperialism; colonialism
individual rights, principle of, 99
Ingenieros, José, 30–33, 72, 77, 181,
   198
Ingram, Avrea, 145

Insurrexit (student center), 79, 103
intellectuals: influence of, xii, 198;
   leadership of, 79; in Reform generation, 30–31
International Monetary Fund, 177
International Student Conference
   (ISC), 147
International Student Congress
   (Mexico, 1921), 70
international student meetings, 42–
   43, 70, 89
International Union of Students
   (IUS), 147–148, 175–177
Intransigents, splinter party, 161
Irigoyen, Hipólito, 26–27, 41–43,
   47–48, 52–54, 59, 65, 67–68,
   102–103, 188; decree of, following Reform struggle, 53–55; failure of, 63–64; first administration
   of, 63–64; resignation of, 91–92;
   second term, 89–90

Jesuits, 4, 52
Jiménez, Marcos Pérez, vii
Johnson, John J., xviii
Justo, Augustín P., 82, 88, 92, 101,
   106, 108, 119
Justo, Juan B., 26, 33, 51
Justo government (of Augustín P.),
   89, 97–98, 102; repressions under,
   114; struggle against, 110

"Khrushchev line," 174
Kling, Merle, xviii
Korn, Alejandro, 30, 66, 101

labor unions, student relationships
   with, 179–180; see also working
   class
laissez-faire politics, 24
La Nación (pub.), 136, 171
La Pampa, University of, 5
La Plata, University of, 5, 17, 29–
   30, 35, 65–67, 70, 96, 121–122,
   127–129, 137, 144
La Prensa (pub.), 47, 91, 136
Las Alumnas Democráticas de la
   Facultad de Derecho, 127

Laski, Harold, xii
Latin America: Communism and, 174–177; Reform movement spreads to, 55; university student as revolutionary in, 201
Lattendorf, Abel Alexis, 144–145, 193
La universidad del porvenir (Ingenieros), 32
La Vanguardia (pub.), 46
La Voz del Interior (pub.), 46
law: drop-outs in, 18; emphasis on, 15
Law Directive Council, 81; *see also* Directive Council
leadership: education and, 11–12; qualities of, 193–194; socio-economic background and, x, 10, 194; students' responsibility for, 195–196
League of Nations, 63
Legión Cívica Argentina, 104, 108, 125
Lejarraga, Pablo, 95, 101, 189, 193, 202
Lenin, Vladimir Ilyich, 28, 181
"Ley Avellaneda" (National Law), 8–9, 159; *see also* Article 28
liberal groups, rise of, 34
Liga de Estudiantes Humanistas, 150, 166; *see also* Humanistas
Liga de la Juventud Católica Argentina, 160
Liga Patriótica, 76, 83, 105
Lima: 1912 meetings in, 49; Popular University of, 70
Lipset, Seymour Martin, xii–xiv, xvii
Lista Humanista, 170
Lista Reformista, 170
Lista Unica Reformista, 169
Lista Universitaria, 169
Littoral, University of, 67, 80, 96, 113, 129, 144
Lonardi, Gen. Eduardo, 158–160
Lopez, Germán O., 128, 130
Loudet, Osvaldo, 29, 42, 58, 137
Lugones, Leopoldo, 30–32

McCarthy, Joseph R., 176
Maini, Atilio Dell'Oro, 160–161
Marcha de la Constitución y la Libertad, 128, 134
Marines, U.S., in Nicaragua, 73
Maritain, Jacques, 167
Martínez Paz, Enrique, 44, 54
Martínez Zuviría, Gustavo, 121, 123
Marx, Karl, 25, 33, 181
Marxist-Leninist theories, 28, 102–103, 168, 172, 176
materialism, versus idealism, 56, 70–72
Matienzo, José Nicolás, 42–43, 45
May Zubiría, Alberto, 100–101
meat-packing plants, 24
medicine: drop-outs in, 18; emphasis on, 15
Mexican Revolution (1910), 27
Mexico, International Student Congress in, 1921, 70
middle class, political pressure of, 26
militarism, 103; economic nationalism and, 106–107
military groups, control by, 189–190
Mills, C. Wright, 181
Mitre, Bartolomé, 4, 11
modernization, reform and, 27–29, 50–51
Monner Sans, José María, 32, 137
Monroe Doctrine, 72
Montevideo, 1908 meetings in, 49
Monthly Review (pub.), 181
Moreno, Nicolás Besio, 121
Mosca, Enrique, 131
Movimiento de Acción Popular, 169
Movimiento Estudiantil de Reforma Universitaria de Veterinaria, 169
Movimiento Reformista de Agronomía, 169
Movimiento Social Cristiano, 170
Movimiento Unidad Estudiantil de Agronomía y Movimiento Unidad Estudiantil de Veterinaria, 169

Movimiento Universitario de Agronomía, 169
Movimiento Universitario de Centro, 170–171, 200
Movimiento Universitario Humanista, 167
Movimiento Universitario Reformista, 170
Mussolini, Benito, 104, 120, 132

Nación, La (pub.), 136, 171
National Chamber of Deputies, 33, 165
National Congress, 17, 137–138, 162–163, 189
nationalism: defined by del Mazo, 77; versus imperialism, 71; Perón and, 150; Reform movement and, 56; rise of, 24–29, 31; social responsibility and, 31; versus ultra-nationalism, 76
National Law No. 1597, *see* "Ley Avellaneda"
national politics, Reformistas and, 101; *see also* political activism; political parties
National Student Association (NSA), 173
national student federations, xiii, 29
National University of the Littoral, *see* Littoral, University of
Nazism, 111–113
negativism, in post-Perón period, 192–193
Negro, American, 178–179
Nicaragua, U.S. invasion of, 73
Nores, Antonio, 44–46, 52, 54
Northeast, University of the, 5
Nosotros (pub.), 47

October Revolution, Russia, 26
Odena, Isidro, 100–101, 189, 193, 202
oil companies, foreign-owned, 177–178
older students, percentage of, 12
oligarchy, rise of, 24–25

Organización de Estudiantes Humanistas Argentinos, 168
Orgaz, Arturo, 34, 41, 137
Orgaz, Jorge, 96
Ortíz, Raúl Scalabrini, 107
Ortiz, Roberto, 88, 111

Palacios, Alfredo L., 17, 30, 34, 46, 68, 72, 97, 107, 121, 135, 137, 157, 181, 198
Pan-American Union, 72
Partido Demócrata Progresista, 26
Partido Nacional Reformista, 81
Partido Socialista Internacionalista, 26
patriotism, 76; see also ultra-nationalist groups
Paz, Enrique Martínez, 44, 54
Peace Corps, vii
Pearl Harbor attack, 111
Peco, José, 95, 97, 101, 121, 137
Pérez Jiménez, Marcos, vii
Perón, Eva (Evita), 131, 138, 143
Perón, Juan D., 8, 16, 126–151, 155–156, 182, 193; as anti-intellectual, 133; downfall of, 148–149, 155; elected president (1946), 134; pro-Axis sympathies, 133; proletariat support, 130–131, 179–180; purge of professors, 121–124, 129–130, 136–137; "stooges" of, 135; student opposition to, 140, 191, 198–199; student strikes and, 146
Perón regime: character of, 135–136; exile groups and, 144–145; opposition to, 137, 140, 143, 191, 198; summary of, 149
Peronistas, youth and, 200
Peru, university reform in, 64, 69–70
Plaza de Mayo, revolt of, Buenos Aires, 91, 158
political activism: career and, 11; educational quality and, xiv; of professors, 17; of students, xii–xiii, 3, 17; tradition of, ix
political anarchy, 30

political consciousness, 11–12
political corruption, 64–65
political leader, xii, 193–194
political parties, 13–14; Reform of
1918 and, 58–59; rise of, 25–26;
student and, xi, 198
Ponce, Aníbal, 181
popular front, against Fascism, 108
population growth, 24
positivism, professors and, 65–66,
71
Potter, David M., xvii
Prensa, La (pub.), 47, 91, 136
*Primer Congreso Ibero-Americano
de Estudiantes,* 110
private economy, principle of, 99
professional men, unemployment
among, 15–16
professors: arrest of (October 1945),
129–130; dismissal of in 1918 Reform movement, 60; in First Student Congress reform program,
50; government repression of, 95;
influence of, xii, 198; in 1918
student strike, 41; Peronist purge
of, 121–124, 129–130, 136–137;
political activism of, 17; "positivist," 65–66; return to academic
position, 125; right to hold dissident opinions, 33; salaries of,
17; student relations, 199; teaching improvements by, 50
proletariat, Perón and, 179–180
purges, Perón regime, 121–124,
129–130, 136–137

racial equality, 105
Radical party and Radicals, 26–27,
63–64, 77, 87–88, 90, 97, 102,
111, 134–135, 189, 198; Communists and, 174; in Democratic
Union, 131; election victory, 1916,
49; Frondizi and, 161; Peronists
and, 156; student membership in,
190; support of Reformistas by,
59; youth and, 200
railroad system, 24
Ramírez, Gen. Pedro P., 120, 126

Ramos, Juan P., 104
Rawson, Gen. Arturo, 120
Reconstruction period, Argentina,
155–182
Reform ideal, challenge to, 204
Reformistas (reform group), 43, 45,
47–48, 54–55, 57, 83–84, 181;
Anarchists and, 59; anti-imperialism of, 71–72, 102; careers of
after graduation, 195; and Catholic universities, 159–160; challenges for, 203–205; Communism and, 172; compromise with,
53; in counter-Reform, 81; "democratization" and, 49; dictatorship and, 74, 102; dismissal from
UBA, 82–83; dominant role of,
200; economic nationalism and,
106; emerging philosophy of, 77,
84, 89, 149; end of achievements
by, 64–65; future of, 205–206;
Humanistas and, 166–168 (*see
also* Humanistas); idealism of,
56; internal discord in, 150–151;
Jesuit influence and, 52; labor
unions and, 179; of La Plata, 66;
lasting importance of, 56; in Latin
American Union, 72–73; in "militant political life," 114–115; national politics and, 101; Nazism-
Fascism issue and, 113; negativism of, 192–193; in 1918 Reform
movement, 40–41 (*see also* Reform Movement); opposition to
Article 28, 161–165, 167, 182,
192–193, 199; in Perón regime,
139, 149; Peruvian, 70; philosophy of, 77, 84, 89, 149; popular
front and, 109; in post-Perón period, 160; racial equality of, 105;
repression of following revolution of 1930, 93–95; social justice
and, 190; solidarity among, 67–
68; support for Socialists and
Radicals, 58–59; ultra-nationalism
and, 105–106; university autonomy and, 161; university enrollment restriction and, 204; in Uni-

versity of Littoral, 67; university extension and, 75; university seen as agent of change by, 50; and World War II, 112, 124; youth and, 201
Reform Movement (1918–1930), 63–84; counter-Reform and, 80, 94; intellectual activity in, 30–31, 79; key aspect of, 54–55; in La Plata, 66–67; see also University Reform Movement
Reform of 1918, 18, 187; extension of to other Argentine cities, 68; political parties and, 58–59
Reform publications, 97
Renovación (pub.), 97, 132
Renovación Reformista, 170
Revista de derecho y ciencias sociales (pub.), 13–14
Revista de filosofía (pub.), 31, 47
Revista jurídica (pub.), 112
revolutionary ideas, 9
Revolution of September 1930, 89–90
Ripa Alberdi, Héctor, 66–67, 70–71
Rivadavia, Bernardino, 4
Roca, Deodoro, 33–34, 44, 54, 58, 67, 73, 100–101, 106–107, 181, 198, 202
Roca-Runciman trade, 106
Rockefeller Foundation, 181
Rojas, Ricardo, 30–32
Romano, Nicolás, 121
Romero, José Luis, xvii, 158–159, 161, 163
Rosas, Juan Manuel de, viii, 4, 23, 87, 103
Russian Revolution, 26; see also Bolshevik Revolution

Sáenz, Mario, 95, 101
Sáenz Peña, Roque, 26, 49, 112
Sáenz Peña electoral reform law, 49, 93, 127
Sagitario (pub.), 79
Salamanca, University of, 6
salaries, professors', 17

Salinas, José S., 40, 42, 45, 48, 53, 59, 68–69
Sánchez, Luis Alberto, 9
Sánchez Viamonte, Carlos, 79, 81, 83–84, 101, 124–125, 135, 137, 151, 181, 189
Sandino, Augusto César, 73
Sanguinetti, Florentino V., xvii, 75, 79, 81, 83–84, 101, 137, 162, 193
Sanguinetti, Horacio J., xvii
San Martin, Gen. José de, 138
Sans, José María Monner, 32, 137
Santa Fe, University of, 29
Sarmiento, Domingo Faustino, 4, 11
Sartre, Jean-Paul, xii
Sayago, Gumersindo, 41–42, 58, 137
Scalabrini Ortíz, Raúl, 107
Second National Student Congress (Buenos Aires, 1932), 98–101, 104, 108, 176
Second Pan-American Scientific Congress, 31–32
secret police, Perón regime, 135–136, 158
Segundo Congreso Latinoamericano de Estudiantes (La Plata, 1957), 176
Selser, Gregorio, 176–177
Semana Tragica (January 1919), 74–76
Shils, Edward, xii
"shock troops," Uriburu and, 104
Silvert, Kalman H., x, 18, 201
Sindicato Español Universitario, 175
Sindicato Universitario Argentino, 126
Sindicato Universitario de Derecho, 170
Siperman, Arnoldo, 172
Sixth International Conference of Students (Ceylon, 1956), 175
Socialists and Socialist Party, 26, 46, 75, 77, 88, 90, 101, 108, 111, 130, 134, 157, 198; Communists and, 174; Peronists and, 156; student members of, 190; support of Reformistas by, 59; youth and, 200

social justice, suport for, 77
social life, off-campus, 10
social mobility, university degree and, 11
social status, 11
society, change of by Reformistas, 100
socio-economic class: of student leaders, x, 194; in University of Buenos Aires, 10
solidarity: continental, 109; expansion of, 109–110; of students with working class, 56–57, 74–77, 99, 179
South, University of the, 5, 194
Soviet Union, Communist movement and, 147
Spanish-American War, 176
Spanish colonial tradition: break with, 48; glorification of, 103
Spanish University Syndicate, 175
Steinbeck, John, 181
strike, student, see student strikes
student center, 13
student federations, 109–110
student manifesto (1930), 90
student movement: fragmentation of in 1920's, 78–79; history of, 3–19; 1960 crisis in, 182; political parties and, 198; political tendency of, 200
student politics, effect of, 17, 55, 198–200; see also political activism
student publications, 34, 46–47, 79, 97, 112
students: anti-dictatorship creed of, 189; anti-imperialism of, 71–73; arrests and imprisonment of (1930), 93–95; arrests by Peronists, 129–130; attacks on Uriburu regime, 96–97; Communists and, 98, 141–142; Conservatives and, 87–115; dismissal from University of Buenos Aires, 82–83; harassment of by Peronist mobs, 132; as "hot-eyed revolutionary," 201; increasing political role of, 196–

197; influence of professors and political leaders on, xii, 198; labor unions and, 179–180; in Latin American revolution, 89–90; leadership of, x, 193–196; in 1918 Reform, 40–41; older, 12; participation of in university administration, 49–50, 53–54, 65; political activism of, xii–xiii, 3, 17; political parties and, xi, 198; postgraduation activity of, xiv, 195; in post-Perón era, 159; prestige of, xi, 11; "professional," x, 193; rejection of Perón's advice, 127; relations with professors, 198–199; repression of in Perón regime, 122; responsibilities of, 195–196; in revolution of 1930, 91–95; right of to dissident ideas, 33; seizure of Córdoba University buildings by, 53; socio-economic survey of, x, 10, 194; solidarity of, 89; solidarity with urban workers, 56–57, 99, 179; violence of, 47, 192
student strikes, 13; in Littoral University, 67; of 1918, 40–43; of 1954, 146; nationwide, 45–46; university (1954), 146, 188; violence and, 47
Superior Council (*Consejo Superior*), 7, 43, 54
super-patriots, 76; see also ultra-nationalist groups
Supreme Court of Argentina, 135
Susini, Telémaco, 52, 54

Taborda, Saúl Alejandro, 34, 44, 58, 100
Tamborini, José, 131
Tarbell, Ida, 182
Third International Conference of Students (Copenhagen, 1953), 147–148
Third National Student Congress (Córdoba, October 1942), 113–114
Toubes, Amanda, 145, 193

Trejo y Sanabria, Father Fernando, 4
Trotskyism, 171
Tucumán, University of, 5, 67–68, 144

UBA, *see* Buenos Aires, University of
ULP, *see* La Plata, University of
ultra-liberalism, rise of, 35
ultra-nationalist groups, 75–76, 103–105; and March of 1945, 129; opposition to, 89; in Perón regime, 122–123, 134; in World War II, 125, 134
unemployment, among professional men, 15–16
Unidad Programática Estudiantil, 170
Unión Cívica de la Juventud, 25–26
Unión Cívica Radical, 26
Unión Cívica Radical del Pueblo, 156
Unión Cívica Radical Intransigente, 156
Unión Democrática, 131, 134, 142
Unión Lation Americana, 72–73, 107
Unión Universitaria, 67
Unión Universitaria de La Plata, 178
Unión Universitaria Nacionalista, 104
United States: "colonialism" of, 107; criticism of, 178; expansionist and exploitative policies of, 71; student activism in, vii; in World War II, 112–113
United States National Student Association, 179
university: anti-government activity in, 138; anti-Reform groups in, 157; autonomy of, *see* university autonomy; democratization of, 49; drop-out rates in, 18; growth in size of, 29; nationalism and, 31; national issues and, 201–202;

October 1945 intervention in, 129–130; "politicization" of, 102; student participation in administration of, 49–50, 53–54, 65
University Assembly, 7
university autonomy, 8–9, 93–94, 159; new era of, 158; Peronist attack on, 128; in post-Perón era, 158; principle of, 50; Reformistas and, 161; in World War II, 134
university degree, prestige of, 11–12
university extension, principle of, 75–76, 179
university federation, 14
university organization, Peronist, 159
University Reform movement, viii, 23, 187; antecedents of, 23–35; versus Conservatives, 34–35; Córdoba Reform of 1918, 39–60; in Unión Democrática, 131; *see also* Córdoba Reform; Reform
university strike (October 1954), 146, 188; *see also* student strikes
university system, newness of, 6
unregulated attendance, 50, 65
urban workers, student solidarity with, 56–57, 99, 179
Uriburu, Gen. José F., 87–89, 92–94, 98, 101, 104, 108, 119, 198
Uriburu government: Reform professors and, 95; repressions of, 114; struggle against, 110; student attacks on, 96–97
Urquiza, Justo José, 4
Uruguay, exile groups in, 144
Uruguayan universities, student representation in, 49

Valdés, Horacio, 41–42
Veblen, Thorstein, 182
Versailles Treaty, 72
Viamente, Carlos Sánchez, 79, 81, 83–84, 101, 124–125, 135, 137, 151, 181, 189
Villareal, Juan Manuel, 95
Villegas, Daniel Cosío, 70

violence: results of, 192; in student strikes, 47

War College, 83
Washington, S. Walter, xi
Watson, Guillermo, 42, 49, 58, 193
Weinschelbaum, Ernesto, 148
Whitaker, Arthur P., 188
Williams, Tennessee, 181
Wilsonian democracy, 31
Wirth, John D., xvii
women: political life of, 150; student support of suffrage for, 127
working class: Perón and, 149–150; student solidarity with, 56–57, 74–77, 99, 179
World Bank, 177

World War I, 26–27, 31, 63, 71–72, 74; Argentine youth and, 113; Reform movement and, 114; university groups at end of, 124
World War II, 88–89, 111, 121, 146; Argentina as ally in, 123; Communism and, 176; Perón and, 133–134, 142–143; proletariat during, 130; ultra-nationalist groups and, 124–125; university autonomy and, 134; U.S. entry into, 112–113

Zubiría, Alberto May, 100–101
Zuviría, Gustavo Martínez, 121, 123